The Transit of Civilization

THE TRANSIT OF CIVILIZATION
FROM ENGLAND TO AMERICA IN THE SEVENTEENTH CENTURY

BY

EDWARD EGGLESTON

With a New Introduction by Arthur M. Schlesinger

Beacon Press *Beacon Hill* *Boston*

First published in 1900 by D. Appleton & Co.
First published as a Beacon Paperback in 1959
Library of Congress Catalog Card Number: 59–11792
Printed in the United States of America

The introduction by Arthur M. Schlesinger that appears in this volume was originally delivered as a paper before the Massachusetts Historical Society on April 12, 1956.

To Frances My Wife

INTRODUCTION

Evolution of a Historian

Edward Eggleston, well known to an earlier generation as author of the popular novel, The Hoosier Schoolmaster, *appears here in his less familiar guise of a social and cultural historian. American historical writers have arrived at their calling in strange and divers ways. Today they are usually the products of graduate schools; but until the latter part of the nineteenth century, when professional training first became available, they were self-taught. Moreover, they nearly always cultivated history as an afterthought, since they felt the need to attain a firm financial footing before chancing the uncertain rewards of scholarship. Of Eggleston's contemporaries, for example, John Bach McMaster started out as a civil engineer, James Schouler made a prior reputation as a legal writer, George Bancroft devoted many years of his life to politics and the public service, and James Ford Rhodes was a retired industrialist. Francis Parkman and Henry Adams, both born to wealth, were the shining exceptions, though Adams served briefly and regretfully as a Harvard professor of history.*

Fortunately, history is not a recondite subject girt with impregnable barriers; hence it was possible for men of studious bent, insight and critical acumen to make significant contributions, as all these men did. Moreover, unlike most of their successors of the so-called scientific school, they preferred the large canvas to the miniature, the rounded treatment to the monograph, and they strove to interest the general public rather than communicate only with fellow students.

Of this eminent company, Edward Eggleston was a worthy member. Turning to historical writing later in life than the others, he also brought to it an extraordinarily rich endowment. Born on December 10, 1837, at Vevay, a backwoods hamlet on the Indiana bank of the Ohio River, he was the son of Joseph Cary Eggleston, of colonial Virginia ancestry, who had migrated from the Old Dominion three years before to practice law in the rude settlement. Edward's mother, Mary Jane Craig, was the daughter of a nearby farmer and former Indian fighter, who had crossed the Alleghenies in 1781 and built the first blockhouse on the Indiana side of the stream. Little wonder that the Eggleston children found "the daring adventures of the generation before us" far more absorbing than the storybook account of Little Red Ridinghood and the wolf.

The youth obtained most of his education outside the classroom, probably no handicap in view of the bad teaching in country schools. He was a voracious reader, levying upon his father's library, which outnumbered any in the vicinity, and borrowing additional books whenever he could. He also spent long periods on the Craig farm, where he shared in tending the apple orchard as well as slaughtering pigs, rendering lard and making soap. "In many households," he recalled in after years, "the old customs still held sway; the wool was carded, spun, dyed, woven, cut and made up in the house . . . ."

From infancy he imbibed a belief in a hidebound form of Methodism, which was heightened when his mother, four years after her husband's death in 1846, married a Methodist minister, William Terrell. This union caused the family to reside from time to time in various parts of Indiana — at New Albany and Madison as well as Vevay. In 1854, Edward paid a visit lasting over a year to his Eggleston relatives in Virginia. There he encountered a more genial mode of life, but found nothing in slavery, even in the patriarchal form practiced by his kinsfolk, to alter his deep aversion to the institution. During these years he declined several opportunities to attend college, believing, so he avowed in retrospect, that colleges were for youngsters who were unable or unwilling to educate themselves.

Already in 1852, at the age of fifteen, he had struck out for himself, clerking in a Madison grocery store, the first of a bewildering variety of occupations. Then, early in 1856, impelled by his deep-seated piety, he ventured his first sermon, at Milton, just across the river in Kentucky, with such success that the presiding elder of the Madison District licensed him to preach regularly. Almost at once an attack of tuberculosis sent him off to the rugged Territory of Minnesota, where for three months he earned his keep and restored his lungs by working in a surveyor's gang and breaking the prairie with oxen. Later in 1856 he embarked upon his ministerial duties as a Methodist itinerant in southeastern Indiana, riding circuit through the dark forest and exhorting the unregenerate to repentance. Ill health, however, obliged him the next spring to return to Minnesota. There he spent the following nine years mostly as a parson, but occasionally sampling other means of livelihood, such as Bible agent, soap manufacturer, book peddler, insurance salesman and exhibitor of magic-lantern slides.

Almost fortuitously Eggleston drifted into magazine writing. In 1860 he contributed to the Ladies' Repository in Cincinnati an essay on "Béranger, the Poet of the People," a by-product of his omnivorous reading, and in 1864 he followed it with an article on "An Incident of the Indian Massacres of 1862." This vein was a more natural one for him to exploit, and since it fell in with his desire to provide more virile literary matter for children, it led him the next year to write a series on Indian lore and pioneer life for the Little Corporal, a juvenile periodical published in Chicago. In 1866 he moved to the Midwest metropolis to become a member of its staff, and the following year he assumed additional duties as editor of the Sunday School Teacher. As though he were not sufficiently busy, he also contributed a Saturday column of local comment to the Chicago Evening Journal for a while, sent regular weekly articles on Western affairs to the Independent magazine in New York and somehow found time also to lecture on miscellaneous topics in various parts of the country.

Well launched now on his writing career, this son of the Middle Border responded eagerly when the Independent in 1870 invited him to New York to join its editorial board. In that bracing literary capital, he tried his hand for the first time at fiction for adults when, after more than a year on the Independent, he became editor of Hearth and Home and serialized The Hoosier Schoolmaster in its pages late in 1871. The book, faithfully depicting the Indiana of Eggleston's childhood, holds a special niche in American letters as one of the earliest novels to strike the note of realism. It sold 20,000 copies within a year and has continued to sell ever since.

Emboldened by this success, Eggleston retired from the magazine *in the fall of 1872 to devote all his time to authorship. Soon he was turning out other novels treating Midwestern themes with similar fidelity:* The End of the World *(1872);* The Mystery of Metropolisville *(1873);* The Circuit Rider *(1874) — dedicated "To My Comrades of Other Years, the Brave and Self-sacrificing Men with Whom I Had the Honor to be Associated in a Frontier Ministry" — and* Roxy *(1878). Adept at keeping many balls in the air, Eggleston at the same time continued to write copiously for various periodicals, made the first of his four journeys to Europe and took a final fling at the pulpit. He had long been cooling toward the fervid orthodoxy of his youth, and from 1875 to 1879 he presided over a creedless church in Brooklyn until his theological liberalism proved too much for powerful elements of the congregation. During the last two years of this pastorate he also collaborated with his daughter Elizabeth (Mrs. Elwin Seelye) — always known to the family as Lillie — on a set of biographies of famous Indians. This, his first excursion into American history at the adult level, sharpened his interest in the nation's past and opened his eyes to the possibilities of original work in that field.*

It was during Eggleston's second visit abroad in 1880 that he decided to undertake the ambitious project of a "History of Life in the United States." Doubtless his foreign wanderings had whetted his perceptions of cultural differences between the European peoples on the two sides of the water and had made him eager to search into the underlying causes. Other factors, however, were more fundamental. As he wrote Lillie, "I am ripe for it. Everything in my life seems to have prepared me for it."

Indeed, few if any men of letters of his day had partaken so abundantly of the many-sidedness of American civilization. "In my early life," so Eggleston recapitulated to an Outlook *interviewer upon the appearance of the first volume of the projected series, "I rapidly changed from one social environment to another" — from town to country, from a new free state to an old slave state, from the primitive Hoosier backwoods to the still rawer Minnesota frontier where the railroad had not yet penetrated and all travel was "by boat or wagon." In a very real sense, he felt that "I have known colonial life, having been among people of different manners and dialect. I can imagine in the colonies the same collision and the same contact with Indian* life." Moreover, his many shifts of occupation had acquainted him with all sorts and conditions of humanity. By the same token, he had explored successive religious frontiers and hence could enter understandingly into the theological dissensions that beset the early comers to America. Finally, his change of residence to the Atlantic seaboard enabled him to view these experiences at a focal distance.

In so far as other historians influenced Eggleston, his model was the Frenchman, Augustin Thierry, whom he had first come across in an article by John Stuart Mill and then read in the original. Thierry's emphasis on the neglected role of the "popular classes" in medieval France, his concern with conveying to the reader "the atmosphere of the period," his belief that history should also be literature, all reinforced Eggleston's ideas of what he wished to do. Of his United States contemporaries, he doubtless found inspiration in the example of his old friend Moses Coit Tyler, the social historian of colonial literature; and none other than the great Francis Parkman had blessed his venture by saying, "You are the only man in America that can write a history of life in the United States; you are the only man who has seen so many forms of our life."

Actually, Eggleston's imaginative writings had also foreshadowed his plunge into history. In the preface to *The Mystery of Metropolisville* in 1873, he had demanded that novels "be the truest of books" and declared that to this end he sought to make his own stories "of value as a contribution to the history of civilization in America." And some years later, reflecting on these literary progeny, he considered that what particularly distinguished them was that the "characters were all treated in their relation to social conditions." It was not a far cry from realistic fiction to realistic history — the sort that obliged the author, as he was to say in the initial volume of his undertaking, to treat the past not "otherwise than unreverently. Here," he went on, with an eye on superpatriots and ancestor worshippers among his readers, "are no forefathers or foremothers, but simply English men and women of the seventeenth century, with the faults and fanaticisms as well as the virtures of their age."

In Eggleston's letter to Lillie in June, 1880, announcing his scheme, he wrote almost lyrically, "What chapters I can write on 'Religious Life in New England,' 'The Great Kentucky Revival,' 'Flight of

Emigrants Across the Mountains,' 'Indian Wars and Cabin Life in the Interior,' 'Early Fur Traders,' 'The Old Gentry in the South,' 'Social Changes of the Revolution,'" and so on. But Eggleston, even at forty-two, did not allow sufficient time to complete so formidable a task, considering the thoroughness with which he planned to do it as well as the many other activities, including the writing of three more novels, that he allowed to divert his energies. In the end he finished only two installments of the vast enterprise and did not carry it beyond the limits of the seventeenth century.

Taking advantage of his European sojourn, he hunted material in the Bibliothèque Nationale, the British Museum and other collections in Paris and London, jotting down his findings and thoughts in two notebooks. These entries included chapter headings and tentative passages as well as subject indexes and references to further sources. Returning to New York in September, 1880, he resumed his spadework, principally at the Astor Library. His snail-like progress caused him moments of despondency. "New Eng. history & all colonial history is a horrible labyrinth," he groaned in a letter to Lillie at the end of four months. In a trial draft he had set down 4000 words on the Pilgrims in England and their flight to Holland, and he gloomily foresaw reaching "the settlement of Boston in the course of ten or fifteen years of work." By early 1882 he was pursuing his quarry in Cambridge, Massachusetts, where the learned Harvard librarian and bibliographer, Justin Winsor, helped steer his research. "The Harvard people whom I have met treat me most kindly," he reported, though some of them candidly admitted to him that until then they had never heard of him or his writings.

The next year Eggleston built a commodious field-stone library alongside his summer place at Lake George, where in due course he gathered some 10,000 volumes, eagerly scrutinizing the latest auction catalogues to acquire rare items. It proved an excellent working collection, and he found he could accomplish more there in the few months away from the heat and buzz of the city than in the whole wintertime. Through self-education he was now able to use seven languages in his researches.

Ferris Greenslet, then a young boy, remembers him at this time as a tall, slender man "with a shock of iron-grey hair and beard that stood out from the oval of his face at least five fingers' breadth in every direction, with the nose of Socrates below bright black eyes." *L. Frank Tooker of the* Century Magazine *described his head, evidently Eggleston's outstanding feature, as "most leonine" with "a deep-toned voice that so easily might have become a leonine roar, but never did." The vicissitudes of an unusually varied life had in fact left him "the most genial and kindly of men."*

In a third trip abroad, in 1885-86, Eggleston was elated to discover in the British Museum and the Public Record Office documents that apparently had escaped the eye of fellow historians, notably material on Bacon's Rebellion and other early Virginia developments. He also tramped in the north of England, where he visited Scrooby and Austerfield, whence the Pilgrims had set forth on their wanderings. Hearing from America that John Fiske was preparing a five-volume history of the United States, he confided in a letter to Lillie, "It will be popular, well-written, and lacking in nothing but correctness & fullness of information. I know we have no public sufficiently intellectual to justify the spending my resources on such a work as I am doing but I am compelled by internal forces to do it."

Back in his native land once more, he burrowed into the treasures of the Historical Society of Pennsylvania in Philadelphia, with his wife by his side transcribing manuscripts in "her nice antique hand." At various times he also combed the holdings of the Library of Congress, the Boston Public Library, the New York State Library at Albany, the Peabody Institute at Baltimore and the historical societies of Massachusetts, New York, Maryland and Virginia, besides private repositories at home and abroad. In 1889 he visited the Virginia farm where Jamestown had once stood, finding handwrought nails and bits of early glass, and tracing the ground plan of the first English settlement by means of the hearth bricks strewn about the field. "There is really no other way of writing vividly and familiarly," he commented in the Outlook *interview, "except by saturating one's self."*

Not long after entering upon his Sisyphean labors, Eggleston, whose habit had always been to rush into print, submitted some of his preliminary conclusions to the public. In November, 1882, he began a series of thirteen articles in the Century Magazine, *which in the next eight years treated such topics as "Husbandry in Colonial Times," "Social Life in the Colonies" and "The Colonists at Home." Early in 1883, at Justin Winsor's invitation, he read a paper on the colonial Indians before the Harvard Historical Society and was secretly irked when a member remarked that he had contributed nothing new. "It is one thing," he exploded to Lillie, "to unearth new facts as Mr. Deane does — it is quite another to see what the facts collectively amount to, & to mass them so as to carry that impression in its wholeness into the mind of the reader."*

The experience may have made him resolve to dig deeper, however. In any event, such criticisms did not prevent Eggleston from being included in the notable group of scholars who assembled at Saratoga in September, 1884, to organize the American Historical Association, which at once became the country's foremost agency for the advancement of research and writing in the historical field. As further evidence of the respect in which he was held, the official report of the Association's gathering in 1890 noted that "Mr. Eggleston's remarks upon various papers read in the convention were, by general consent, one of the most valuable features of the entire meeting." Nonetheless, he could never quite reconcile himself to this "new school of historians, men of large and accurate scholarship," who, thanks to German training or example, "dump the crude ore of history into ponderous sentences."

As still another offshoot of his interest in the American past, Eggleston published a school history of the United States in 1888, paralleling it the next year with one for more elementary pupils. His conscience occasionally pricked him for this distraction from his primary task, but he comforted himself with the belief that his texts would greatly improve upon the manuals currently in use. Besides, he seized the opportunity to inject his thesis of the key importance of "changes in modes of living" in "the progress of civilization." In any case he badly needed the money, and the two ventures actually yielded him the largest income he had ever enjoyed. Moreover, he discovered he had not lost face with the scholarly world, for Columbia College in 1892 invited him to deliver a series of public lectures on "The Culture-History of the American People."

"Poor history!" Eggleston lamented in a letter to Lillie in March,

1894, "no one man's life is long enough for it, certainly not the life of a sickish man like myself with a dozen other irons and no wealth to come and go on." Another embarrassment was the fact that, after nearly a decade and a half of amassing data on the first century of English settlement, he found himself with more than enough to fill two volumes on that single period alone. One student has estimated that at this rate of progress it would have required thirty-eight more volumes to carry the story to 1900. Driven by fear that "the darkness of age and death" might overtake him, Eggleston bent his energies to putting this initial material into published form.

Early in 1896, a heart ailment tempted him to go South for a rest, but, as he wrote his daughter Allegra, "only grim death itself will make me let go of my work." To render doubly certain that the volume in hand contained no errors, he engaged Victor H. Paltsits of the Lenox Library, later a scholar in his own right, to check his references, verify dates and quotations, and extend other assistance. In November the book appeared under the title The Beginners of a Nation, a History of the Source and Rise of the Earliest English Settlements in America with Special Reference to the Life and Character of the People and the half-title A History of Life in the United States. It bridges the years from the origins of Jamestown to about 1650 when, as the author held, "The compactness of English settlement and the prolific increase of English people decided the fate of North America."

After a much-needed but quick vacation at Old Point Comfort, Virginia, Eggleston returned to his toils, though "a kind of pen-paralysis" slowed his pace for a time. Finding it necessary to eke out his previous researches, he spent the months from April to September, 1897, delving in the libraries of New York as well as in his Lake George collection, then hied off for a protracted sojourn in Washington to run down additional sources. "Nobody knows we are here," he wrote Lillie, "and we are having a good quiet time."

Ill health, now further complicated by failing eyesight, continued to plague him — he lost ten pounds during his Washington stay — and he dolefully informed Lillie early in 1899 that his work was creeping "on all fours." By keeping doggedly at it, however, he finished the second volume in November of the following year. To *this new portion of* A History of Life in the United States *he gave the arresting title* The Transit of Civilization from England to America in the Seventeenth Century. *Unlike the first volume, it covers the full span to 1700 except for Pennsylvania and the Carolinas, which he optimistically reserved for later treatment. Inasmuch as the book deals with a wholly different kind of subject matter, it possesses a completeness which enables it to stand alone.*

Of the two works, The Beginners of a Nation *received greater critical acclaim at the time. It was better constructed, and, what probably counted for more, it treated thoughtfully and luminously what was currently accepted as the orthodox content of history. The author's principal concern was with the English background of colonization, the hardships of the early settlers, their theological doctrines and schisms, and the peopling of new colonies from the older ones. Though deploring a "paroxysm of citations," Eggleston came close to committing the offense by amplifying many of his points in "Elucidations" at the end of each chapter, where, however, they could easily be ignored.*

Herbert L. Osgood's review in the American Historical Review *reflected the general academic reception. While he denied that the volume offered many unfamiliar facts or a "distinctly new point of view," he praised Eggleston's delineation of men and events as "realistic" and termed his style of writing as "of such beauty and force as to make the book at once a history and a contribution to literature." This was no slight accolade from a professionally trained scholar who within a few years was himself to produce a monumental treatise on the legal and institutional aspects of seventeenth-century America.*

The Transit of Civilization, *on the other hand, was a trail-breaking book, dealing with material hitherto off the beaten track. Of contemporary writers in America, Henry Adams had made a bow to social and intellectual aspects of the past by opening his* History of the United States during the Administrations of Thomas Jefferson and James Madison *with six acute chapters of that nature and then happily forgetting all about the matter until his four concluding chapters eight volumes later. Somewhat closer to Eggleston's conception was John Bach McMaster, who began publishing his* History of the People of the United States from the Revolution to the Civil

War in 1883 and had produced five portly installments of the full set of eight before Eggleston brought out his Transit of Civilization.

Eggleston, however, had preceded McMaster in the field of social history with the first of his articles on colonial life in the Century Magazine; and, in any event, the two men addressed themselves to quite different stages of American development: one, the period of infancy; the other, that of young manhood. But what was more significant, they held very different ideas of how to evoke the past. McMaster generally sought to let the facts speak for themselves, and his unadorned account often reads like a poorly digested notebook. To an inquirer he tartly remarked, "It is not the business of the historian to be a philosopher." And despite the implications of the word People in the title of his work, he gave nearly three-quarters of his space to politics, diplomacy and war.

Eggleston, who took even greater care than McMaster to authenticate his data, considered that the historian should seek to clothe the bare bones with the flesh and blood of interpretation. The historian, he believed, should try to look beneath and behind the facts, to penetrate to "the history that underlies history." The resulting interpretation should arise out of the student's complete identification with the age, but must not preclude him from utilizing such insights as were afforded by the perspective of his own day. Eggleston, moreover, deliberately played down the role of government in society as actually wielding less influence than a multitude of more urgent concerns of life.

As the name suggests, The Transit of Civilization centers on the "mental furniture" the English newcomers carried with them to America and the modifications wrought by wilderness conditions. In a wide-ranging survey, Eggleston considers such aspects of life as the colonists' scientific conceptions, their belief in an ever-present invisible world (which tended to be as real to them as the material world), their medical notions and practices, their religious and moral outlook, the persistence of class distinctions in law and custom, the popular distrust of lawyers, the neologisms and other changes in English speech, the modes of education and the "literature below literature that has to do with the hopes and fears, the beliefs and aspirations of uncritical people." While noting that "Men may live at the same time without being intellectual contemporaries," he stresses the fact that even the better informed shared much of the credulity of the rank and file. Some of them indeed lent it the high sanction of their erudition. Eggleston again appended "Elucidations" to his chapters to provide significant supporting data.

This second volume of *A History of Life in the United States* nonplused the learned reviewers. Barrett Wendell, a literary scholar and author of a biography of Cotton Mather, passed judgment on it in the *American Historical Review*. After his well-known manner, he cavalierly pronounced it the product of intellectual indigestion induced by too much browsing in libraries; but despite this and other animadversions, he nevertheless granted that "it really points the way to a kind of American history which in time may flood our past with revivifying light."

Charles M. Andrews, who would presently rival Osgood as an authority on colonial America, greeted the work in the *Political Science Quarterly* with similar mixed feelings. With good reason he, like Wendell, accounted it a bundle of essays rather than a unified whole; and while saying he considered these disquisitions "interesting and readable," he chided the author for inaccuracies concerning the English antecedents of certain colonial land and educational practices. Obedient to the historical canons of the time, he barely mentioned Eggleston's discussions of pseudo-science, medical customs, intellectual concerns and the like, which made up two-thirds of the book, though he cautiously surmised they "may be thoroughly sound and scholarly." Upon further reflection, Andrews several years later referred again in much the same manner to the "valuable chapters on out-of-the-way subjects."

Today, however, with our different criterion of the scope of history, the essence of Eggleston's achievement may be said to lie in his discerning accounts of these very "out-of-the-way subjects," no longer considered freakish and off center. Though scholars since his time have piled up detailed studies of many of the same themes, Eggleston's pioneering effort still shines through with a special glow of its own. From this longer perspective, for example, the late Carl Van Doren, American historian and man of letters, termed the work "erudite, humane, and graceful"; Ferris Greenslet, the biographer, has called *it the best of all of Eggleston's many writings, "a learned, vividly written, yeasty book"; and Michael Kraus, weighing the two Eggleston volumes in his* History of American History, *has declared, more restrainedly, that they are still informative, better written than most historical treatises and "not as well known as they should be."*

Eggleston delivered his valedictory to the historical profession in December, 1900, in his presidential address to the American Historical Association, which he was too ill to present in person. He chose as his title "The New History," and in a somewhat disjointed discourse that betrayed his declining powers he reiterated the convictions that had served as the guiding star of his scholarly labors. Paying tribute to Thierry, Michelet, Macaulay, Green and other European historians for their attention to the common life, he decried "drum and trumpet history" as outmoded and unworthy of the serious student and pleaded instead for a "history of culture, the real history of men and women." He died two years later on September 2, 1902.

But neither Eggleston's example nor that of McMaster wrought any immediate transformation in American historical writing. The grip of political and military history continued too strong in academic groves to be easily dislodged. It was not until the 1920's that the thirteen-volume co-operative History of American Life, *breaking sharply with the older point of view, began publication and that Charles and Mary Beard brought out their* Rise of American Civilization, *with many other students also turning to the field. A full generation after Eggleston's pioneering achievement, his vision of a "New History" thus came at last to fulfillment.*

The Transit of Civilization *hence is well worth reading today, not only for its intrinsic interest and engaging style, but also because it was a notable milestone in the history of American historiography.*

ARTHUR M. SCHLESINGER

Note to the Reader: *For fuller information on Edward Eggleston's life, see* The First of the Hoosiers *(Philadelphia 1903) by his brother George Cary Eggleston, and the scholarly biography* Edward Eggleston *(New York, 1946) by William Peirce Randel. For a somewhat different estimate of "Edward Eggleston: Pioneer in Social History," see Charles Hirschfeld's essay in* Historiography and Urbanization *(Baltimore, 1941), edited by Eric F. Goldman. The quotations from Eggleston's correspondence in the present account came from the latter two sources.*

A. M. S.

PREFACE.

PREFACE.

IN seeking to give a history of the civilization of the seventeenth century there was little help in anything American, and, to my surprise, I found long ago that I could not count on anything English. There were many books on Shakespeare, more or less good when they were not bad, and there was Masson's ponderous Life and Times of John Milton in six octavo volumes. These afforded something, but the civilization of the century was not told in any of them. It became necessary to build a description from the ground. The complex states of knowing and thinking, of feeling and passion, must be explained. The little world as seen by the man of the seventeenth century must be understood. Its sun, moon, and planets were flames of fire without gravity, revolved about the earth by countless angels; its God governed this one little world with mock majesty. Its heaven, its horrible hell of material fire blown by the mouth of God, its chained demons whose fetters might be loosed, its damnation of infants were to be appreciated and expounded. The inhumanity of punishments and of sport in that day, the mixture made of religion and revenge—these and a hundred other things went to make up the traits of the century. To explain the things in this other age in which I found myself it was necessary to go to England. To understand England one must understand the Continent; to make this out one must often thread his way to antiquity. The use of Latin by nearly all scholars made the world's knowledge more or less common to all. My little corner widened out into a part of all human history.

Eclipses, parhelia, comets, were danger signals hung out in the heavens as warnings. Logic was the only implement for the discovery of truth. Observation was in its birth throes. Medicines were recognized by signaturism; on this slender basis what a towering structure was built! Right and wrong were thought of only as the result of direct revelation; they had not yet found standing room in the great theater of natural knowledge. Until we understand these things we write the history of the seventeenth century in vain. It is the last age which sought knowledge of physical things by deduction. The next century brought philosophy and philosophy dawned into science.

We must apply to the seventeenth century the severe canons of history; people with ancestors will be disappointed. We can not make out in the seventeenth century the great destiny of Virginia in the eighteenth. We must not be sure that the future greatness of later New England is wrapped up in the peculiarly narrow and forbidding husk of the later seventeenth century. Nor can commercial greatness be predicted of New York; nor did Pennsylvania show signs of the great industries developed from her coal fields. The causes of greatness are not always traceable. Where least looked for may develop the next group of statesmen and authors, of inventors and great merchants. We may write history, but we may not prophesy.

JOSHUA'S ROCK, LAKE GEORGE, *November, 1900.*

CONTENTS.

THE TRANSIT OF CIVILIZATION.

CHAPTER THE FIRST.

MENTAL OUTFIT OF THE EARLY COLONISTS.

I.

The first English-Americans.

WHAT are loosely spoken of as national characteristics are probably a result not so much of heredity as of controlling traditions. Seminal ideas received in childhood, standards of feeling and thinking and living handed down from one overlapping generation to another, make the man English or French or German in the rudimentary outfit of his mind. A gradual change in fundamental notions produces the difference between the character of a nation at an early epoch and that of the same people in a later age. In taking account of the mental furniture which the early English emigrants carried aboard ship with them, we shall gain a knowledge of what may be called the original investment from which has been developed Anglo-Saxon culture in America. The mother country of the United States was England in the first half of the seventeenth century, or, at most, England before the Revolution of 1688. From the English spoken in the days of the Stuart kings came

CHAP. I.

our primitive speech, and the opinions, prejudices, and modes of thinking of the English in that day lay at the bottom of what intellectual life there was in the colonies. Some seventeenth-century characteristics, long since lost or obscured in England, may yet be recognized in the folk-lore and folk-speech, the superstitions and beliefs of people in America. The number of English who crossed the seas before the middle of the century was above thirty thousand. Those who survived the first rude outset of pioneer life, with their fast-multiplying progeny, numbered probably fifty thousand in 1650, and this population was about halved between the colonies on the Chesapeake waters and those to the northward of the Dutch settlement on the New England coast. To these early comers it is due that the speech, the usages, the institutions, and the binding traditions of the United States are English.

II.

Milton and Shakespeare.

In reckoning the mental outfit of the first comers we should only mislead ourselves by recalling the names of Jonson and Shakespeare and the other lights that were shining when the Susan Constant and her two little consorts sailed out of the Thames to bear a company of English people to the James River. Nor will it avail much to remember that Milton was a Puritan at the same time with Cotton and Hooker and Winthrop. The emigrants had no considerable part in the higher intellectual life of the age; the great artistic passions of Shakespeare and Milton touched them not at any point. Bacon's contribution to the art of finding truth did not belong to them. Men may live in the same time without being intellectual contemporaries.

III.

The Copernican system.

The science that touched the popular imagination in the seventeenth century was astronomy. "God gave to man an upright face that he might view the stars and learn astronomy," according to a couplet of the time. As then accepted astronomy was a jumble of the prevalent Ptolemaic theory of the universe with the world at the center, and of the odds and ends of mediæval astrology —moon-signs, zodiac-signs, horoscopes, ominous eclipses followed by devastating fires, and comets presaging disaster and the death of princes, with the mystical doctrine of the dominance of planets over plants, minerals, and diseases. The Copernican system, which essayed to displace the "firm-set earth" from that central position in the universe it had so long occupied, made headway slowly. In the interval between the landing of the Jamestown gold hunters and that of the Plymouth Pilgrims, the great Kepler, working in obscurity, developed the three principles which are the foundations of modern astronomy. It was two years before the beginning of the Plymouth settlement that, in poverty and neglect, he wrote: "Fare-

Wilkin's works, 271.

CHAP. I.

well, Ptolemy! I am turning back to Aristarchus under the lead of Copernicus"; and in the loneliness of his convictions he said in the same year, "My book may well wait a hundred years for a reader, since God himself for six thousand years awaited a discoverer." After Virginia and New England were securely settled, Galileo was imprisoned for demonstrating the earth's motion regardless of the time-honored opinion of Joshua the son of Nun and the indubitable witness of everybody's senses. As the middle of the century approached, one finds Copernicanism spoken of as "the theory that has so stirred all our modern wits." In strictly orthodox circles, in good society, and among the people generally, the sun, the moon, the planets, and the fixed stars continued to revolve round the earth as aforetime to lighten the paths of men or at least to twinkle on them, to lord it over plants and animals, to indicate the nature of diseases, and to foretell to the expert the fortunes of the future. The rhetoric of colonial preachers still turned the universe of fiery lights about the solid earth. In 1666 and afterward one may read between the lines in the non-committal writings of some Harvard mathematicians a possible preference for Copernicanism. Throughout the century the English-American colonists with a few exceptions rested undisturbed in the notion that the center of universal motion was the earth, and that the heavenly bodies were imponderable flames hung up for the convenience of man.

Kepler, De Cometis, p. 98.

Ibid., Harmonicus Mundi, 178, 179.

Note 1.

Howell's Letters, vol. iii, ix, and Sir T. Browne's Vulgar Errors, book vi, chap. v.

Note 2.

Note 3.

CHAP. I.

IV.

Astrology.

The interest in astronomy was mainly practical; the stars were thought to exert a controlling influence on human affairs. Kepler himself lived in part by casting horoscopes for princes, as Tycho had done before him; it is by such scullion work that the world in every age contrives to degrade its superior men and dissipate their energies. John Winthrop, the younger, Governor of Connecticut, a fellow of the Royal Society and a man of much learning, as learning was then understood, possessed some of the works on astrology so much esteemed at that time. Among these is a book with astrological figures set one on each page with the lower half of the page blank. These diagrams are for every four minutes of time, and by means of them "any reasonable artist" in such things "may give judgment of a question." On one page some reasonable artist has essayed to find out, by casting a horoscope, what was the ailment afflicting one Alice Wilkins in 1656. Medicines were administered when the moon was in the proper sign, and the almanacs of the eighteenth century told the farmer to cut his brushwood in certain signs of the zodiac and in the decrease of the moon, that it might not grow again, but to cut firewood in the increase. Timber to last must be cut in the last quarter of the moon. So Tusser, in his Points of Good Husbandry, says, "The moon in the wane gather fruit for to last." The Rev. Jared Elliot,

A Table of the Astrological Houses of the Heaven, 1654.

Note 4.

Note 5.

CHAP. I.

the leading colonial writer on agriculture in the middle of the eighteenth century, shows great respect to the zodiac, and the prosperity of the Pennsylvania German was attributed to his regard for the moon's phases. In many regions to-day the moon rules the planting of potatoes, the cutting of hair, and the killing of pigs; and women wean their infants in the proper sign of the zodiac. These are the ragged remnants of the ancient and complicated science of astrology which survived from the middle ages, and which with much other strange baggage of the sort crossed the wide seas with the emigrants to America.

Note 6.

V.

Comets and other portents.

Most people knew little of the complicated mysteries of horoscopes, and they understood less of the jargon of astrology. But the unlearned kept pace with the learned in looking with religious dread upon comets. "Experience Attests and reason Asserts that they have served for sad Prologues to tragical Epilogues." The words are those of perhaps the earliest American writer on astronomy; the opinion was that of the world at large in his time. On the science of prognostication by comets learned men disagreed. "Some," says the writer we have just quoted, "put much trust or vertue in the tail, terming it the Ignomon." Naturally enough a comet "operated most powerfully" on the people to whom it was "vertical"

Alexander Nowell, Cambridge Almanac, 1666.

Note 7.

Nowell, as above.

CHAP. I.

—that is to say, over whose heads the body of it passed. Some thought that comets were themselves agents of mischief, drying up the moisture of Nature and thus producing droughts and pestilential fevers, and inflaming the anger of princes; as they were supposed to be in combustion they excited the air to tempests, and thus raised great waves and inundated the earth. The winds driven into caves, and by some means imprisoned in the earth, made the ground quake in their endeavors to get out, said the astrologers. Others believed that they were but a sort of celestial weather signal hung out to give warning of the imminence of calamities ordained by God. Yet others believed that, in the phrase of the time, they were "both effectual and significant." It was noted in New England that when John Cotton, the great ecclesiastical luminary of the first generation, drew near his end, a comet appeared which "went out" soon after the preacher's death. The blight of 1665, that put an end to the hope of prosperity from wheat-raising in Massachusetts, was heralded by "a great and blazing comet," which, like all portents and omens, lacked definiteness, for it was "accompanied with many sad effects" beside. John Hull, the pine-tree shilling-maker, calls the attention of a correspondent to the comet of 1680 with a pious ejaculation of alarm: "The Lord fit us and you for all his will and pleasure." A protagonist of Puritanism in its decline was Increase Mather. He was a pessimist with a keen relish

Spencer, Of Natural Prodigies, 14.

Compare Kepler's De Cometis, 104, 105.

Compare Kepler, as above, 107, 108.

John Edwards, Cometomania, p. 3, 1684.

Josselyn, Chron. Obs. *sub anno.*

Compare the horoscope of an eclipse in Chauncey's Cambridge, Mass., Almanac for 1663.

CHAP. I.

for the supernatural and sensational. Nothing delighted him more than calamities past, present, or potential. The brilliant comet of 1680 was a call from heaven for a man of his genius; he re-enforced it by a sermon entitled "Heaven's Alarm to the World." When two years later another blazing star burst upon a world that had not yet had time to recover its equanimity, Mather proceeded to expound this also in "The Latter Sign Discoursed of," and then followed these with a book, for which he borrowed the title "Kometographia." In this the accidents by land and sea, the disasters of pestilence, famine, war, and assassination, that had ever come trailing after any comet, were once more rehearsed, as they had been rehearsed in other times by other sensational moralists. The notable comet of 1680, which set so many watchdogs baying at the sky, alarmed the Dutch dwellers on the upper Hudson, as we may see in a letter dispatched by their usual post, an Indian runner, to New York. In this they mention the "Dreadful comett starr" "with a very fyery Tail or Streemer." "Undoubtedly God threatens us," is their inference, and they crave permission of superior authority in New York to cause "the Domine" to proclaim in the church "a day of fasting and humiliation."

Am. Antiq. Soc. Trans., iii, 247. Compare D'Ewe's Autobiography, i, 123, and Royal MSS. Comm. Rept., xii, p. vii. Acct. book of Sir D. Fleming.

Doc. Hist., N. Y., iii, 882.

Note 8.

On the eve of Bacon's rebellion in Virginia, in 1676, the people were warned, to no good purpose apparently, by signs in the heavens, in the air, and out of the earth. To a comet "streaming like a

The Beginning, Progress, and

horse taile westwards" there was added "fflights of pigeons in breadth nigh a quarter of the midhemisphere, and of their length was no visible end." This ought to have been enough to frighten even the easy-going Virginians of that time out of their sins, but comet and pigeons were re-enforced by a third omen—strange swarms of flies "rising out of spigot holes in the earth"; no doubt what are now known as the seventeen-year locusts. Not only comets, but eclipses, parhelia, or "multiplied suns," and other unusual phenomena were beheld with awe. In auroras the colonists saw swords of flame brandished, and fiery horsemen charging in ghostly battle. There was always the chance that a particularly brilliant display of northern lights might prove an awful forerunner, not of war and famine, but of the combustion of the earth and the crack of doom itself. Rainbows, on the other hand, were recorded with a "Laus Deo." The people of Boston were comforted by a rainbow after the unlucky outcome of an expedition against Port Royal in 1707, but nothing else came of it. The rainbow which raised all hopes at the outset of an expedition, in 1711, also played Boston false.

CHAP. I.

Conclusion of Bacon's Rebellion, by T. M., Force, i. Note 9.

Compare Evelyn's Diary, i, 264, and Henry King's sermon at Pavl's Crosse, 1621, p. 15.

Lambert's New Haven, 190.

Compare The Rainbow, a sermon at Pavl's Crosse, 1617, by Bourne.

Sewall's Diary, ii, 189, 314, 318.

VI.

Spontaneous generation.

From Greek and Roman antiquity down at least to the middle of the seventeenth century no scientific proposition was more universally received than that insects and some birds, fishes, and

CHAP. I.

reptiles were generated by putrefaction, or, to turn the proposition round, that all putrefaction produced life. From the bodies of decaying horses came hornets; but kine in decomposition produced honeybees. Ovid says that this was known by experience, and later writers quoted his verses on the subject and saved themselves the necessity of observation. The practical bee-keeper of the seventeenth century did not read the classics, or Gesner or Mouffet, or any of the other innumerable Latin treatises on animal life, but he did look into his hive occasionally, and he knew that a bee came from a "little worm" in the comb. Bees taken from England to Virginia and New England prospered. But the traveler Josselyn entertained the hope that, when the carnivorous animals should have been exterminated, American bees might be produced from dead bullocks, after the approved scientific formula. Some kinds of wasps had their origin in the decay of apples and pears; the most superficial observer might find them to his sorrow issuing from the fruit. Minnows were produced from foam, carp came from putrid slime, the oyster, the nautilus, and other shellfish from different kinds of putrescence mixed sometimes with mud, sometimes combined with the sand of the sea bottom. So far did Nature carry this economy that even the discarded tails of New England tadpoles were not suffered to go to waste: out of them were formed the water newts, as Josselyn takes pains to explain. Lord Bacon, who floun-

Note 10.

Porta, Magia Nat., liber xv, caput iv.

ders like a stranded leviathan when he seeks to explore the coasts of physical science, suggests that toads come from the corruption of water mixed with mud; to "old snow" he attributes the generation of those red larvæ or "worms" which are yet believed by the unlearned to have "snowed down." A chemist of that day, whose work was reprinted by the Royal Society, says of fermenting bread dough that "unless it were bridled and restrained by . . . Artificial Fire it would proceed to vitality and produce worms." It was held in Elizabeth's time, and long before and after, that parasites were bred from the body on which they lived. As late as 1676, when Bacon, the Virginia rebel, in his last illness found himself obliged to cast his discarded garments directly into the fire, the presence of the parasites was thought to be one of the results of his disease and a divine judgment on him for rebellion, though the case is sufficiently explained by the fact that he had been dwelling in Indian wigwams a few weeks before. The persistence of vitality was held then as the persistence of force is now; "no one living creature corrupts without the production of another," was an accepted maxim. Lord Bacon states it more cautiously: "Briefly, most things putrefied bring forth insects of various names."

Bacon's Natural History, *passim.*

Otto Tachenius, His Clavis, 6.

Note 11.

Comp. Tiraboschi, ii, 430, on the production of fossil trees.

Note 12.

VII.

If there was much lack of book learning in the generation of English people that sprung up first

Migration of birds.

CHAP. I.

on American soil, there was some gain in a life in which exigent wants compelled a habit of shrewd observation. For centuries strange theories had prevailed among learned and unlearned regarding the origin of those far-wandering waterfowl whose distant resting places were yet undiscovered. Following the analogy of the accepted theory regarding the production of "insects," including frogs, mice, and snakes, there were those who derived many birds from wood rotting in the water, or from decaying fruits. Others said that some birds grew on trees, and proved it by showing the shells of the nuts from which the bird had emerged. The so-called barnacle goose had been held for centuries to develop from the shellfish barnacle which clings to the bottom of a ship or a water-soaked timber. More than one writer of standing testified to the metamorphosis on the evidence of his own senses, at least he had found a barnacle all befeathered and ready to take flight. Easy-going casuists treated the barnacle goose as a fish by virtue of its marine origin, and it was served up to monks and other self-indulgent fasters on Fridays. Such a myth could not be long held in solution by American tradition; barnacle geese were not found, and the unlearned pioneer seeking his meat by prowling along the reedy shores of rivers, ponds, and estuaries with a great fowling piece six or seven feet long in the barrel came to know the life habits of waterfowl better than any of that procession of philosophers who with pedantic learning copied

Note 13.

incredibilities from one Latin book to another down the ages. One bit of ornithology of that time crossed the seas, and perhaps by virtue of its absurdity was able to hold its own in America for two hundred years. The annual disappearance of migratory birds and their return in the spring demanded explanation, and in old British folk-lore it was held that such birds were accustomed to lie hid in caves, rocks, and hollow trees. In Cornwall it was reported that swallows out of season had been "found sitting in old deepe Tynne—workes and holes in the Sea Cliffes." Olaus Magnus, a banished Scandinavian bishop living at Rome, published in the sixteenth century a work learned in form but as full of things unbelievable as the writings of the much-venerated Pliny. He told on the never-to-be-questioned authority of fishermen that they had drawn up torpid swallows in their nets which came to life on warming. He even gave all the details of their taking refuge for the winter in the clay at the bottom of the river. Once this fond story of the fishermen got itself printed in Latin and authenticated by a bishop, it became a scientific fact. The new notion almost crowded out the old folk-theory of hibernation in caves and holes, and held its own for two centuries, to be reluctantly discarded almost in our time. The revelations of the telescope made the moon seem near, and Bishop Godwin formed a new theory of hibernation in the satellites, which was elaborated by Charles Morton, an Oxford scholar,

Burton's Anat., ii, 2, 3.

Carew's Cornwall, 1602, fol. 23.

Historiæ de Gentibus Septentrionalibus, 418, abridgment.

Note 14.

Note 15. Morton in Harleiam

CHAP. I.

Miscell., Park's edition, vol. ii, 581. But see same suggestion in Godwin's Voyage to the Moon, 1638. And compare Wilkin's works, 134.

whose old age was passed in Massachusetts. He preached a sermon from a text in Jeremiah, from which he deduced a winter home for all kinds of migratory birds among the newly revealed mountains and valleys of the moon. If that were thought too far away for wing travel, Morton was willing to split the difference by suggesting that the earth might have some smaller satellites—little undiscovered gull islands in the heavens for the birds to roost upon. After Morton's death, omnivorous and marvel-loving Cotton Mather appropriated this hypothesis as a piece of flotsam, and wrote a letter to the Royal Society in which he suggested that the prodigious flights of pigeons in the colonies rendered probable the existence of an unseen, near-at-hand satellite, from which came these myriads of birds, and to which they were wont to retreat again. But the English colonists who touched elbows with Nature, and had larger opportunities for observation than their island ancestors, came to accept the annual migration of the disappearing birds before the middle of the eighteenth century. There were, however, learned pundits in Philadelphia as late as 1800, who followed Olaus in wintering their swallows in the bottoms of the rivers.

VIII.

Other phases of thought regarding animals and plants.

Classification, which is at once the result of knowledge and an instrument of investigation, was infantile and unstable even among the learned.

Fishes, including, of course, sea mammals, had been divided into round and long; to these Harrison adds shelled fishes and legged fishes. Popular classification is always rough, but in that day nobody held firmly to the cardinal division of the vertebrate animals. The beaver and otter were even divided transversely in classification; their hind quarters were counted with the fishes. In ecclesiastical regulations it was not always thought worth while to make two bites of a beaver; Lorrainers and Savoyards, as well as Canadian woodsmen, ate freely of his flesh on fish days, making sure that the meat of so aquatic an animal with so flat a tail could not be flesh. The interest in animal life was unscientific, being mainly an interest in the marvelous stories of the basilisk hatched from a cock's egg brooded by a toad, of the unicorn with a horn eight or ten feet long growing out of his head, of the salamander that endured the fire, of the phœnix that lived five hundred years, of the common hare that changed sex in alternate years, of men that were metamorphosed into wolves in Ireland, of wolves that struck men dumb by seeing them first, of swans that sing before dying, and so on and on. Wonders were not wanting among American animals; the unicorn was observed on the Hudson, and many half-human creatures, reported by early voyagers, dwelt along the seacoast from Cape Ann eastward. Sometimes these were seen at night dancing in groups about a fire on the shore; one daring Triton swimming in Casco Bay

CHAP. I.

Holinshed, i, 377.

Russell's Boke of Nurture, Early English Text Society, v, 153, and note from Topsell.

Salmon's English Physician, 324.

Harrison, Holinsh., i, 379.

On Unicorns, Brown's Travels, in Harris Voyages, ii, 524. Ray in same, 554.

Hakewill's Apologie, "Of divers opinions justly suspected though commonly received," lib. c, 1, sect. 5.

Two Voyages, 25.

CHAP. I.

Compare Browne's Vulgar Errors generally and Shakespeare in many places.

made bold to grasp the side of a canoe and got his hand lopped off with a hatchet. Narrating these occurrences, Josselyn meditates that "there are many stranger things in the world than are to be seen between London and Stanes." We are accustomed to see popular credulity controlled by scientific skepticism, but in the seventeenth century the learned looked for scientific knowledge primarily in the writings of the ancients, sacred and profane, and devoured most of the atrocious stories accumulated by Pliny, "the greatest gull of antiquity." When modern light began to dawn and science tried to observe, it was not mainly the ordinary and the regular that were noted; members of the new Royal Society and others thought to learn from the monstrosities and marvels; New England ministers acted as soothsayers and expounded the hidden meaning of monstrous births, and even played showmen to exhibit these ghastly messages from the Almighty.

Comp. Sewall's Diary, ii, 493.

IX.

The world invisible.

The world invisible as conceived in every age is a reflection of the familiar material world; the image is often inverted: it may be exaggerated, glorified, distorted, but it is still their own old world mirrored in the clouds of heaven. Even the love of rank and ostentation in the seventeenth century—the snobbery of the age—projected itself into heavenly arrangements. In a day when idle serving men stood about the halls of a country gentleman merely to lend dignity to the master, when one no greater than a high sheriff thought it unfit to perform his functions without a squad of liveried retainers at his heels, when a bishop in Christian humility rode about with sometimes a hundred and fifty horsemen clanking after him, and when kingly state was multitudinous in proportion, the majesty of Almighty God required myriads of attendants. Milton thinks thus of God:

Sonnet xix.

> His State
> Is Kingly. Thousands at his bidding speed
> And post o'er Land and Ocean without rest.

And the prose of Bishop Hall is almost as lofty as Milton's verse, when it contemplates "those next-to-infinite numbers of mighty and majestical spirits, wherewith the great God of heaven hath furnished his throne and footstool." Human arithmetic had no terms by which to tell the number of those who "are numerable only to God who made them." The uncountable angels were employed in keeping the universe in motion, as many eminent writers knew partly by intuition, but also by metaphysical demonstration. The busy angels turned round the crystalline spheres from the outer *primum mobile*, just this side the immovable abode of God, to the nethermost of all that carried the moon about in her lagging revolutions. Besides this duty of keeping the lights of heaven burning and turning, "these mighty

The Invisible World, ed. 1659, p. 15.

As above, p. 18.

The good angels.

Digby's Peripatetical Institutions, 362, 398.

Hakewill's Apologie, 85, 86.

CHAP. I.

angels" produced those "strange concussations of the earth" which are so alarming and "direfull prodigies in the skie," about which it was not deemed safe to speculate. Hall relates that one philosopher was stricken dead for venturing to reason about thunderstorms. It was angelic agency that caused a corpse, in that believing age, to bleed when touched by the guilty hand of the murderer. Angels gave warnings and revelations by dreams, by mental impressions and by apparitions; and they even fought for men against the spirits of the underworld. Of such stuff as this the great Puritan poet wrought the splendid fabric of his epic. To contemporary readers Paradise Lost had as much of history as of poetry. It was an imaginative rendering of the picturesque mythology of the seventeenth century, a mythology destined to grow dim in the gray morning light of the critical century that followed.

Hall's Invisible World, 39, and *passim.*

Increase Mather's Illustrious Providences.

X.

The evil angels.

The American settlers lived in a different world from that which they had left in England, and their conceptions of the invisible could not escape modification. Far removed from the ostentatious conventions of the old civilization, the minds of the colonists could no longer form vivid pictures of heavenly retinues. One finds few allusions to angelic agency in their writings; thunderbolts which Bishop Hall, "the English Seneca," as he

Note 16.

was called, ascribes to good angels, Cotton Mather, the New England Seneca, will have to be the work of devils; on this hypothesis he easily explains the disproportionate number of churches that suffered from lightning. The popular belief of the time in the active meddling of evil spirits was not weakened by a life passed in coast settlements, between a wide and wild sea and an impenetrable forest filled with beasts and devil-worshipers. Diabolical disturbances occurred rather early in all the colonies, and they were particularly rife in New England, where the imagination was set on edge by theological speculation. In 1637 Jane Hawkins, the Boston midwife and dispenser of quackery oil of mandrakes, was diligently examined on suspicion of familiarity with the devil. Eight years later a man from Virginia, reported to have skill in necromancy, was "blown up" in Boston Harbor, and strange to say it was accounted a marvel that he could never afterward be found. Yet more diabolical was it that men in fiery shapes, or "fire in the shape of men," walked the water near where the ship had exploded. In the settlement on the Connecticut devils were particularly active. Hartford, Stratford, Fairfield, and New Haven had witch trials, and in some instances the ordeal of swimming the witch to see whether she could float was resorted to. Springfield was accounted "infamous by reason of the witches there," as the traveler Josselyn tells us. More than one Long Island town had its shallows

Cotton's Way of the Churches Cleared, 91. Savage's Winthrop, i, 313, 316, ii, 10, 11.

Mass. Rec., 12, March, 1637.

Winthrop, ii, 185. Hutch. Papers, 136.

Increase Mather's Providences, 96–99, and other authorities.

Comp. Mass. Rec., iii, 295, 347. Hutch. Mass., i, 179. Wonder-working Providences, iii, 2. S. Side Signal, Nov. 13, 1880.

CHAP. I.

stirred by witchcraft accusations. Boston brought its first witch to trial in 1648, and in 1656 the wife of one of the magistrates was "hanged for a witch only for having more wit than her neighbors," as was said at the time. In 1654 a shipmaster sailing with emigrants to Maryland encountered two months of stormy weather, such weather as only "the malevolence of witches" could get up. The crew selected a little old woman of suitable appearance, one Mary Lee, whom they examined "with strictest scrutiny, guilty or not guilty." The poor old body was hanged "out of hand," and all her possessions were huddled into the sea with her, but the hungry tempest would not be quieted by the hideous sacrifice. There were sporadic witch excitements sooner or later in nearly every colony; miniature reflections of what was passing at the time in Europe.

Barber's N. Y. Coll., 462.

Mass. Rec., iii, 123.

Letters of Missionaries, 91.

Md. Council Proceedings, 306-308.

Comp. Gatford's Public Good, 12, where is a loose statement of same fact.

Comp., e. g., Ridgely's Annals of Annapolis, 58 ff. and others.

XI.

Witchcraft.

The ancient belief in witchcraft, though never extinct, passed through a sort of renascence in the religious excitements of the sixteenth century. As early as 1548 newborn Protestant zeal against superstition began to attack all kinds of sorcery, and there was also opposition to various popular superstitions in Catholic countries. The charms by which women sought to mitigate the sorrows of childbearing were special subjects of ecclesiastical inquisition in England in the first year of Elizabeth's reign. The tendency of this was to make a

Note 17.

Cranmer's Articles of Visitation, 2. Edw. VI, Sparrow's Coll., 31.

witch of every midwife and wise woman who encouraged her patients by little quackeries. The trial of a supposed witch by weighing her wizened form in the balances against the huge church Bible bound in heavy boards with metal clasps, or by tying her thumbs and her toes together crosswise to see whether she would float when put into the water, attracted a concourse of people and spread abroad the horrible superstition. "Swimming witches" became a favorite amusement of the brutal populace. "Our Countrey people," says an English writer in 1718, "are still as fond of it as they are of Baiting a Bear or a Bull." The notoriety and outcry served for a sort of devil's advertisement; the afflicted were everywhere set to brooding on the probability that some malicious neighbor or some doted old woman of uncanny aspect had laid them under a spell. The attempt to put down witchery by the infliction of the death penalty served to breed new alarms, new accusations, and fresh executions. In the time of the civil war and the Commonwealth there were infectious witch panics in England. In Essex and Sussex alone two hundred persons were prosecuted for witchcraft, and half of them were executed. Medical skill was dangerous in a time of suspicion. Meric Casaubon saw a clever woman doctor driven from a town because she had benefited a lunatic patient. It was evident to the populace that nothing less than sorcery could relieve a demoniac. In 1646 James Howell wrote: "There have been

But compare Reprouacion de las Supersticiones, by P. Liruelo, of Salamanca, 1547, and others.

Art. Visitation, I Eliz., Sparrow's Coll., 180.

Note 18.

Fr. Hutchinson, Hist. Essay on Witchcr., 137, 138.

Casaubon's Enthusiasme, 1656, p. 100.

Familiar Letters, 398.

CHAP. I.

Commentaire sur Beccaria, ix.

more witches Arraign'd and Executed heer lately than ever were in this Island since the Creation." "All the tribunals of Christian Europe resounded with such condemnations," says Voltaire of this period. The poor Turks had never a witch or demoniac among them, a proof positive that their religion was false; the devil sparing his own. It was estimated, on the other hand, that the judges of Christian lands had sent more than a hundred thousand people to death on the gallows or at the stake for the crime of witchcraft.

XII.

Descended from hobgoblins.

The classic dignity of Milton's evil angels, when marshaled "in battailous aspect," is the work of the poet. The sprites of popular fancy in that age were groveling and grotesque. They made silly contracts with doting crones whom they persuaded to write their names with their own blood in a book, and that without any valuable consideration; they held burlesque religious exercises and dug up dead men's bones to enchant with. They were of the sort that masqueraded as dogs and cats, and hares and toads. They haunted houses for the mere fun of terrifying the inmates; they took possession of hysterical people and talked nonsense from their lips, and they tangled the manes of horses in the night for mere wanton deviltry. The antipathies of these demons were equally incomprehensible. They could be frightened away by hanging up lucky stones with natural holes in them, or discarded horseshoes, or better still by burying "witch-jugs" full of horseshoe nails under a threshold, or by the hanging up of fresh bays about a house. They were sometimes known to the witches who were their familiars by such names as Pluck, Vinegar Tom, Catch, Hard-name, Jarmara, Elemauzer, Pyewacket, Peckin-the-Crown, and Smack. Sprites like these are not primarily the offspring of theological speculation; they resemble the gnomes, trolls, and brownies, the Hudekins, Robin Goodfellows, and Friar Rushs of the tales and ballads. They have floated down from ancient heathen times on the stream of nursery and fireside folk-lore. But they had ceased to be regarded with awed amusement as were their progenitors the gnomes and fairies. They had come to be denounced from pulpits and accused of grewsome and horrible acts suited to their new position as Christian devils.

Notes and Queries, vol. vi, No. 151, p. 271.

Mather's Providences, chap. v.

Retrospective Review, v, 122.

Hutch., Hist. Essay on Witchcraft, 1718, p. 103.

See Wright's Literature and Superstition of England, vol. ii, essay x; and Comp. Douce's Shakespeare, i, 382–394.

XIII.

This grotesque superstition could not be disentangled from the creed of the time. Jurists like the astute Coke and the conscientious Sir Matthew Hale, and even such philosophers as Lord Bacon and Sir Thomas Browne, were helpless to rid themselves of it. It was part of what we may call the fixed intellect of the age. The people who first saw on the stage Shakespeare's "secret, black,

Realism of devils.

See A Tryal of Witches, 1664, before Sir Matthew Hale, especially Sir T. Browne's

CHAP. I.

and midnight hags" were no doubt touched with a ghastlier horror than the æsthetic shudder this apparition affords in later times, for the diabolical dance of witches concocting infernal spells had then the force of daring realism. "That there are evill spirits," says Bishop Hall, "is no lesse certaine then that there are men. . . . That evill spirits have given certaine proofes of their presence with men, both in visible apparitions and in the possessions of places and bodies, is no lesse manifest then that we have soules." But God had "bound up the evill Angels in chaines of darknesse." This was to restrain them from frightening God's "weake creatures" by "those frequent and horrible appearances which they would otherwise make." It was God's pleasure sometimes to "loosen or lengthen" the chains and permit these diabolonians "to exhibit themselves under some assumed shapes unto men," which gives the eminent casuist occasion to discuss "what our deportment should be" when a devil whose chain has been temporarily slackened "exhibits" himself to us. This very materialistic conception of the devils in chains like mastiffs is not peculiar to Hall. It was a trait of thought at the time. It occurs more than once in Increase Mather, as "the Lord doth sometimes lengthen the chain which the infernal lions are bound fast in," and so on. In the trials at Salem we repeatedly come upon the expression in a grossly literal sense.

testimony, p. 41, and Hale's Charge, 55, 56.

Note 19.

Hall's Cases of Conscience, Dec. 3, Case I.

Illustrious Providences, ed. 1856, p. 120.

See Upham in many places.

XIV.

Haunted houses.

The notion of house-haunting demons—a superstition the most nearly a survival from the days of the elves and brownies—crossed the sea with the early emigrants. One such spirit in Newbury in New Hampshire, in 1679, threw sticks and stones on the roof of the house, lifted up the bedstead from the floor, threw the bedstaff out the window, threw a cat at the mistress of the house and beat the goodman over the head with a broom, made the pole on which the kettles were hung to dance up and down in the chimney, tossed a potlid into the fire, set a chair in the middle of the table when dinner was served, seasoned the victuals with ashes, filled a pair of shoes with hot ashes, ran away with an inkhorn, threw a ladder against a door, and put an awl into the bed. It played a hundred other lively pranks until "it pleased God to shorten the chain of this wicked demon." While the chain was shortening the disheartened demon was heard to cry six times over, "Alas! me knock no more!" In Hartford, in 1683, there was a gentle devil with a taste for flinging corncobs through the windows and down the chimney. Stones and sticks were sometimes thrown, but softly so as to do no serious harm. When the occupant of the haunted house returned to its owner a chest of clothes unjustly detained, no more corncobs were thrown. In Portsmouth it rained stones outdoors and in at the house of George Walton, and, what is curi

Mather's Providences, 101, 110, ed. 1856.

CHAP. I.

Comp. burning of Bingen by devils, Inc. Mather's Cases of Conscience, 18, and other stories, ibid., *passim*.

ous, some of these stones were hot. Glass windows were shattered, and a stirrup iron traveled off on its own motion without horse or rider and was never again seen. Sometimes a hollow whistling sound was heard. This whistling devil amused himself like a true brownie by hanging the haycocks up in the trees and decorating the kitchen "all up and down" with wisps of hay. Sometimes the chains were sufficiently lengthened for a New England demon to become visible. One appeared as a "black-a-moor child," another as a woman clad in green safeguard, short blue cloak, and white cap. Once the black cat, so dear to tradition, appeared and was shot at; again the head of a man was seen swimming through the water, followed a little way off by the tail of a white cat. These American devils with their undiabolical sense of humor have at least a family likeness to the mischievous elves, pucks, brownies, and other "tricksy sprites" with which the English imagination peopled lonesome glens and the dark corners of their houses in primitive times. Whether the later demons were creatures of excited fancy or of imposture, or both, they were cast in molds supplied by ancient tradition.

Note 20.

XV.

Demoniacal possession.

The phenomena known in later times as hysteria, and as mesmerism and hypnotism, were not yet recognized to be due to natural causes. The infinitely delicate shadings by which mental sanity passes without any line of demarcation into madness could not then be imagined. A belief in demoniacal possession was almost unavoidable. That men and women might be "obsessed with cacodemons," in the pedantic phrase of the time, had the sanction of the ages, of religion, and of science itself. Only the most hardy intellects ventured to question an opinion so well supported.

Inc. Mather, Cases of Conscience concerning Witchcraft, 31.

In the Massachusetts town of Groton, in 1671, occurred a case of well-defined hysteria. The village minister naturally concluded that the violent contortions and "ravings" of the patient, Elizabeth Knap, "represented a dark resemblance to hellish torments." When in one of her fits she cried out, "What cheer, old man?" to whom could she be speaking if not to the devil? Like many other hysterical sufferers, she was susceptible to hypnotic suggestion, and in answer to leading questions she was able to remember having made the compact with Satan always presupposed in such cases. This in saner moments she retracted, as she did also accusations of witchcraft made against others in reply to probing inquiries. She once described to the shuddering bystanders a witch visible to her at that moment, having a dog's body and a woman's head, running through the room and climbing up the chimney. Good Parson Willard and others present found all this so exciting that they, though unable to see the apparition, could detect the imprint of a dog's foot in the clay daubing of the chimney.

S. A. Green's Groton in Witchcraft Times.

CHAP. I.

XVI.

Agency of religious fervor.

Worst element of all in this delusion was the mistaken zeal of the clergy. Ministers of differing creeds agreed in believing that the palpable evidences of spiritual existence afforded by witchcraft might serve to vanquish the ever-present skepticism regarding the supernatural. Squalid tales gathered at witch trials, many of them foul and revolting as well as unbelievable, were disseminated as religious reading, in hope that they might prove a means of grace by revulsion. If any man had the courage to question the supernatural character of these disgusting apparitions, he found himself gazetted in the authoritative writings of eminent divines as a Sadducee, a patron of witches, and a witch advocate; if he took a neutral position for safety, averring the existence of witchcraft but denying the possibility of proving it in particular cases, he was dubbed a "nullibist." This in America as well as in England. A new case of witchcraft did not excite pity, but something like exultation; the Sadducees were again confounded. The Puritan ram's horn of Increase Mather answered across the seas to the bugle of Glanvill, chaplain in ordinary to Charles II, and late in the century the good Richard Baxter himself re-echoed Cotton Mather's shout of victory amid the horrors of the judicial massacre at Salem. Reports of continental witch trials were translated for the edification of Englishmen. By this array of frightful diabolism it was

Glanvill's Sadducismus Triumphatus, and I. Mather's Providences, *passim*. Comp. Sprengel's Geschichte der Arzneikunde, edition 1803, iv, 341, note 4.

hoped that the swelling tide of gross immorality might be checked and religion promoted, for the appeal of religion in that day was to fear rather than to aspiration; the peril of trying to kindle altar fires with embers from hell was not understood.

XVII.

The Salem Witchcraft.

Salem village, an outlying suburb, two or three miles from Salem proper, was almost a frontier town in 1692. Men still wore buckskin breeches and hats with a brim narrow in front and long behind. Wolves, bears, and catamounts were trapped. Some of the settlers had participated in the desperate battle at the Narragansetts' town sixteen years before. The sword and the rapier were still worn at the side, the fowling piece six and seven feet in length was in use. Men had been killed by the Indians in the bounds of Salem within three years. Education was generally neglected; even men of substance were sometimes unable to write. The old patriarchs who had made the settlement had just died off; the community had lost its steadfast guides. New clergymen had come in and new magistrates, not with the education of England, but with the scantier training of New England—a training in which the felling axe was more important than the Latin grammar. The new clergy, men of the second and third generations, were, with a few exceptions, profoundly impressed with the necessity of believing anything ghostly or horrible; the supernatural was the basis of their piety. Increase Mather, the bishop by brevet of New England, had published books on the ominous eclipses of 1680 and 1682, and another in 1686 on Illustrious Providences, which was a storehouse of those dragons' teeth that bore such ample fruit in 1692. His abler but less judicious son, Cotton, had issued a book on "Memorable Providences relating to witchcraft and Possessions." It had come to a second edition in the very year before the horrors of Salem.

The village of Salem had the elements needed for a witchcraft mania—a quarrel between minister and people; a circle of young girls from eleven to twenty, including some who worked as helps, who met at the minister's house and practiced together folk-sorcery and that kind of divining that has been the amusement of such for ages. These girls soon began to manifest symptoms of hysteria and hypnotism; one or two married women also had "fits" in sympathy with them. A doctor called to attend them decided that they were afflicted by "an evil hand." There was some heartless and heedless imposture, no doubt, in what followed, but there was also much of self-deception.

The glimpses of the infernal world that we get in Salem are highly incredible. The witches say prayers to a tall black man with a high-crowned hat—always with a high-crowned hat. They ride on sticks and poles, sometimes they are on brooms, and sometimes three are on one pole. One relates that a pole carrying two broke, but, by holding fast to the one in front of her, the witch got safe to her destination. The witches fondle yellow birds, suckling them between their fingers, and one day a girl cries out in meeting that a yellow bird sits on the minister's hat as it hangs on a pin on the pulpit. The witch usually sits on the great cross-beam of the meetinghouse, fondling the yellow bird. One man was seen to nurse two black pigs at his breasts. Sometimes a hog, sometimes a black dog, appears and says, "Serve me." Then the dog or pig "looks like a man," and this man has a yellow bird. Cats naturally abound, white cats and red cats and cats without color. Once a man struck with a rapier at a place designated by one of the girls, and she declared the cat dead and the floor to be all covered with blood. But no one else saw it. This is probably hypnotism, hardly imposture. A great mass of such inconsequent and paltry foolery was believed, not alone by owl-blasted children, but by Stoughton and the other judges, and by pious Samuel Sewall himself, more's the pity! Where is the motive? What prompted the most eminent Christians and leading citizens to prefer so base a life—companions to cats and dogs and devils? Why did this torture of innocent children, this mischief-working witchcraft with endless perdition at the tail of it, give pleasure to rational creatures? The court never once thought to ask.

CHAP. I.

The trial scenes were perdition. The "afflicted children" screamed, went into spasms, shouted, charged the prisoners with torturing them, and their apparent torments were frightful. They laid to the charge of the accused unheard-of deviltries, such as the killing of wives long dead, attempting to choke aged grandparents, and what not besides. Husbands in some instances turned against wives, in others they adhered to them, were accused themselves, and died with them.

The trials were accompanied by great cruelties. Officers of the law were allowed to plunder the estates of the accused of all movable property. The prisoners had to pay their jail expenses, and many families were utterly impoverished. Prisoners were cast into the dungeon and were "fettered." Goodman Hutchinson complained of certain prisoners for tormenting his wife; additional fetters were put on them, after which Mrs. Hutchinson was "tolerable well." Some were tortured to make them confess; lads were laid neck and heels until the blood gushed from their noses. These were accredited practices at the time. Several died in prison.

The very skill of the accused was against them. One very neat woman walked miles over dirty roads without showing any mud. "I scorn to be drabbled," she said, and she was hanged for her cleanliness. George Burroughs, the minister, was a strong man, much addicted to gymnastics. He carried barrels of cider by inserting his fingers into the bunghole, and held a seven-foot gun at arm's length. He was the devil's man, away with him to the gallows! The first people in the colony became involved. Twenty in all were executed, four or five at a time. Their bodies were ignominiously thrust into holes at the place where they were executed and were scantly covered.

There were brave men and women among them. Giles Corey, an eccentric old man, had at first signed an affidavit of uncertainty about his wife, a woman of piety, and, strange to say, an entire unbeliever in witchcraft. Two of his sons-in-law turned against her, two were for her. But when old Giles was accused he stiffened his neck. He would save his property, which was considerable and might be compromised; he would will it all to his two faithful sons-in-law. He would prove his steadfastness. He made a will, perfect in every part, giving his property to the sons-in-law, and then totally refused to plead and was slowly pressed to death. The constancy of the old man did much to overthrow the partisans of witchcraft. Joseph Putnam, a young man of twenty-two, declared his detestation of the doctrine. He kept some one of his horses bridled and saddled for six months. He armed all his family, and it was understood that he must be taken, if taken at all, pistol in hand. When the mania was at its height he refused to have his child baptized in the village, but carried it to Salem.

The excitement had risen with every arrest. More than fifty badgered souls had confessed that they were witches. Some had fled the country. But the wide extent of the accusations produced a change in the minds of the people. They knew not who would be struck at next. The governor, at length, refused to call the special court together, and after a tedious confinement a hundred and fifty were released by proclamation. The population of Salem had decreased, its business had suffered, and perhaps it never recovered its prosperity. Slowly the people got over the delusion and came to realize the incalculable and irretrievable harm that had been wrought. Judge Sewall, at a general fast, handed up to the minister to be read a humble confession, and stood while it was read. He annually kept a private day of humiliation. Honor to his memory! The twelve jurymen also signed an affecting paper asking to be forgiven. Cotton Mather, who had been very conspicuous and had published a book about it, never acknowledged himself wrong in this or any other matter. From the time it became unpopular he speaks of the witchcraft trials in a far-away manner, as if they were wholly the work of some one else. He was never forgiven, and probably never ought to have been.

Note 21.

The revulsion was complete. No witches were tried or hanged or "swimmed" in America after the Salem trials. In half a lifetime more the ardor of the English people visibly abated, and few witches were thereafter arrested in England.

ELUCIDATIONS.

Note 1, page 4.

In 1638 there was published anonymously the voyage of Domingo Gonzales to the moon, in which clever bit Godwin, Bishop of Hereford, anticipated some of the traits of Bergerac's A Voyage to the Moon, of Robinson Crusoe, of Gulliver's Travels, of Peter Wilkins and his Flying Wife, and even of Mr. Stockton's Negative Gravity, to say nothing of Hans Pfaal, in which Poe imitated the story with purpose aforethought—and I know not how many tales besides. But what interests us most is that under cover of a fantastic story, said to have been written about 1603, the bishop declares himself on the side of Copernicus and Galileo, and suggests the doctrine of gravity propounded by Newton at a later period. On time of writing Antony à Wood, Ath. Oxon., i, 582, second edition, Hallam, part iii, chapter vii, Wilkins, Bishop of Chester, an able mathematician, published anonymously in 1640 two treatises, the first to prove that "the moon may be a world," the second arguing that the earth is a planet. They are reprinted in his mathematical works. See a character of Wilkins in the life of Seth, Bishop of Salisbury, 27. As late as 1660 Peacham's Compleat Gentleman gives an account of the ancient system of Ptolemy, and does not think it worth while to inform the polite reader that any other notion of the universe had ever been suggested.

Note 2, page 4.

George Sandys, who died in 1643, and who was the poet secretary to the Virginia colony, wrote in his old age of the firmament·

> With such undiscerned swiftness hurl'd
> About the steadfast center of the world,
> Against whose rapid course the restless sun
> And wand'ring flames in varied motions run.
> Which heat, light, life infuse, time, night and day
> Distinguish, in our human bodies sway, etc.

Note 3, page 4.

In 1666 Samuel Danforth published, in Cambridge, Mass., a book entitled An Astronomical Description of the Late Comet or Blazing Star. It was reprinted in London. He maintained that its orbit was elliptical, and that its center of motion was not the earth—a long stride toward Copernicus. He proved that it was a celestial luminary by its size, its parallax, its duration, its visibility in many countries, etc., and concludes that it is a "planetick or erratick body." It was observed without instruments. Alex-

CHAP. I.

ander Nowell, a Harvard graduate of the previous year, published an almanac in which he argues in opposition to the old notion that planets have no light of their own, and in 1667 he issued a little booklet which I have not seen, Josselyn's Voyages to New England, 47–52, if indeed Josselyn has not confused the almanac with an imaginary booklet. In 1674 a thesis for the master's degree at Harvard affirmed the old opinion that the starry heavens were of fire, but in 1688 it was maintained that the material of the celestial and terrestrial bodies were the same, which may have been as far in the direction of the new astronomy as it was safe to go at that time. Young's Subjects for Master's Degree, 15. On the notion of the heavenly bodies as free from gravitation, compare Hakewill's Apologie, 1630: "They are not subject to the qualities of heat and cold, or drought and moisture, nor yet to weight and lightnesse which arise from those qualities," p. 73. "Light bodies naturally moove vpward and heavy downwarde, that which is neither light nor heavy is rather disposed to a circular motion," etc., p. 86. See a passage on pp. 85 and 86 on the various hypotheses of celestial motion. In the entire discussion this English divine, learned in the lore of the day, does not think it worth while to mention Copernicus or Tycho, or either of his own great contemporaries, Kepler or Galileo. The Copernican theory was a stone rejected of the builders.

Note 4, page 5.

The calculation is based on the "decumbiture or the time when sickness envaded or ceased [seized] on Allice Wilkins," which was January 11, 1656, at 6 P. M. This is the only American case of which I know any record. "That ye pty is really sick is evident in yt the lord of ye ascendant is not in essential dignity, but in his detriment & in ye six house and is in configuration with bad planets, thein freindly aspects which signifye the disease will not bee exceeding greate. And in yt there is a melancholly signe in the six house, and his lord of a melancholly nature, we may judge the rise of the desease to proceed from melancholly, and all so choler doth much abound and the bloud corrupted with melancholly humorus the pts affected are these, viz., the heart and back." So runs on our astrologer until "the stone of the kidneys" is somewhat suddenly hit upon as the disease. The book is in the Winthrop collection in the New York Society Library. There was formerly care taken to administer medicine when the "sign came right"; laxatives were to be given when the moon was in Libra or other favorable constellations, and the approach of Saturn was to be guarded against because that malign planet congealed the humors and remedies in the body. Aristotelis Secretum Secretorum, folio xxv, 1528, in Latin black letter. This work, attributed to Aristotle, was often printed in Latin, and was translated into English in the reign of Henry VIII.

Note 5, page 5.

Porta in liber, xiv, caput iii, under the title Vt aves tenescant, explains that meat exposed to the rays of the moon became more tender, this tenderness being but a form of putrefaction. So wood more rapidly decays, and fruits mature, in the moonshine.

Note 6, page 6.

Archdeacon Hakewill, in his Apologie, traces the regulation of farm processes by the changes of the moon to Pliny and Aristotle, and even to Hesiod. Hakewill mentions the moon's supposed influence on lunatics, the selenite, a stone whose light is said to wax and wane with the moon, the tides, etc. "The physitian in opening a veine hath ever an eie to the sign then raigning." Edition of 1630, pp. 71 and 72. "Mr. Camden observes that the towne of Shrewesbery suffered twice most grievous losse of life by fire within the compasse of fiftie years vpon two severall eclypses of the sunne in Aries," p. 151. Hakewill thinks the stars "not signes only," but "causes of immoderate cold or heat, drought or moysture, lightning, thunder, raging windes, inundations, earthquakes, and consequently of famine and pestilence"; but he admits that "the prognostication . . . is very vncertane." The popularity of astrology in the seventeenth century is manifest from the frequent references to it, and from the great number of books published on the subject. The doctrine of correspondence connected astrology closely with every other science. Some of the clergy opposed it. See, for example, Henry King's sermon at St. Paul's, 1621, p. 25, and, earlier, Hall's Satires. liber ii, satire vii. As early as 1577, indeed, the Bishop of Winchester, writing to Sir W. More, says that he would gladly know the opinion of astrologers relative to the "tayled star." He would "gladly learn what they find in the lower heavens, for to the higher they never will ascend." Losely MSS., 491. The reader may compare Hakewill's Apologie, 126, 128, edition of 1630. The troublous time of the great rebellion led many in England to see signs in the heavens, and brought about an increase of interest in astrology. The opinions prevailing more and more among the best-informed men of the time are set forth

CHAP. I.

briefly and with much moderation in the Spanish work Magia Natural, o Ciencia de Filosofia Ocvlta, written by Castrillo, a Jesuit, and published 1649. See especially chapter xi of the first part, in which Castrillo concludes that "the movements or aspects of the heavens are not certain indications of free acts and contingent consequences, for these are subject to changes independently of them." Folio 17, reverse.

Note 7, page 6.

These words are attributed to Danforth by Josselyn. Danforth's book on the comet of 1666 I have not seen. But I find the passage in Nowell's Cambridge Almanac of 1666, the date of the London edition of Danforth. I have therefore credited them to Nowell.

Note 8, page 8.

The discussion of the significance of comets by Kepler in his De Cometis, published in 1619, is an interesting example of a great mind deriding the vulgar astrological notions on the subject, and yet feeling a necessity for some rational explanation of the generally believed connection between comets and disasters. His explanation seems to the modern mind insufficient enough, and he was himself little content with it. "Haec igitur est, si vlla est, naturalis connexio horum euentuum cum Cometa." It would have been but a short step from this to the rejection of calamitous comets, head and tail. The works that treat of the ominous character of comets were a considerable element in the literature of Europe in the seventeenth century. Christiani, in 1633, declares that man but a stranger in history who denies that God threatens this "worn-out world" by means of dreadful comets, multiplied by suns, and other portentous phenomena. The passage is quoted by Voëtius in his Excertatio de Prognosticus Cometarum, 1665. Voëtius lays stress on the universal consent both of learned and vulgar to the bad reputation of comets. Dr. John Spencer, afterward Dean of Ely, protested in a learned and liberal little book that comets were not ominous. In this Discourse concerning Prodigies, 1663, this large-minded divine maintains that God has no use for "any such winding and squint-ey'd Oracles" as those of the heathen. He aptly characterizes the traditionary science of that day in a single phrase: "A Series of many Assertours which (like persons in the dark) shut their eyes and take care onely to hold fast by those which went before them." First edition, p. 72. The ridicule in Boileau's Arrêt Burlesque in 1671 shows that the belief in such portents was waning. Œuvres de Boileau, edition of 1821, iii, 120. The notable comet of 1680, which brought the English colonists to the point of talking about reforming their morals, brought forth Pierre Bayle's work, into which he built a great many other thlngs besides comets. It also awakened discussion in Mexico. Sigurenza y Gorgora, a Mexican priest, published in 1681 his Manifesto filosofico contra los Cometas, in which he opposed the popular dread.

Note 9, page 9.

The larva of this insect, known to us as the army worm, was regarded with similar wonder in Massachusetts. In the probably unique copy of a New England almanac for 1649, preserved in the New York Public Library, an appearance of them in 1646 is set down in the chronology of marvelous events, as is also a great flight of pigeons. The conventional bit of verse at the foot of one of the pages is devoted to these omens, ending with the couplet:

> But suddenly to flight they all prepare,
> No man knows how unless it was by pray'r.

There will soon be left no living eyewitness of the flights of wild pigeons which were seen in the colonies and continued to occur occasionally in the Ohio Valley a little later than the middle of the nineteenth century. Let me here record my personal testimony that no account which I have seen gives an adequate conception of the incredible size of these vast flocks, which followed one another at short intervals sometimes during an entire day. The apparition seems not to have been so frequent in Virginia as elsewhere, and it was the more terrible in 1675 because it had last occurred before the great Indian massacre of 1644.

Note 10, page 10.

See the strange notions on the propagation of bees in the Insectorum of Movertus, 1634, pp. 12, 13. He says that rustic experience confirms the opinión of famous men that bees are bred from the putrefaction of bulls, oxen, cows, and calves. Kings and leaders among the bees are produced from the brain and spinal marrow, common bees from the flesh. My copy of Movertus has on the margin a note in the handwriting of the learned Vossius, who died in 1649. This is much nearer the truth. Vossius says that the "seed" of the "king" bee, laid in single cells, is like a poppy seed, and from it the little grubs are produced. Movertus, or, as his name is in English, Mouffet, was the first authoritative writer on insects in England. His work was translated in 1658 into English, but I have not had access to an English version. Butler's Feminine Monarchie, published in 1634, the same year with Movertus, shows how much the practical bee-keeper knew

CHAP. I.

that was not suspected by the man of science. Butler holds the principal bee to be a female, but does not know that she was the only fertile female. He knows the drones to be males, and he does not mention the spontaneous generation of bees from bullocks, which had come down from more than two thousand years on the authority of Aristotle and other classic writers. John Baptist Porta, in his Magia Naturalis, 1644, page 53, quotes from Ovid a passage about bodies that in wasting are changed to little animals—in parva animalia verti—and this of the birth of flower-gathering bees from the waste of slaughtered beeves:

> "deputri viscere passim
> Florilegae nascuntur apes."

This passage suggests the absence of any considerable power of scientific observation in centuries preceding the eighteenth. A recent French writer says of the seventeenth: "L'esprit d'observation et à fortiori d'expérimentation, qui nous semble si natural à l'homme d'étude, était à peine né. . . . Quand quelque fait contredisait trop ouvertement la théorie, ils s'en tiraient par une subtilité." Folet, Molière, et la Médecine, 61.

Note 11, page 11.

The Gentleman Instructed, 1713, p. 316: "He shews us what our idoliz'd Bodies are by the Infection of Lice, Worms, and Toads they produce." Movertus, Insectorum Theatrum, 1634, explains the rise of differing parasites on various parts of the human body, p. 260: "Ex humoribus carne adipe, sudoribusque corruptis ortum habent omnes pediculi; et pro loci humorisque natura longe differunt." The generation of such parasites he regards as an unmistakable sign of misery and sometimes an inevitable scourge of God. This was the notion that Nathaniel Bacon's opponents made the most of in Virginia. On vital products of the putrid humors of the human body, see Levinus Lemnius De Miracvlis Occvltis Natvræ, liber iv, page 403 (1604). Lemnius says that snakes are produced from the decay of the spinal marrow.

> Art can beget bees, hornets, beetles, wasps,
> Out of the carcases . . . of creatures;
> Yea, scorpions of an herb, being rightly placed.
>
> Ben Jonson's Alchemist, act ii, scene 1.

Note 12. page 11.

Lord Bacon's Natural History, section 696, discusses the generation of insects. Moths originate, he says, in woolen fabrics, especially those in a moist condition. Bacon had got as far as to suppose that creatures spontaneously generated sometimes reproduce their kind by procreation. Compare section 900. Dade's Almanac for 1684 says that an unusual number of frogs, flies, locusts, and so on, is a sign of a pestilential season. "For these creatures, being ingendered of Putrefaction, shew a general disposition of the Year and constitution of the Aire to Putrefaction." In one of the early volumes of the Royal Society's Transactions is a proposition to produce cochineal dye in England by generation of insects from putrefaction. Sir Kenelm Digby, then much esteemed, says that the earth at the outset was most "aptly tempered and dispos'd" and "brought forth perfect animals; as it now being barrener, of its own accord, produces such as we call insecta, as Mice and Frogs, and sometimes new fashion'd Animals." Peripatetical Institutions, appendix 356, 357. The underlying thought in science and theology was that the world was "worn out" or in decay, and the general effect was a paralyzing pessimism. It was not worth while to do anything notable so near the world's end, as there would be "scarcely any posterity to inherit its memory." See Milton's University oration in Masson, i, 230, and Hakewill's Apologie, generally with others on "great sickness and malice of the times." On spontaneous generation compare Browne's Vulgar Errors, 78, 107, 109, 193, and especially on p. 148 his allusion to "the receipt to make Mice out of Wheat . . . which Helmont hath delivered." Increase Mather in his Illustrious Providences says that demons can make insects, no seminal virtue being required. Compare also Early English Text Society, v, 229, on the generation of eels. But a new spirit of wholesome scientific skepticism was born in the seventeenth century. The first to question the "equivocal generation" of insects, so far as I know, was Aramatori, in a letter written in 1625. Tiraboschi, Letteratura Italiana, xiv, 433. Meantime Dr. William Harvey, one of the first scientific minds of the world, took up the subject of generation and published his researches in 1651. In these his genius struck out the great truth that every animal is from the egg. In regard to insects and their spontaneous generation he speaks ambiguously, but the portion of his work devoted to the generation of insects was destroyed or lost in the civil war, and we can never know just how far he had advanced. See Dr. Ent's letter in Willis's translation of Harvey's works, Sydenham Society, 148, and the passages in Harvey on Generation, 170, 456. Werner Rolfink, of Jena, the most learned of German anatomists, and a follower of Harvey, published a textbook on chemistry in 1661 in which he rejected palingenesis.

CHAP. I.

Sprengel's Geschichte der Arzneikunde, iv, 364. About this time the infant Royal Society of London was listening to papers on "the equivocal generation of insects," on "the making of insects with cheese and sack," and on "the generation of insects out of dead cantharides"; but there was one paper whose title implies true experimentation "of Flesh not breeding Worms when secured from fly-blowings." Sprat's Royal Society, 198, 223. The times were ripening for a great discoverer who should, in spite of Aristotle, extinguish the ancient error and clear the way for modern biology. In 1686 Redi, a Franciscan monk, and also an enthusiastic advocate of Harvey's doctrines, published his experiments, showing that "none were generated by putrefaction as the ancients believed." Even so great a naturalist as John Ray was rather slow to receive so surprising a conclusion. Transactions of the Royal Society, Abridgment ii, 765. But though Redi conceded in the spirit of the old philosophy that the "vegetable soul of the plant" might produce the anomalous little creatures found in excrescences, his general conclusion is a broad one: "Venga tutta dalla Semenza reale, e vera della piante degli animali stessi, i quali col mezzo dal proprio seme loro Spezia conservano." Opere, iii, 15.

Note 13, page 12.

Salmon's English Physician, or the Druggist's Shop Opened, 1693: "For a long time it was a received Opinion, that they [the barnacle geese] were bred out of old rotten Wood . . . by the enforming power of water: afterwards that they were bred out of certain Shells, which bred upon or stuck to these pieces of Timber, which by means of Sea-weed are fastened thereto by the holes of the rotten Wood, as Michael Mejer writes." Salmon gives here a long list of authorities, and proceeds: "Gerarde in his History of Plants, 1588, tells us what he had seen with his Eyes and touched with his hands . . . Shells in shape like those of a Muscle . . . out of which in time comes the shape and form of a Bird, which when it is perfectly formed the shell opens, and the Bird comes forth, hanging by the Bill; in short space after it comes to maturity and falls into the Sea where it gets Feathers." But the notion had been contested, and Salmon gives some statements in opposition, citing strong words from the closing part of Fabius Columna's Phytobasanos, pp. 507–511. For another convinced eyewitness see Harrison in Holinshed, i, 67, 374, edition of 1807. Compare Bury wills, Camden Society, 243, and Sir R. Murray in Abridgment of Philosophical Transactions, iii, 853, and Dr. T. Robinson, the same, number 172, p. 1036. For a modern treatment of the question, Muller's Science of Language, ii, lecture xiii. Lovell's History of Animals, 1661, cites Gesner on this subject, and Douce's Shakespeare, i, 24, refers to Gaspar Schot's Physica Curiosa. The evolution of the barnacle into a goose was not the only absurdity of the sort credited. Lovell's History of Animals and Minerals, 1661, says under "bistard," or bustard: "Some report that they generate by the month by eructation of sperme." On the barnacle compare Dr. Andrew D. White's Warfare of Science and Theology, 36, where the Strasburg edition of Mandeville of 1484 is mentioned as having pictured illustrations both of birds and of beasts produced in the fruit of trees. Bishop Hall proposes for the arms of an upstart boaster of an ancestry traceable to the Conqueror—

> The Scottish barnacle (if I might choose)
> That of a worme doth waxe a winged goose.
>
> —Liber iv, Satire ii.

In Porta's Magia Naturalis, liber ii, caput iii, is an account of birds produced from the putrefying fruits of trees, and a section entitled Aves é lignorum putrefactione. In this is given, after Gesner, all the details of the spontaneous production of worms in wood that presently have a head, feet, wings, and tail feathers, and grow to the bigness of geese and fly away. Garden sage in decay will also produce birds. One finds in the Manuscript Commission, Eleventh Report, part iii, 27, that Colonel Solomon Richard had observed the barnacle geese to arrive in Ireland on the 21st of August for twenty years with their young, and supposed them to have bred in the isles of Scotland. Richard lived in the later seventeenth century.

Note 14, page 13.

The first appearance in English dress of what we may call the Scandinavian myth of the swallow is, I believe, in Richard Carew's Survey of Cornwall, 1602, folio 25, reverse. "Olaus Magnus," says Carew, "maketh a farre stranger report. For he saith that in the North parts of the world as Summer weareth out they clap mouth to mouth, wing to wing, legge in legge, and so after a sweete singing fall down into certaine great lakes or pooles amongst the canes from whence the next spring they receive a new resurrection. The fishermen in winter doe sometimes light on these swallows congealed in clods of a Slymie substance," etc. Carew also mentions confirmatory accounts received from a Venetian ambassador employed in Poland, and from travelers. In an epitome of Olaus, published in 1562, the swallows are seen in the fishermen's net. Burton's Anatomy of Melancholy, ii, 2, 3, cites both Olaus and Carew, but Burton is staggered by the statement of Peter Martyr that swallows and Spanish kites were flying in Egypt in December and January. An early paper before the Royal Society is entitled "Relation of swallows living after they have been frozen under the water." Sprat, 199. Samuel Johnson, whose chief merit was that he could translate a thing into Latin-English, says "the swallows conglobulate themselves," and so fall down. White, of Selbourne, struggled with the question of the hibernation of swallows; unable to verify the Scandinavian notion of torpor in the mud at the bottom of rivers and pools, he finally accepts in part the older English belief. He says that "many of the swallow kind do not depart from this island, but lay themselves up in holes and caverns, and do, insect-like and bat-like, come forth at mild times, and then retire again into their latebrae or lurking places." The letter from which this was taken was written in 1772. I am indebted to Mrs. Ripley Hitchcock for calling my attention to White's discussion of the question, and for this list of references to Mr. Burrough's edition: i, 35, 49, 81, 91, 149, 156, 175; ii, 1, 41, 83, 140, 147, 158, 164. Kalm found the Scandinavian theory prevalent among the descendants of the old Swedish colony on the Delaware. The Dutch at Albany held the other theory of repose in holes in the rocks, while the Canadians and English settlers had somehow come to believe in migration. Kalm's Travels, ii, 146. But the theory of torpidity was held by the Philadelphia naturalist Barton, in the latter part of the eighteenth century. Ord's Life of Wilson, 191. According to William Bartram, "very celebrated men" were able to believe in it in 1792, and I have somewhere seen a paper, published in Philadelphia as late as 1800, combating the very tough delusion that swallows hibernated in the water. In the American Philosophical Transactions, vi, p. 59 (1801), is a story thirty years old told by Colonel Antes of a swallow taken out of the slime in February. Salmon, whose English Physician, or the Druggist's Shop Opened, is dated 1693, does not mention either of the theories of hibernation so much discussed earlier and later. He treats the swallow, the throstle, and the fieldfare as migratory, on the authority of Aldrovandus and Peter Martyr. Dante held to migration: "Come le augei che vernan lungo il Nilo." Purgatory, xxiv, line 63. It probably holds good of the Latin races that they knew the facts from their residence on the Mediterranean.

Chap. I.

Note 15, page 13.

Charles Morton was perhaps the most accomplished scholar that came to New England in the colonial period. He arrived in 1686, and was appointed vice-president of Harvard College, with the expectation of being made president. He read lectures on philosophy at his home in Charlestown which attracted so many from the college that he found it wise to desist. He died in 1698. See an account of him, 2 Massachusetts Historical Collection, i, 158–162, and Quincy's History of Harvard College, i, *passim.*

Note 16, page 18.

Richard, in his Dissertation sur la Possession des corps . . . par les démons, Amiens, 1746, attributes to the Anabaptists the opinion that the word angel is only the name of an office, and that scriptural angels are subjective apparitions, or rather "les bonne ou les mauvaises pensées." Dufresnoy's Recueil de Dissertations sur les Apparitions, tome ii, part i, page 196. No such opinion, I think, existed among the New England Puritans; but good angels were not so conspicuous in the theology of the colonies generally as were bad demons. Cotton Mather had great hopes of what good angels might do for him, but that was wholly personal, and born of an imagination that could not be contained within limits. Wendell's Life of Mather.

Note 17, page 20.

See the remarks of Sprengel on the increase of demonism after the Reformation, Geschichte der Arzneikunde, iii, 273, 274. Luther inherited the traditions of the humble class from which he sprang, and set the first Protestant example of extreme faith in witchcraft, berating the medical men who traced diseases to natural causes, most of which he himself attributed to the devil. He advised that an afflicted child should be cast into the river Mulde, and complained afterward that he was not obeyed. After the Reformation melancholy and hysterical women could no longer relieve their morbid sense of culpability by a meritorious pilgrimage. Perhaps this sort of faith cure was the greatest benefit of the old religion lost by the Lutheran revolution. Puritanism sometimes drove such brain-sick creatures to stark madness.

Note 18, page 21.

The entirely unlawful ordeal by water was retained in Protestant England after that which gave it virtue, the prayers of the priest in tying the thumbs and toes together and his solemn adjuration to the water, was suppressed. The wise King James, in his Demonology, felt bound to find another reason for the witch's floating. According to that Solomon, the water rejected her for having renounced baptism in her bargain with the devil. A full account of the ancient ordeal by water as practiced on the Con-

Chap. I.

tinent is given by a Dutch writer, Scheltema, in his Geschiedenis der Heksenprocessen, pp. 69 and 70, and the note in the appendix, 18 and 19, where also the mode of exorcising devils is described. The English witch-finders in the seventeenth century not only lacked the prayers and adjurations of the priests, but the rack having been disused, they were compelled to substitute the torture of enforced vigils and incessant walking to wring confessions from their victims. Both Scheltema and Hutchinson express their belief that the mode of holding the rope had much to do with the witch's floating. See an account of "swimming" a man and a woman at Hartford, Conn., in Mather's Illustrious Providences. Mather strongly disapproves of the custom, which was obsolete in the south of Europe in his time. It was also opposed by all the German academies. Mather cites Sprenger that it had formerly been used for those accused of other crimes. "The devil is in it," he says. The declaration of Chief-Justice Parker, in 1712, that if any supposed witch should thereafter die in the dangerous ordeal, those who put her into the water would be held guilty of willful murder, is commonly said to have put an end to the rare sport of baiting old women in England; but, according to Hutchinson, it appears to have been still in vogue some years later. A man was "swam for a wizard" in Suffolk, England, as late as 1825. Hone's Every Day Book, i, 942, quoting London Times of July 19, 1825. It is to the credit of Increase Mather that he insists that witch confessions should be voluntary.

Note 19, page 24.

As late as June 14, 1711, Addison printed in The Spectator, No. 117, his famous essay on witchcraft. "I believe in general," he says, "that there is and has been such a thing as witchcraft, but at the same time can give no credit to any particular instances of it." The politic position taken by Montesquieu in his Esprit des Lois, 1747, livre xii, ch. v, was not very different from Addison's; and Blackstone puts himself under shelter of Addison and Montesquieu; Commentaries, book iv, chapter iv. It was those who believed thus in evil spirits generally, but refused the evidence in particular cases, that Glanvill calls "nullibists" or no-where-ists.

Note 20, page 26.

In Browne's Vulgar Errors, 148, it is set down to be considered "whether the brains of Cats be attended with such destructive malignities as Dioscorides and others put upon them." See a passage on this subject in Parey's works, book 21, chapter xxxiv. It is to be remembered that though Paré was not an

English writer, his works were translated into English and his name spelled Parey.

Note 21, page 34.

I have not thought it necessary to fall into what Milton calls a "paroxysm of citations" on this subject. I have given authorities on specific points in passing, but the witch literature of the seventeenth century is oppressively vast. Some of the Continental writers are referred to in Scheltma's Heksenprocessen, others in Sprengel's Geschichte der Arzneikunde; there is a list of English writers in the Retrospective Review, v, and the late Justin Winsor printed a pamphlet bibliography of American witchcraft. Francis Hutchinson's work is the best on witchcraft generally. No subject within the scope of history can be more dreary to the student of original authorities, more revolting to humane feelings, or more disgusting in many of its details. Upham's Salem Witchcraft, with an account of Salem village, is the only work on the witches in Salem on which one can depend. It has no chapters and no index worthy of the name, and is utterly exasperating, but it is a full account of the witchcraft ordered and made clear. Upham did not know how to make a book, he did not know the subtle laws of mind, but the external facts are well given. I have had recourse to nearly all the other data as well, from Cotton Mather and Calef down.

CHAPTER THE SECOND.

DIGRESSION CONCERNING MEDICAL NOTIONS AT THE PERIOD OF SETTLEMENT.

I.

CHAP. II.

The circulation of the blood.

Harvey's Prelectiones Anatomiæ Universalis, 72–80, and Exercitatio de Motu Cordis, Frankfort, 1628.

To the historian of medicine the early seventeenth century seems a period of brilliant discovery, for, in 1616, while Virginia was yet in its birth throes, William Harvey first expounded to his students the circulation of the blood, which he published to the world twelve years later. But to the student of culture history the stubborn resistance offered to this capital discovery is one of the many signs of the thralldom of the age to tradition. So unusual was the spectacle of a man questioning the conclusions of the ancients that Harvey was accounted "crack-brained," his practice declined, and a pack of "barking dogs," as he calls them, were soon baying at him. "Would you have us believe that you know something that Aristotle did not know?" demanded one adversary, Dr. Primrose. "Aristotle observed everything," he adds, "and no one should dare to come after him." The voice of Primrose is the voice of that age. It is said that no man over forty years old accepted Harvey's new physiology. Half a century after Harvey's discovery the medical faculty of Paris,

Aubrey quoted in Prefatory Memoir to the reprint of Exercitatio. Comp. the Life by Willis in Harvey's works.

Quoted by Folet in Molière et

noted for its spotless orthodoxy, solemnly petitioned the French king to prohibit the teaching of the circulation, as a doctrine contrary to the authority of Aristotle. Against the plated hulk of this conservatism Boileau let fly a broadside of derision in the shape of a burlesque decree, in which among other things the court "forbids the blood to be any longer vagabond, wandering and circulating about the body, on pain of being wholly given over to the faculty of Paris to be let without measure." Harvey "gave to anatomy its most illustrious discovery, . . . and to philosophy its first real alliance with experience," says a German writer, and we like to linger over the story of the most shining intellectual achievement of the century. But its relation to anatomical knowledge in America in the seventeenth century is small. It is probable that few of the earlier doctors and chirurgeons who came to the colonies were interested in the question raised by Harvey. It is certainly improbable that anything new in science ever came into possession of the barbers and bloodletters and bonesetters who practiced the rougher sort of surgery and physic in England and the pioneer settlements of America, nor would novelties of any sort influence the practice of traditional medicine by the preacher of the parish or some jack-at-all-trades who served as justice of the peace, medical adviser, and neighborhood wiseacre. Still less would there be any advance in that "kitchen physic," as the colonists were accustomed to call it, that was so

la Médecine, 81. Comp. Revue Scientifique, Nov., 1893, on La Circulation et ses Detracteurs.

Œuvres de Boileau, ed. 1821, iii, 120. Earlier form of the Arrêt Burlesque.

Isensee, Geschichte der Medecin, I. Theil, 255.

CHAP. II.

liberally dispensed by midwives and knowing house mothers who revered neither Galen nor Hippocrates, but followed mediæval traditions and employed remedies that may have been older than the father of medicine himself. In 1660 the circulation of the blood was argued in a master's thesis at Harvard, which institution seems to have been about that time hospitable to new opinions in science. This was thirty-two years after Harvey's treatise had appeared. The circulation of the blood was still a question at Harvard in 1699.

Subjects for Master's Degrees at Harvard, 17.

II.

Humorism.

Note 1.

That which one age tells to another seems to men truth fundamental. From antiquity it had been told and retold with much formality that the human body consisted of four elements—earth, air, fire, and water—and that it contained just four humors or liquids corresponding neatly in number with the four elements. These humors were bile or choler, blood, melancholy or black bile, and phlegm. In the mystical science of that time a mysterious relation or correspondence was supposed to exist between each of the several elements and one of the four humors. Anne Bradstreet, the beginner of New England poetry, sets it forth in rhyme, that choler was the daughter of fire, blood of air, melancholy of earth, and phlegm of water. Disease came from an excess of one or another humor, or from a humor's being too cold

Note 2. Aphorisms of Hippocrates. Paulus Ægineta, b. vii, sec. 2. Comp. especially extracts from Aëtius in Adams's Commentary on P. Ægineta,

or too hot, or too moist or too dry. The four humors, offspring of the four elements, had these four qualities, cold, heat, moisture, and dryness, which were something other than what we mean by these terms. Each of these qualities might exist in either one of four degrees of intensity, not only in the humors but in the food and remedies. A writer in 1603 estimates the possible mixtures and wrong-goings of the four humors at eighty thousand. This afforded a system of diagnosis fairly bewildering and impressive to the patient. The belief that the humors wrongly mixed or tempered affected the mood of a sufferer was a commonplace of the literature of the period. "Humor . . . some time hath his hour with every man," says Shakespeare's Portia to Brutus. Certain forms of speech that gave expression to humoral theories still persist as petrifactions of extinct notions. The words humor, temperament, bilious, choleric, atrabilious, melancholy, phlegmatic, and others, are veritable fossils of the Galenic age. The numerous simples, such as sassafras and sarsaparilla, that are yet decocted to remove morbid humors and "purify the blood," are but remains of Galenism, and nostrums that restore health by invigorating the liver show the survival in folk-science of the old physiology that gave supremacy to that organ, or of the theory of ancient medicine that "the liver is made up from the roots of the veins" and that it was the center of life, the desires of the soul being there seated.

Sydenham Soc., iii, 6, and old medical literature generally.

Note 3.

Sprengel's Geschichte der Arzneikunde, v. 251, citing Sanctorius.

Julius Cæsar, ii, 1.

Note 4.

For example, Aretæus of Cappadocia on Acute Diseases, ii, vii, Sydenham Soc. edition.

CHAP. II.

III.

Common remedies.

Note 5.

Compare Molière's Malade Imaginaire, third interlude. Adams's Paulus Ægineta, iii, 483 and ff. Comp. Maurice Raynaud, Les Médecins au Temps de Molière, p. 181, and Folet, 87. Hippocrates, Aphorisms, vi, 47. Paulus Ægineta, b. vi, sec. 40, with Adams's Commentary, ii, 320. Comp. Rhazes on Smallpox, 37. Raynaud, Les Médecins au Temps de Molière, 180.

The physicians of the seventeenth century were acquainted with the properties of many valuable simples. They had a set of astringents and cathartics handed down from antiquity. Some of the latter are so drastic that nothing could have justified their use but the necessity for evacuating humors which had a depraved way of going wrong and sending up poisonous vapors to the brain, to the injury of those imaginary "animal spirits" which played a leading part in the physiology of the age. The several purgative remedies were supposed to act specifically, each on one or more particular humor; one thing was needed for phlegm and quite another to remove the black bile that weighed on the spirits of a hypochondriac. The favorite and perhaps the most destructive remedy of that time was venesection. Hippocrates had used it with caution, thinking it best in the spring time. Galen forbade bloodletting in the case of persons under fourteen or over seventy years old. But in the seventeenth century it was inflicted on men, women, and children for almost every pathological offense. Louis XIII was bled forty-seven times in twelve months. Infants of three days and men past eighty were thus depleted: the "peccant" humors had to be expelled. Venesection was supposed to be local in its effects and a vein was opened in the head for troubles in the head. The French when depleting generally opened a vein on each side of the body, supposing in their ignorance of the circulation that otherwise it would require twenty-four hours to restore by some process an equilibrium. The great surgeon Paré drew seven pounds of blood, troy weight, from a man in four days; and there was a case in England of almost as severe a treatment inflicted on a man seventy-six years of age. Bleeding was used by barbers and other humble practitioners. In the American colonies it was practiced by the half-taught chirurgeon, as well as by clergymen and other medical amateurs and dabblers, to whom the old almanacs pointed out the proper time of the moon for letting blood according to the age of the patient.

Comp. C. Sprengell on the Sentences of Celsus, *passim*. Howell's Letters, i, 2, Letter xxi.

Note 6.

Parey (Paré), works, lib. 10, c. xiv, and Deodati's Letter in Appx. to Hakewill. Compare Medicine in Mass., 43.

IV.

Medical sects.

The great medical controversies which the early seventeenth century had received by way of legacy from past ages wakened few echoes in America. The Latin countries generally held to Greek and Arabian traditions, while the Germans were following the insurgent Paracelsus and the chemical school—doctors of fire, or pyrotechnics, as they called themselves. But the seventeenth century was a period of approach and attempted reconciliation. Pott, the English physician who was sent to Virginia in its early years, was thought all the better qualified because he had studied in the Low Countries, and was acquainted with chemistry. He

Sprengel, Geschichte der Arzneikunde, iv, 341, note. Browne's Vulgar Errors, 72.

CHAP. II.

appears to have combined Galenical with the chemical methods, and there were other eclectics at the time. Some stiff Galenists in England were suspected of using spagyric methods surreptitiously. If any allusion to medical sects was made in the newly planted colonies, no record of it has come down to us; the people, in their necessities, availed themselves eagerly of any science or promising quackery or ignorant folk-physic that offered relief, reserving all their polemics for theology. One finds remedies dating back to Galen and Hippocrates standing on the family medicine shelf of nearly every plantation house of Virginia; the Oriental bezoar stone of somebody in the middle ages and the ancient dittany of the Greeks were prescribed by colonial doctors. But in the little medical libraries Glauber's Chemistry holds up its head alongside of Galen's Art of Physic, and even the Unlearned Chemist ventures to keep company with Ambrose Paré's Surgery. In New England, as in Virginia, Barrough's Method of Phisicke was the accepted handbook for nearly a hundred years. Wigglesworth had Barrough with Harvey and Culpepper; but it is significant that several Paracelsian books, such as the Basilica Chymica, were their friendly shelf neighbors. One is forced to conclude from the collections of books that colonial medicine at least was rather inclusive. Governor Winthrop, of Connecticut, whose influence must have modified medical practice in New England, appears to have belonged to the chemical

Hakewill's Apol., iii, v, pp. 244, 245.

J. Clayton to Royal Society.

See Force's reprint.

William and Mary Qrly., ii, 170. MS. county records in Va. State Library generally.

J. W. Deane's Sketch of Wigglesworth. Inventories of books generally.

school, and to have held strongly to hermetic medicine of various kinds.

V.

Signaturism.

The doctrine of signatures, so often ascribed to Paracelsus and strongly upheld by him, pervaded medical theory in the colonies. The notion was, indeed, as old as Hippocrates himself, and probably yet more ancient, since it is found in the primitive medical theory of savages. But writers of the Paracelsian school of the sixteenth century amplified, emphasized, intricated, and mysticized the doctrine in such a way as to make it seem almost an original discovery of their own time. Theories were accepted in that day for poetic rather than scientific reasons. Whatever thought was reached by symbolism, or uttered obscurely or mystically, impressed the susceptible imagination of the age. The imagination then held the place of authority that rightly belongs to the judgment. The later and elaborate doctrine of signatures was a part of the prevalent philosophy of correspondences. It was related to the influence of the planets on plants and minerals, which influence was shown by color and other qualities and had to do with medical properties. It was a part also of an obscure theory of sympathy and antipathy existing in inanimate things—a doctrine suggested apparently by the magnet. It belonged to the overshadowing supernaturalism of the time,

Note 7.

Note 8.

CHAP. II.

and to the geocentric and homocentric notions of the universe that gave value to things only in their relation to man. The world was a cosmic pharmacy; God had placed a signature on each substance to indicate the disease it was good for. What was necessary was to read the label, to note the indications of odor, color, form, and other marks. The resemblance was often wholly external. "Like by like is to be cured—that is, similar ulcers by similar forms," says Paracelsus. The porosity of the leaves of St. John's-wort, and the spots which resembled perforations of the leaf, left no doubt of the value of the plant in all cases of abrasion, external or internal. The illusory appearance of holes in its leaves showed it good for hallucinations, madness, and assaults of the devil. This curious theory of medicine is to be detected in many of the remedies prescribed in the colonies, and is yet more evident in the popular modes of healing.

De Cutis Apertionibus, folio 62.

VI.

Dr. Stafford's paper.

We may see the influence of the theory of signatures on English medicine in actual transit to the colonies by examining a paper sent by Dr. Stafford, of London, to Winthrop, Governor of Connecticut, the most noted master of medicine in the early colonial period. In this paper are remedies which must have been often prescribed in New England. Stafford cured "madnesse" with St. John's-wort "sometimes in five days." Paracelsus had treated the fibers of its leaves as a signature, showing that this plant was good to drive away "phantasms and specters." But the doctrine of "curing by the assimulate" was perhaps present even in superstitions before the time of Paracelsus; the water of St. John's-wort was used to drive away devils, and the herbs St. John's-wort and rue were blessed after a prescribed form, wrapped in a "hallowed paper," and carried about "to be smelled at" against all "invasions of the devil." The inhabitants of North Wales put sprigs of it over their doors as an antidote to demons. Stafford gave sweet milk with salt for "jaunders." Milk, being white, cleared black humors. This was "contraries cured by contraries," but Stafford used both methods in one remedy; he added saffron to his milk and salt for jaundice, and this was "curing by the assimulate," a yellow remedy for a yellow disease. If a patient were torn by pains in the breast or limbs, Stafford cured like by like; he bade him wear a "wild catt's skin on the place grieved." But our London doctor's masterpiece, as communicated to Connecticut, appears to have been his "black powder" against smallpox and other eruptive diseases. It was made of toads because toads were believed to be poisonous, and all poison drew poison to itself, and thus cured disease, as the author of the Triumphal Chariot of Antimony had long before proved. This also was one mode of curing by the assimulate. But the warts on the toad were perhaps regarded as a specific divine indorsement

Paracelsus, Opera, fol. 191 ff. The Book of Quinte Essence, E. E. Text Soc., p. 19.

Hall's Cases of Consc., Dec. 3, Case I, citing Thesaurum Exorcismorum.

Barton's Med. and Phys. Journal, May, i, pt. ii, 60.

Note 9.

Compare Adams's Paulus Ægineta, ii, 207. Basilius Valentinus.

CHAP. II.

of his value against eruptions. "In the month of March," says Stafford, with the usual particularity of time, "take toads as many as you will alive; putt them in an earthen pott, so that it may be half full; cover it with a broad tyle or Iron plate; then overwhelme the pott so that the bottome may be uppermost; putt charcoales round about it and over it. . . . Sett it on fire and lett it burne out and extinguish of itselfe; when it is cold take out the toades; and in an Iron mortar pound them very well." By a second roasting this brown toad powder was reduced to a black, innocuous animal charcoal. "Moderate the dose according to the strength of the partie," says Stafford gravely. A toad boiled in oil, "after the toad has fasted two or three days," he recommends for king's evil. With an exactitude characteristic of the medicine of the day he mixes a plaster not with simple hog's lard, but with "barrow's grease." Subtlety of this sort pervaded every department of thought; the little that was known of science had rather dazed than clarified vision.

Note 10.

O. W. Holmes, Mass. Hist. Soc. Proc., 1862, pp. 379–382.

VII.

Weapon ointment and sympathetic powder.

Beside the doctrine of signatures and a superstitious etiquette in the preparation of remedies, there were other curious results of the mystical tendency in the medicine of the time—the weapon ointment derived from the Rosicrucians, for example. It was compounded of many absurdities; there was pulverized bloodstone, a cure by likes, and there was also moss taken from the skull of a dead man unburied and other ghastly ingredients. This precious unguent was applied, not to the wound, but to the weapon or implement that had produced it. The weapon was then carefully bandaged, to protect it from the air. It was the wound, however, that was healed; the cures are well attested, as impossible cures usually are. Experiment proved that "a more homely and familiar ointment" would serve the turn just as well, and moreover, in that day of emblemism, the ointment proved quite as efficacious when applied to an image of the offending weapon. To the Rosicrucians was attributed also a similar cure which came into great notoriety in England in the middle of the seventeenth century. This was the widely famous sympathetic powder made of vitriol with much ceremonial precision. The powder stopped hæmorrhages either from disease or wounds. It was applied to the blood after it had issued from the wound or to the blood-stained garment. Winthrop, of Connecticut, imported the latest books on the subject of this powder, which may well have come into use in a new country where surgical cases were not infrequent. Before Winthrop's time, and after, German writers on medicine attempted to give a scientific basis to the weapon ointment and powder of sympathy by attributing their operation to magnetism, a term that has covered more ignorance than any other ever invented. The philosopher Kenelm Digby, a con-

CHAP. II. Note 11.

Sprengel, Geschichte der Arzneikunde, iv, 345.

E. g., De Pulvere Sympathetica, 1650.

Sprengel, as above, iv, 345, 346.

Note 12.

CHAP. II.

temporary of Winthrop, made himself the protagonist of the powder in a treatise on the subject. Lord Bacon was in some doubt about the weapon ointment, but he rather inclined to believe in its cures, because a distinguished lady had similarly relieved him of warts by rubbing them with a rind of pork, which was then hung up, fat side to the sun, to waste vicariously away, carrying his warts into non-existence with it. Roberti, the Jesuit, believed that such cures took place, but ascribed them to the devil; all these cures that were wrought without "contaction," including the home-made witchcraft for curing warts, Bishop Hall accounted damnable sorceries. Of such necromancy, this cure of warts with a rind of pork has alone survived to modern times. The rag-bag of folk-medicine is filled with the cast-off clothes of science.

Bacon's Nat. Hist., 997.

Hall's Cases of Conscience, 232, note.

Note 13.

VIII.

The seventeenth century lay in the penumbra of the middle ages, and the long-sought potable gold of the alchemists was yet in request; it even enjoyed a revival. Almost everything precious and rare was accounted of medicinal virtue, and it was inferred that gold as the most precious metal would be the most valuable remedy if it could be taken in liquid form. The known usefulness of mercurial remedies was attributed to the fact that mercury was the densest of liquids. Gold was the densest metal then known, and it

Potable gold.

Burton's Anat. of Melancholy, sec. 1, 3.

Note 14.

was easily decided, by the process of using fancy to give fluidity to logic, that if it could be reduced to drinkable consistency it would be the most valuable of medicaments. There was a yet more convincing way of proving its medicinal value by the process of presumption, so much used by hermetic philosophers. The sun and gold were related in the mystical thought of the time; the sun as chief luminary was "lord in the property" of gold. "There is not found among things above or things beneath," says Glauber, "a greater harmony and friendship than that between the sun, gold, man, and wine." The easy logic of the time found in this transcendental fancy a "therefore" potent enough to make gold a universal remedy for human maladies, where the recovery was not "contrary to the unfathomable counsel of God." Gold was even administered in its solid state; Arabic doctors had prescribed leaf gold, and it held place in several compounds. Fragments and leaves of gold were seethed with meats, and the broth used to clear the heart and raise the strength and vital spirits of invalids beyond all conception. But the hermetic writers thought the use of leaf gold a coarse application of a metal which they were fond of styling "the lower Sun." Preparations professing to be potable gold and tincture of gold were in much request and frequently administered in the seventeenth century. On the other hand, their efficacy was warmly debated. The alchemists held that three drops at the highest taken in wine or

Note 15.

Glauber, De Auro Potabile, 3, and Georgius Phaedro, Vom Stein der Weisen, 1624, 394–397.

Note 16.

Note 17.

Lemnius, De Miraculis Occvlt. Nat., 1604, pp. 309, 310.

Phaedro Von Rodach.

CHAP. II.

beer would cure the most serious illness. Of its nature it is more than enough for us to know that it was triplex, being vegetable, animal, and mineral; it was one thing chosen out of all others, of a livid color, metallic, limpid and fluid, hot and moist, watery and swarthy, a living oil and a living tincture, a mineral stone and a water of life of wonderful efficacy. So spake the admiring alchemist.

Geber, quoted in De Via Universali.

John Winthrop the younger, of whom we have spoken, was a man of an eager and curious mind, fond of peering into the occult. He dabbled in alchemy as well as astrology, and on his shelves were many of the latest works on potable gold. A poet of his time says of him:

> Were there a Balsam, which all wounds could cure,
> 'Twas in this Asculapian hand be sure.

He left a son Wait who inherited his father's fondness for prescribing, and who like his father was an adept in panaceas, and was believed to have golden secrets and secrets more precious than gold, "unknown to Hippocrates and Helmont." Doubtless many New-Englanders were dosed by the revered Winthrops with the tincture of the sun, potable gold, made by marrying in some fashion the "masculine gold" to the "feminine mercury," and possessing all virtues—vegetable, mineral, and animal—"destroying the Root and Seminaries of all malignant and poisonous diseases."

Green's Medicine in Massachusetts, quoting Cotton Mather.

Note 18.

IX.

Theriac and remedies of serpent's flesh.

Weapon ointment, sympathetic powder, potable gold, were much thought of, but the authorized pharmacopœias ignored these Gothic medicines that traced their origin to alchemists and Rosicrucians. Yet the notion of a universal antidote was in regular medicine as well. Primitive science, having no reins on the imagination, longs for perfection, seeks the universal, and dreams of great discoveries. Back through a long line of medical writers we may trace the belief in the virtues of theriac and mithridate to Galen and into the centuries before Galen. The accepted story of its origin is that Mithridates, King of Pontus, by a series of experiments on criminals, had found out, or thought he had found out, what medicaments would neutralize various poisons. These he put together for a universal antidote. Andromachus, physician to Nero, changed the constitution of the remedy somewhat, adding the flesh of the viper, probably on the principle of curing like by like. This remedy of Andromachus was the famous theriac which was so much lauded by Galen and which imposed itself even on modern times. It was expelled from the British Pharmacopœia only in the middle of the eighteenth century by a bare majority of one vote in the college. It contained more than sixty ingredients, and was commonly known in England as Venice treacle. Not only all poisons but many diseases were supposed to be

Galen, De Theriaca ad Pisonem, and De Antidotis Epitomes. Adams, Paulus Ægineta, iii, 528.

CHAP. II.

Maranta, De Theriaca et Mithridatio, 1576.

Note 19.

conquerable by this universal remedy. Numerous other preparations of viper's flesh were in use; things poisonous were thought to contain much virtue. What theriac was used in the colonies was no doubt made abroad. In less complicated preparations the American rattlesnake was made to take the place held for thousands of years by its rival in virulence, the European viper. The flesh of the rattlesnake was fed to the infirm, perhaps in broths as the viper was given for ages, and as the Scotch used the adder. His gall mixed with chalk was made into "snake balls" and given internally; his heart was dried and powdered and drunk in wine or beer to cure the venom of the snake, on the ancient principle of curing by likes. In Virginia the oil of the snake was recommended for gout, while in frosty New England the fat was, if we may believe Josselyn, "very sovraign for frozen limbs . . . and sprains." The American backwoodsman of to-day, perhaps unconsciously, uses a homely substitute for the viper wine or theriacal wine of other times when he soaks the flesh of the rattlesnake in spirits to make "bitters" against rheumatism.

Comp. Adams on P. Ægineta, iii, 121. Judd's Hadley, 361. Josselyn's Two Voyages, 114.

Byrd's Westover Papers, 66.

Joannes Juvenis, De Medicamentis, 240, and Salmon's Eng. Physician, 763.

X.

Bezoar.

There was yet another universal antidote recognized in the regular medicine of the time. The bezoar or bezar stone was a concretion taken from the intestines of wild goats and other animals. That brought from the Orient was accounted most valuable. It was used at first in the East as an amulet; there were other remedies of olden times that served their purpose just as well when worn about the person as when taken medicinally. A "stone" found in so unusual a place excited wonder, and there grew up a mythical notion of its origin. This particular wild goat, in the opinion of the sixteenth century, indulged itself on occasion in a diet of poisonous snakes. To cool the burning produced in its stomach by this debauch, the creature plunged into the water. On coming out it sought and ate of health-giving herbs, and as a result the bezoar was concreted in its vitals. The cost of the bezoar, the "queen of poisons," was great. "If you take too much, your purse will soon complain," says a medical writer in 1661. The concretions of the "mountain goat" were the original bezoar, but any intestinal formation of the kind came to be considered bezoar. In Java the viscera of the porcupine were eagerly searched for such deposits, and one of these worthless things called a *pedro porco* was sold for the price of pearls. There were ruminants in Chili and Peru that yielded bezoars, which ranked second to those of the East; Mexico contributed a lower grade still. Finding these stones valuable, the shrewd Indians learned to counterfeit them, and as they were of all sizes, colors, and forms, and there was no test of fineness, there were others than natives who knew how to sophisticate, so that the famous powder magisterial

CHAP. II.

Monardes, Eng. ed., page 3, and Acosta, livre 4, chap. xiii.

Tanner's Art of Physic, 515.

Note 20.

Castrillo, chap. xxvi.

CHAP. II.

of bezoar often probably contained nothing of the kind. The remedy was used in the colonies. Clayton, the parson who was in Virginia before 1690, tells of a skillful woman physician there who gave pulverized "oriental bezoar stone" in the case of a man bitten by a rattlesnake and followed it with a decoction of dittany, the same at least in name with that ancient remedy which Venus applied to the wound of her son Æneas, and to which the wild goats in those knowing times resorted when the winged arrows of the hunters were sticking in their sides. We get a notion of the persistence of medical tradition when we find administered in Virginia an antidote brought into Europe from the East in the middle ages and an orthodox simple derived from the remotest Greek antiquity, and both of them probably without merit.

Æneid, xii, 412.

Note 21.

Comp. Hatfield House MSS., v, 3.

XI.

American herbs.

This magic of dittany has much instruction for us who study the genesis of colonial medicine. Not only Cretan dittany, but white dittany as well, was esteemed efficacious against the poison of "serpents, mad dogs, and venomous beasts." Medical theory was very expansive. Because the plant that grew on the Cretan mountain sides was fabled to expel the barbed arrows that remained in the wounds of the wild goats, Cretan dittany and white dittany were accounted potent not only to cure poison, but to extract bits of wood or bone from wounds, and to remove foreign bodies of all sorts, and even to assist in parturition. Dittany was such an antagonist to poison that Gerarde is quoted as saying, "The very smell driveth away venomous beasts, and doth astonish them." Whether the Virginia doctors mentioned in the preceding section cured the rattlesnake's bite by using Cretan or white dittany, or perhaps by neither, is not certain, for by a curious process the name and virtues of dittany had before this time been transferred to American pennyroyal, which appears to have been still more astonishing to a snake than dittany. Captain Silas Taylor told the learned Royal Society, ever eager in that day to hear of marvelous discoveries from returning travelers, that in 1657 he had held to the nose of an unwilling rattlesnake the bruised leaves of "wild pennyroyal, or dittany, of Virginia." The serpent was killed by the antidote in half an hour. Other virtues of dittany were ascribed to pennyroyal in New York; here it was also used against rattlesnakes. But the name dittany, or American dittany, was presently settled by early Virginia botanists on *Cunila Americana*, and the miraculous virtues ascribed to Cretan dittany anciently, and later to European species and to pennyroyal, were finally attached to the so-called American dittany.

Royal Soc. Phil. Trans., Abridgment, ii, 811.

Gowan's Wooley, 43, 44.

Meehan's Monthly, Nov., 1897, on American dittany.

Glover in Phil. Trans., Abridgment, iii, 572.

It was by such processes that many American herbs became medicinal. A fancied resemblance caused the name of a European plant to be transferred, sometimes to more than one American spe-

CHAP. II.

Note 22.

Glover to Royal Society, Abridgment, iii, 570.

Two Voyages to New England, 61.

cies, and with the name was carried over the traditional virtues. Favorite herbs were transplanted from English gardens to those of colonial house mothers, who even took pains to cultivate in America the wild plants they had been wont to pluck for simples from English hedgerows. But the seeds of English weeds emigrated by smuggling themselves with better company, and the hardy vagabonds of English roadsides gained an easy advantage over the feebler natives of the American banks. Herbs from Europe soon put on the airs of native Americans. There was no lack, therefore, of old acquaintances for simples, and the wild woods were full of new plants and animals presumed to be of pharmaceutical value, for the idealism of the time denied that anything was superfluous. "We have the Scriptures to back it," says Josselyn, "that God created nothing in vain."

XII.

Botanical researches

Comp. Tiraboschi, Storia della Letteratura Italiana, xiv, 424, 431.

Note 23.

Compare Latham's Life of Sydenham,

The search for new remedies in the bewildering jumble of hitherto unknown plants revealed by the discovery of America gave a new interest to botany, which was the foremost of the biological sciences in the seventeenth and eighteenth centuries. Jesuit missionaries in South America learned from the natives the medicinal value of the bark of the cinchona tree, in 1632, and it was at length introduced into European medicine. This was the greatest trophy of botanical research in the New World, though the Old World met the discovery with stubborn prejudice and resistance. The brilliant results achieved in malarial diseases by the use of Jesuits' or Peruvian bark after its general introduction into Europe, about the middle of the century, probably awakened expectation of similar discoveries in North America. The traveler Josselyn, who arrived in New England in 1663, was an assiduous herb gatherer; he examined the weeds and woods and wild beasts to find novel remedies, and he has recorded for us the popular applications of many new substances. Glover, and Clayton the parson, and the botanist Bannister, were observing Virginia plants in the latter part of the seventeenth century. In the eighteenth there were several eminent native botanists, and others came from Europe. To three of these—Kalm, a Swede; Schöpf, a German; and Castiglione, an Italian—we owe the most careful observations, not only of the plants but of social conditions in America.

CHAP. II.

p. lxxv ff. Comp. Œuvres de Bayle, i, 267, 268.

Note 24.

XIII.

Signaturism in America.

But the popular use of American plants and animals did not depend on botanical research. The general belief was that all things were made with reference to man. The wild woods were full of creatures whose value was written on each of them in the language of signatures, if the seeker for simples could only manage to decipher the

CHAP. II.

label with which it had been considerately tagged at the creation. If we look into Josselyn's list of American remedies, we shall see how much painful observation and investigation had been saved by this shopkeeper scheme of Nature. The bark of the board-pine was naturally good for the skin; rosin gathered on the bark was used for outward application; turpentine procured by incisions was "excellent to heal wounds and cuts." Even cosmetic applications were probably suggested in the same way; green pine cones having a corrugated surface were good to remove wrinkles from the face; water distilled from them was "laid on with cloths." The familiar kidney bean, first known to Europeans in the gardens of the American savages, was "good to strengthen the kidneys," as anybody might know at sight. The signature might be "internal" as well as external, and very opposite deductions were sometimes made. The French thought that the mottled eggs of the American turkey bred leprosy, but the English colonists thought that the similar eggs of the turkey buzzard were able to "restore decayed nature exceedingly." From some association of symbolism the brains of the shark and jelly from the head of the drumfish were thought to assist in obstetric cases. Brickell, a medical man, records the fact that the pit of the Carolina haw was thought serviceable in cases of "the stone, gravel, and dropsy," and he recommends the brains of the screech owl for headache. As in Europe signatur-

Two Voyages, 64, 65, 72.

Two Voyages, 99. Labadists' Journal, 83. Glover in Phil. Trans., Abr., iii, 567. Brickell's Carolina.

ism would seem to have had its first lodgment in the superstitious use of amulets, so in America like cured like when merely worn about the person. In New England the fangs of wolves were strung about the necks of children to save them from fright; and the cast-off skin of the rattlesnake was worn as a girdle to facilitate parturition. The practice must have been pretty general, since we find it in Connecticut and Pennsylvania. No doubt the custom which still obtains in malarial regions of wearing a necklace of caterpillars to cure ague by shuddering, antedates the discovery of Peruvian bark. In the seventeenth century a spider inclosed in a nutshell, wrapped in silk and hung about the neck so as to touch the skin, "did much to drive away intermittent fevers more quickly." In England the patient was sometimes dosed with the spider, and the practice is still known in English folk-medicine. In the valley of the Ohio, spider-web pills are given by rustics to cure ague. The use of spiders in some form against intermittents is more than two thousand years old; Greek physicians, before the beginning of the Christian era, put a plaster of them on the patient's forehead.

It is to be remembered that in the ages before science it was held that in case of recovery there must have been a remedy. Nothing got well of itself. Now we know that the great majority of ills will heal themselves. In every case of spontaneous healing in that time a remedy was looked

Compare Monardes on bloodstone, ed. 1577, folio 18, reverse. Note 25.

König, Regnum Animale, 164. Gentleman's Mag. Library of Pop. Superstitions, 128.

Comp. Longfellow's Evangeline, i, 3.

Lovell's Animals and Minerals, 1661. Adams's Paulus Æg., iii, 49. Compare also König, as above, 164, 165.

CHAP. II.

for, and so nearly everything was believed to be a remedy for something.

XIV.

Animal remedies.

Note 26.

Brickell's Carolina, *passim.* Green's Medicine in Mass., 22, and many others.

Many remedies were in use in the early colonial practice and in Europe that seem to have had nothing to recommend them except an unconfessed notion that disgust was curative, and the belief that nothing was made in vain. Pulverized butterflies, crickets, and grasshoppers are not the worst of these by several degrees. Sowbugs were highly esteemed; earwigs and emmets, which sometimes crept into the ears, were good for deafness and were given in oil; tumblebugs for some reason cured rabies, and bedbugs were valuable in lying-in cases, perhaps from their clinical associations. Even more intimate vermin were given alone or put into compounds. The skins, the viscera, and the dejecta of animals were in use, and many of the most loathsome of these substances were found in the regular pharmacopœias. Human orts and ends were highly prized; the volatile salt of men's bones was especially "homogeneal to humane nature"; the scrapings of human skulls, human fat, and the liquid called mummy distilled from dead bodies were devoutly believed to have much efficacy. It was only as time wore on that organic chemistry arose to deliver the afflicted from the nauseous and the noxious by dumping whole pharmacopœias of vile medicament into the homogeneal sewers.

Note 27.

XV.

Indian remedies.

The colonists fell into a common error of unscientific men: they overestimated the value of the medical hocus-pocus of the savages. In Pennsylvania they were, in 1696, pronounced "as able physicians as any in Europe." Indian physic was in great part empty jugglery against imaginary spirits, but in rough-and-ready surgery the savages had some arts useful in the exigencies of forest life. They had herbs for cathartics and emetics; they taught the colonists the use of various roots which they believed to be antidotes for the bite of the rattlesnake. Byrd is able to name nearly a dozen of these supposed antidotes. One of these, the so-called Seneca snakeroot, came into great reputation in Europe as a general medicine. John Clayton the clergyman collected three hundred species of plants used as remedies by the Indians. Quacks in the colonies soon learned the trick of claiming to have medical secrets from the medicine men of the Indians. As early as the beginning of the eighteenth century this cloak for ignorance and imposture was found convenient, and the "Indian" or "botanical" doctor was already plying his trade.

Watson's Annals, i, 69.

Note 28.

Westover Manuscripts, 42.

Royal Phil. Trans., xli, 143 and ff., 1687.

Lambert's Hist. of New Haven and Milford, 112.

XVI.

Colonial medical men.

It was the usual practice to send out with each "plantation" or settlement a surgeon who knew some physic. One of these was allowed in 1619

CHAP. II.

thirty shillings a month. As money then went, thirty shillings would be equal to nearly as many dollars now. Dr. Pott, a Master of Arts, and both chemist and Galenist in training, a somewhat reckless liver, a councilor, and for a short time a temporary governor, was the only physician in Virginia in 1630. Involved in the factional intrigues of the time, only his medical skill saved him from being hanged out of hand for theft by the arbitrary Sir John Harvey. Harvey could not muster courage to put to death the only competent medical man in the whole colony in a time of epidemic. A like indispensableness probably saved Pratt, a surgeon of Cambridge, Mass., from banishment for free speaking. There were in Virginia a good many rough practitioners of one sort or another; in the manuscript county record books of this early period they are called "chirurgeons." The barber, who practiced minor surgery along with shaving and hairdressing, was a natural outgrowth of the conditions existing in the middle ages. But conditions had changed, and the barber surgeon was in a fair way of extinction from unsuitableness to environment when the colonies were settled. In 1638 a barber surgeon lost his life journeying from Boston to Roxbury in a snowstorm to pull a tooth. In a Virginia inventory of 1640 sixteen kinds of drugs are mixed up with a hone, a razor, a lancet, and four other implements of a surgical barber. In 1652 the surgeons of New Amsterdam petitioned for the exclusive right to

Smith of Nibley MSS.

Comp., for example, Accomac Records, 1633–'39, *passim*, and York Records, 1638, 1639, and 1645.

Note 29.

MSS. Records, Accomac County.

shave. But a trade profession so widely bifurcated could not survive the first generation in a new country. The settler probably shaved himself in preference to seeking a surgeon to do it, and the barber improved his social rank by putting away his razor and hone and setting up in his medical capacity only. As the higher ranks of the profession were mostly unoccupied, the very word surgeon as a professional distinction disappeared from general use in America. Every smatterer breveted himself physician to fill the vacancy. The so-called bonesetters, of whom we hear very early in New England, must have had predecessors in the mother country. Men with no professional training and little education, they appear to have been expert in the mere joiner work of surgery, as their title implies. The art was often transmitted from father to son, and was sometimes believed to be a natural and hereditary gift. In 1652 the Connecticut General Court employed one of these men for the colony. This appointment of a bonesetter-general indicates the rarity of surgeons in the country when those of the first generation had disappeared. Six years later Boston felt some alarm at the number of people resorting thither for "help in physic and surgery," and took measures to prevent the town from becoming responsible for the support of any of these patients. Clayton gives an unflattering account of Virginia physicians in the latter part of the century. They were, no doubt, like all the colonial medical men of the time, mere

CHAP. II.

country-bred doctors, with the training that could be got from an apprenticeship to the half-educated surgeons, their predecessors. Their standard remedy was "crocus metallorum," which indeed, says Clayton, "every house keeps, and if their finger, as the saying is, ake but, they give three or four spoonfuls; if this fail, they give him a second dose, then purge them with fifteen or twenty grains of Rosin of Jalap, afterwards sweat them with Venice Treacle, Powder of Snake Root or Gascoin's Powder." These failing, the case was given up.

Clayton in Force's Tracts.

Note 30.

XVII.

Medical parsons and medical women.

Compare Forsyth, Antiquary's Portfolio, i, 36.

From remote times it fell to the lot of the priest, as the only educated man in the parish, to give medical advice; so that medicine was at one time almost wholly in the hands of the clergy and women. This mediæval usage cast its shadow across the following centuries, and some of the clergy who came to America had a fair acquaintance with the medical knowledge of the time. Robert Paulet, who was sent to Virginia as a parson in 1619, appears to have been highly esteemed as a physician; he refused a place in the governor's council because he could not be spared by the people of his region. Many of the ministers in New England practiced physic, some of them professionally, others apparently gratuitously. There were few educated men in New England or Virginia who did not keep a few medical books and perhaps prescribe for their neighbors. Women had for ages practiced medicine. The dependents in the country houses and the tenants on the estates in England and in Europe generally looked to the wife of the master for medical advice. The same conditions persisted until recently on the large plantations in the Southern States, where the mistress was obliged to have her little stock of drugs and her ready traditional rule of prescription for the ordinary maladies. Professional women physicians were not uncommon. In country places in England the "good woman," as she was called, still lingered; she was "a pretended physician, chirurgeon, and blesser." She claimed especial skill in counteracting the mischief wrought by witches and demons, and this part of her art was sometimes called "white witchcraft." Obstetric cases were wholly in the hands of midwives in the earlier colonial period. It was just about this time that Dr. Peter Chamberlen attempted to organize women practitioners of midwifery in England into a company, with himself at their head as president and examiner. As early as 1655 a midwife was officially appointed in New Amsterdam and a house erected for her. The same class of practitioners were in the other colonies, and it was with difficulty that physicians could acquire a portion of the obstetric practice at a later time. There was also a class of women practitioners in many places who did not confine themselves to any one branch of practice and who gave the officinal remedies of

Roy. Comm. Gawdy MSS., p. 144 and others.

Roll of Royal Coll. of Physicians, i, 195.

Calendar of Dutch MSS., 148. O'Callaghan, New Netherland, 155. Comp. Sewall's Diary, i, preface, xiii, and page 166.

Comp. Watson's Annals of N. Y., 205.

CHAP. II.

Slaughter's History of the Parish quoted in Anderson's Col. Church, iii, 118. Niles, French and Indian Wars, 3. Mass. Hist. Soc. Coll., vi, 199. MSS. Com. 14 Rep't, pt. ii, R. Owen to E. Harley, June, 1638. D'Ewes, Autob., i, 26. Note 31.

the time. Clayton mentions one such doctress in Virginia; Byrd at a later period alludes to another. There is a record that this latter, a Mrs. Livingston, of Fredericksburg, was paid a thousand pounds of tobacco by the parish of St. George "for salivating a poor woman, and promising to cure her again if she should be sick again in twelve Months." In some cases like those of the famous Mrs. Hutchinson, of Boston, the services of a gentlewoman versed in obstetric practice were freely given to her neighbors; the professional doctress of Block Island at a later period was the wife of a rich man. The practice of general medicine by women prevailed in England at the time, and came down from it is hard to say what antiquity, for one of the most famous of all the medical professors of Europe in the eleventh century was a woman.

XVIII.

Decline of medical knowledge.

Green's Medicine in Mass.

Colonial medicine declined in character from the beginning. The physicians of the second generation, like the magistrates and clergymen, had much less education than those who came from England. Besides their lack of general culture they had no proper training; the surgeon sent to Massachusetts in 1629 was obligated to take one or more apprentices to learn his art. This apprenticeship was probably all the teaching received by the native practitioners of the seventeenth century and the early eighteenth. It was complained, in 1647, that medical students in Massachusetts were "forced to fall to practice before ever they saw an Anatomy made." The doctors of America could hardly have ranked with the most rustic chirurgeons in England. As the first generation of the American born came on the stage, ignorant quacks and fanatics grew as rank as the English weeds that flourished in the forest mold of a new continent. "We ought by all means," says a Pennsylvania writer of 1684, "to discountenance all Babylonical Letter-learned physitians both for the Soul and Body." The medicine of the age was bad enough at its best; worse than the Greek medicine whose traditions it revered and sometimes followed. The first influence of the chemical school had been mainly bad; it was only later that good results came from it. But the seventeenth century was none the less a century of advance; in that age modern scientific medicine was born. Harvey's discovery of the circulation of the blood is the starting point, not only of modern medicine, but of experimental science as well. His investigations on the subject of generation gave a philosophical basis to comparative anatomy, and thus broadened the field of human thought. In that century the skill of physicians first learned to cope with malarial disease as a result of the introduction of cinchona, the most important of all modern remedies. But the intellectual progress of the time was a narrow current perceptible in the mid-channel of a wide

The same, 31.

CHAP. II.

and sluggish river whose shore reaches were stagnant marshes and never-changing pools.

ELUCIDATIONS.

Note 1, page 50.

There is a pleasant sentence touching this reverence for the traditional in Harvey's lectures, in which he alludes to the necessity for using the utmost precaution, because he is dealing with an error two thousand years old. "Hinc error 2,000 annorum pridem habitus quare egi obsequatis tabulis quia tam antiqua: a tantis viris culta." Prelectiones, 78.

Note 2, page 50.

> But first they showed their high descent,
> Each eldest daughter to each element,
> Choler was owned by Fire and Blood by Air;
> Earth knew her black swarth child, Water her fair.
> —Anne Bradstreet's Poems, 36.

There were other curious notions about the humors. For example, a physician, writing on Tunbridge water in 1670, speaks of phlegm as "the private excrement of the brain at the mouth and nose." The opinion was no doubt generally held on the authority of Galen's Medical Definitions, in which the mucus from the nostrils is called "an excrement and sediment of the brain." Paré says phlegm is blood half concocted and is fit to nourish the brain. English edition, p. 9.

Note 3, page 51.

This "numeral fetichism" may be plainly traced to Galen, and it is evident also in the theory of the "critical days" in disease which Hippocrates announced and which has been accepted in some form down almost to this day. See, for example, Aphorisms of Hippocrates, section ii, 24; iv, 59, 61, 64; and Adams's references to Galen on these in his edition. Sir Conrad Sprengell's comment on the former of these, in his English translation of the Aphorisms in 1735, shows the vitality of the notion at a late date. Conrad Sprengell reduces the days to periods, and he hesitates to accept the dictum of Hippocrates, that fevers are apt to return unless they leave the patient on odd days. Compare the short work that Kurt Sprengel, at a later day, makes of this very aphorism in his Apologie des Hippocrates, 1788. The ridicule of Molière has not missed a preciosity so delightful as this reverence for number. In the Malade Imaginaire the physician is asked how many grains of salt should be put into an egg.

"Six, eight, ten," is the reply, "in even numbers, as the medicines are to be given in odd numbers." Act ii, sc. ix. Compare also what Philo Judæus says in eulogy of the number seven and its parts: Creation of the World, chap. xxx, and in chap. xxxv, his citation of an elegy by Solon the lawgiver, dividing life into ten periods of seven years. In the following chapter the division of human life by Hippocrates into seven periods is mentioned. This passion for numeration, thousands of years old, emigrated to America. Anne Bradstreet sings of The Four Humors in the Constitution of Man, The Four Ages of Man, The Four Seasons of the Year, and The Four Monarchies. The number four ran in the family; her father, Governor Dudley, wrote of The Four Parts of the World.

Note 4, page 51.

When the words of the text were written I did not know that Maurice Raynaud had remarked the same thing. "Il est digne de remarque que la médecine humorale est restée celle des gens du peuple, dont la langage est si souvent ce qu'était deux cents ans auparavant, celui de la science." Les Médecins au Temps de Molière, 180, note. In 1580 Juan Huarte, a Spanish physician, published Examen de Ingenios para las Sciencias, a work of great popularity which was rendered into many tongues. The English version appeared in 1616 under the title A Triall of Wits. Huarte tried to do what modern phrenology has attempted—to indicate the aptitude of men for different occupations. In chaps. v and vi he explains that all the difference in the character of men's minds is traceable to heat, dryness, and humidity. Dryness is favorable to understanding, heat to imagination, while moisture is essential to memory, which is therefore strongest in the morning.

Note 5, page 52.

In that strange series of notes which we know as Bacon's Natural History, the following remedies are mentioned as familiar cathartics and diuretics of that time: colquintidæ, agaric, black hellebore, scammony, antimony, mechoacan, rhubarb, senna, wormwood, myrobalanes, peach-tree bark, medicines of mercury, salt, oxymel, and pepper. Except mechoacan, peach-tree bark, and perhaps wormwood, all these remedies were known to the Arabians, and all the rest except senna, myrobalanes, and oxymel were, I believe, included in the ancient Greek materia medica. Compare Adams's Paulus Ægineta, vol. iii, *passim*. Clysters and suppositories are mentioned by Bacon. It would seem that purgatives and their opposites were very important elements of Eng-

CHAP. II.

lish medicine in the seventeenth century. Bacon repeats the jest of a famous Jewish physician, who said that English medical men were "like bishops that have the power of binding and loosing, but no more." Advancement of Learning, book ii. The use of cathartics to void humors that might send up vapors to the brain, recalls Vaughan's advice that one should sleep on the right side with the mouth open, and with a hole in the nightcap at the top. Fifteen Directions for Health, p. 13, 1602, Early English Text Society.

Note 6, page 53.

Barrough's The Method of Phisicke directs in certain cases to draw blood out of the middle vein of the forehead, and in another case "you must cut the liuer veine on the arme." Third edition, 1601, pp. 45 and 46. I have also a copy of the seventh edition of this popular manual dated 1634. Its general use in America was probably matched by its authority in England. There is a round denunciation of the practice of venesection by an anti-Galenist in Thomson on the Plague, 1666, pp. 50 and 51. Venesection was not nearly so common in England as in France. In the Historical MSS. Commission, Eleventh Report, Appendix, part v, p. 7, is a letter from Prince Rupert: "I am in noe small paine for our cosin since I heare she hath gott the small poxe. Pray God shee falle not into the Frenchifyed physician's hands, soe lett blode and dye."

Note 7, page 55.

That the doctrine of signatures is more ancient than Paracelsus I have no doubt. The treatise De Dynamdiis, usually enumerated among the works of Galen, and sometimes ascribed to Gariopontus, of the famous medical school of Salerno (a professed compiler from Galen), deduces the therapeutic virtue of substances from color, form, or other characteristics. Œuvres de Ambroise Paré, Introduction par Malgaigne, xxi. Compare also Henderson's School of Salernum, ii. But the editor of Sydenham Society's edition of Paulus Ægineta has in part anticipated this remark, for he says that he has "detected a few traces of the singular doctrine of signatures, so-called, in the works of ancient authorities," iii, 16. Major J. W. Powell, Director of the Bureau of Ethnology of the Smithsonian Institution, tells me that the doctrine of curing by likes is a part of the medical theory of every tribe of American Indians, as it is very curiously of Chinese medicine. The conclusion is not a violent one that it is an element of primitive medicine generally. It was elaborated into an element of philosophy in the later middle ages. Basilius Valentinus, whose Triumph Wagen Antimonii, written about 1500 A. D., appears to have furnished Paracelsus with many germs of theory, pretends that a spider being poisonous can not get away if surrounded by a circle of unicorn's horn which was an ideal antidote to poison. But if any poisonous substance were added to the circle, the spell was broken and the spider escaped. Bread, on the other hand, was strongly attracted by unicorn's horn, both being free from poison, pp. 66 and 67, original edition, 1624. His general principle is stated mystically—"Simile simili gaudet." Paracelsus probably derives from this his dictum "of likes with likes, not contraries against contraries" ("Ex qua recepta sibi proponuntur similium cum similibus non contrariorum ad contraria"), and he adds, "Salt therefore wishes to have its Salt, Mercury its Mercury, and Sulphur its Sulphur"—salt, mercury, and sulphur being the three principal elements in mystic philosophy. Paracelsus, De Cutis Apertionibus, chap. vii, p. 62. Compare Otto Tachenius, His Clavis, p. 2, and see the doctrine of the sympathy of similars stated with a ludicrous mimicry of logic by a learned Galenist, Maranta, in his De Theriaca, liber i, caput iii (1576). Adams, in his edition of the works of Hippocrates, i, 75 ff., on the treatise anciently ascribed to Hippocrates and belonging to his period, On the Places in Man, says: "And he further makes the important remark that, although the general rule of treatment be 'contraria contrariis curantur,' the opposite rule also holds good in some cases, namely, 'Similia similibus curantur.'" Basilius Valentinus, p. 68, recognizes both methods as though this passage were before him, and Paracelsus appears to be denying the first half of it in the extract given above. It is not possible to separate this doctrine of curing by likes from the doctrine of signatures with which it was entangled. One of the best statements of this is to be found in the Magia Natural o Ciencia de Filosofia Secreta, a very intelligent work by Castrillo, a Spanish Jesuit, which bears date 1649. He says that many "modern philosophers" have pretended to find in external forms indications of the occult qualities of things. Plants that show any resemblance to the human head are good for cephalic troubles, as are animals whose heads are remarkable in shape, such as the elephant, the beaver, and others. Animals with eyes notable in any way are remedies for the ills of that organ, and he instances among others the turtle that in dying was believed to shut one eye and open the other, and mentions a stone that showed a pupil within a circle which rendered the vision acute if held in

CHAP. II.

the hand. The whole passage is interesting. Folios 16 and 17. The cure by similitudes is found in the treatment by amulets, and in that form is probably older than in medicine. There seems to be a trace of this mode of thinking in the ancient legend of Telephus, which has served so many poets, including Dante and Chaucer, and which gave anciently the name "telephean" to incurable ulcers. Wounded by Achilles, Telephus could be healed only by rust from the spear that inflicted the injury. A suggestion ot the same feeling among the Semitic nations is perhaps to be found in the brazen serpent of Moses, and in the offering of the Philistines, 1 Samuel, vi.

Note 8, page 55.

From the English version of Jacob Behmen's De Signatura Rerum I quote the following: "Every root as it is in the Earth may be known by the signature for what it is good and profitable, . . . and it is discerned in the leaves and stalk which Planet is Lord in the Property, much more in the Flower: for of what taste the Herb and Root is, even such an Hunger is in it, and such a cure lies therein, for it has such a Salt." Compare the term sulphur applied to rosin: "welchs des Baums Sulphur ist." Triumph Wagen, 230. There was a passion for the mystical and esoteric in science at the end of the middle ages. "Medicine," says Paracelsus, "is not otherwise a science than this that the will of God may be secret and secret may be the will of God." De Naturalibus Rebus, chap. v. Among the manuscripts in my collection is a very clever alchemical Poeme Sur l'elixir Royal in a handwriting of the late seventeenth century. In this, Nature, exhorting the poet to speak of the forces by which Heaven has extracted light from metals, enjoins him to speak esoterically "like a philosopher":

> Parles, m-a-t-elle dit, de ces premiers agens
> Dont la ciel des mêtaux a puise la lumiere,
> Parles en Philosophe, afin que ma matière
> Ne se laisse trouver qu'au plus intelligens.

Note 9, page 57.

Bacon recommended the entrails and skin of a wolf for colic. A case recently occurred in the suburbs of New York city in which a mother administered boiled mice to cure a child of nervous timidity—no doubt a survival of some old English prescription based on "curing by the assimulate." Salmon, in his English Physician, 1693, p. 309, says, "The Flesh and the Liver of a Mad Dog dryed and beaten into Pouder are said to cure the biting of a Mad Dog." He prescribes the spleen of an ox for diseases of that organ, and the lungs of a fox for pulmonary diseases. The list of such remedies might be multiplied. In popular medicine yellow dock is still used for jaundice. In 1708 Lady Otway gives two recipes for curing jaundice made up mostly of yellow substances. In the one she put lemon, turmeric, and saffron; the other consisted of "20 head-lice mixed with nutmeg and sugar and powder of turmerick." Royal Historical MSS. Commission, Tenth Report, Appendix, part iv, 352.

Note 10, page 58.

Stafford appears to claim this as his own nostrum, but the process is given in Paracelsus, who no doubt found it in Basil Valentine, who differs from Stafford in the number of toads. One live poisonous toad—ein lebendige gifftige Kröte—is his prescription. The toad was dried in the sun and burned in a closed kettle, after which it was pulverized. He explains that calcination brought out the inner power or poison of the toad, which being applied, "like its like," drew out. Basil calls it a magnetic cure. Triumph Wagen, edition 1624, 71. See the allusions to this preparation in Emanuel König, Regnum Animale, 1683, 139, where various authorities are cited, and where a mode of preparing the toad for an amulet—nobilissimum amuletum—is given, following Paracelsus and the Basilica Chymica. On the medical uses to which the toad was applied in England compare History of Animals and Minerals, by Robert Lovell, Oxford, 1661, and Salmon's English Physician, 1693. As an antidote to its own poison the red toad was used anciently. See the authorities cited in Adams's Paulus Ægineta, ii, 207.

Note 11, page 59.

It must have been unfortunate to have a prescription of such value in controversy, but the authorities are not agreed as to its ingredients. Moss from the skull of a dead man, *æri derelicta*, was, however, a permanent element. Bacon gives some account of one prescription in his Natural History, section 998. But John Baptist Porta has the prescription given by Paracelsus to the Emperor Maximilian, and received through a courtier by Porta. I give it in English: Two ounces of skull moss, as above; of human flesh, the same; of mummy (a liquor reported to be distilled from dead bodies) and of human blood, each half an ounce; of linseed oil, turpentine, and Armenian bole, each one ounce—pound all together in mortar. Porta's Magia Naturalis, liber viii, caput xii. According to Porta, the weapon was left lying in the ointment. In the text I have followed a different prescription given in Bacon's Natural History. In the selection of ingredients

CHAP. II.

for this preparation the mystical doctrine of curing by similitude is manifest.

Note 12, page 59.

"The operation of this ointment," says the author of a famous pharmacopœia, in 1641, "is by the identity or sameness of the Balsamick spirit, which is the same in a Man and his Blood; for there is no difference but this, in a Man the Spirit actually lives, but in the Blood it is coagulated." Shröder, quoted by Salmon, English Physician, vii, 64. See also Sir Kenelm Digby's Sympathetic Powder generally, and a theory of the action of this powder, or "Zaphyrian Salt," in Howell's Familiar Letters. Jacob's edition, 645. An account of the cure of Howell by this remedy is in supplement ii, 673, 674, and in Digby's A Late Discourse touching the Cure of Wounds by the Powder of Sympathy, 6–11. The sympathetic powder was used for all hæmorrhages and even for other diseases, according to Sprengel. Compare Sir K. Digby on the cure of swelled feet in oxen, Discourse on Sympathetic Powder, 129–132. In the time of their greatest vogue these cures were probably never sanctioned by the strict Galenists. The subject was discussed before the Royal Society in its infancy in a paper intituled Relations of Sympathetic Cures and Trials. Sprat, 199.

Note 13, page 60.

Ambroise Paré, the famous surgeon, had the wholesome scientific skepticism which was wanting in Lord Bacon and most other philosophers of the time. He denounced the weapon ointment as imposture. "Neither if any should let me see the truth of such juggling by the events themselves and my own eyes, would I therefore believe that it were done naturally and by reason, but rather by charms and Magick." Paré's works, old English version, 39. Paré also refused mummy, not knowing what it was made of. Compare the debate in the Glasgow Synod over the curative power of the famous Lee penny. Mitchell's Past in the Present, 159.

Note 14, page 60.

Queen Elizabeth's ambassador to the French court in 1596 was attended in his illness by Lorrayne, a physician of the famous faculty of Montpellier, and another. "They gave him Confectio Alcarmas compounded of musk, amber, gold, pearl, and unicorn's horn," ingredients whose virtues seem to have been deduced from their rarity and costliness. The confectio alkermes, an Arabic remedy, varied in its ingredients. The amber was ambergris. See the formula in the Amsterdam Pharmacopœia of 1636, p. 61, and that in the London Dispensatory as quoted and

CHAP. II.

discussed in Culpepper's Physitian's Library, 1675. The Arabic form of the confection appears to have been less complicated. In the well-known pharmaceutical work of Mesue the younger—John son of Mesue, son of Mech, son of Hely, son of Abdella, King of Damascus—the ingredients in this "confectione alkermes" are fewer, and there are no pearls or ambergris. The costly elements are "good gold," "good musk," and lapis lazuli. My copy of this work is called Mesue Vulgare, perhaps because it is in Italian. It bears date Venice, 1493, and must have been one of the earliest of printed medical works. See K. Sprengel, vol. ii, 361–364, on Mesue the younger. On the tendency to expensive remedies, compare Howell's Familiar Letters, 45. "More operativ then Bezar, of more virtue then Potable Gold or the Elixir of Amber." In Molière's Médecin Malgré Lui, acte iii, scene 2, Sganarelle speaks of a medical preparation: "Oui, c'est un fromage préparé, où il entre de l'or, du corail, et des perles, et quantité des autres choses précieuses." An English confection described by Bassompierre may have been the confectio alkermes spoken of above: "A pie of ambergrease magesterial, of pearl, musk," etc. Bassompierre's Embassy, 36. The bezoardick powder magisterial of the London Dispensatory contained sapphire, ruby, jacinth, emerald, pearls, unicorn's horn, Oriental and American bezoar, musk, ambergris, bone of a stag's heart, kermes, and sixteen other ingredients. "I am afraid to look upon it," says Culpepper. "'Tis a great cordial to revive the Body, but it will bring the purse into a consumption."

The application of a fowl freshly cut open, to cure erysipelas and other diseases, has been practiced in the valley of the Ohio and probably elsewhere within memory. Lorrayne, of the famous faculty of Montpellier, in his treatment of the English ambassador referred to above, made use of "pigeons applied to his side, and all other means that art could devise sufficient to expel the strongest poison and he be not bewicht withal." MSS. at Hatfield House, vi, 112. Manuscripts Commission. "I never heard of but one person bitten in Pennsylvania and New Jersey with the Rattlesnake," says Budd, "and he was helpt of it by two chickens slit assunder and apply'd to the place, which drew out the Poyson." Gowan's edition, p. 71.

Note 15, page 61.

Gold is said by the alchemist to have its origin in the sun. It is called "the under sun," and "an earthly sun endowed by God with an incredible potency, for in it are included all vegetable, animal, and mineral virtues." Potable gold is the "tincture of

CHAP. II.

the sun," and the enthusiastic Glauber talks of "partaking of the fruit of the Sun tree." Compare Phaedro and Glauber *passim.* A large volume would not be sufficient to recount all the virtues of this powerful remedy, in Glauber's opinion. Compare Evelyn's Diary, i, 271.

Note 16, page 61.

The curious and scientific reader may follow if he can the process for making potable gold, the "True tincture of the Sun," in the various works of Glauber, or in De Via Universali he may learn to get both potable gold and the philosopher's stone by "the dry process" or by "the wet process." He may get directions for making the tincture in Glauber's De Auri Tinctura sive Auro Potabili, a German work with a Latin title, dated 1652. Or he may read the Panaceæ Hermeticæ seu Medicinæ Universalis of Johann Gerhard, 1640; but he will find the "most secret mode of compounding the Universal Medicine" in the Arcamun Lullianum. There is a rare tractate, Vom Stein der Weisen, written in the middle of the sixteenth century, by Phaedro von Rodach. These and others are before mc, but, after some wearying of the mind with esoteric phrases in a compound of old German and Latin, I prefer to leave the question of the actual constitution of the most potent universal remedy to special investigators. Fonssagrives, in the Dictionnaire Encyclopédique des Sciences Médicales, under the word "Or," says that a preparation of mercury and chloride of gold constituted the so-called potable gold of the seventeenth century—I do not know on what authority. I am in some doubt whether, after all the complicated hugger-mugger, the alchemists got any gold in their final decoctions. According to Phaedro, it was not so much gold they sought as the subtile spirit of gold that freed men and metals from impurities. Glauber, in his De Auri Tinctura, 1652, took pains to explain how the true could be known from the false and sophisticated potable gold, some of which was nothing but colored water, p. 24. Angelus Sala, though of the Paracelsian school, ridiculed the notion of drinkable gold, and declared that fulminating gold (knallgold) was the only preparation of that metal that had ever been made. Sprengel, Geschichte der Arzneikunde, iv, 557. It has been conjectured that some of the so-called potable gold offered for sale was merely a preparation of mercury. The two metals were allied, in the fancy of the time. In the Ehralter Ritterkrieg Gold calls Mercury "Mein Bruder Mercurio," and yet says that mercury was the female and gold the male. Salmon's English Physician, p. 10, has two recipes for making tincture of gold, one

Chap. II.

with, the other without mercury. More than one writer intimates that there is as much gold left after the liquid essence is drawn off. "Aurum decoctione non atteritur," says Lemnius. But the mere looking at gold coins or at rings, especially if adorned with "stones and lovely gems," recreated the eyes and heart, and a man might be brought to himself when in a collapse by applying gold and saffron to the region of the heart with the third finger of the left hand. Lemnius, Occvltis Naturæ Miraculis, 309, 310.

Note 17, page 61.

An English manuscript in my possession in the handwriting of the seventeenth century gives many directions for alchemical processes to attain the "quintessence" so much sought. Some of these had to be conducted in the earth. Under the title The Essence of wine whereby to Dissolue Gold this occurs: "To the Essence of wine twice circulated (as is elsewhere taught), add Gold & Sett it in digestion in Sand wth a Lamp For 3 months & yu shall finde the Gold dissolued but not irreducibly, never the lesse a quarter of a Spoonfull given at a time to a dying man, tho he be insensible, it will restore him half an hour to perfect sence, as ever he was in all his life."

Note 18, page 62.

The library of Winthrop the younger consisted of more than a thousand volumes. The fraction of it now in the Society Library in New York is less than half. Among these is Hercules Chymicus sive Aurum Potabile, 1641, and Traicte de la Vraye Unique Grand et Universelle Médecine des Anciens, dite des Recens, Or Potabile, 1633. There was also Glauber's Latin Treatise of 1658 on Potable Gold. These were new books. The revival of interest in potable gold in the seventeenth century awakened opposition. Burton, in his Anatomy of Melancholy, says: "Some take it upon them to cure all maladies by one medicine severally applyed, as that Panacea, Aurum potabile, so much controverted in these days." In 1403 an English statute had been passed making it felony to "use any craft of multiplication" to increase the quantity of gold and silver. Statutes at Large, ii, 448. Robert Boyle, in the seventeenth century, in spite of his having written The Sceptical Chemist, thought he had discovered the forgotten secret of the fifteenth century, but he did not print his discovery. Sir Isaac Newton wrote to the Royal Society in praise of Boyle's reticence, fearing that the full disclosure of what the hermetics knew was "not to be communicated without immense damage to the world." In 1689, however, Boyle secured the repeal of the statute forbidding the making of gold. Thus did the dark

CHAP. II.

shadow of mediæval credulity still fall upon the most enlightened minds. Compare Chalmer's Dictionary of Biography, vi, 348, 349.

Note 19, page 64.

The multitudinousness of ancient compounds was perhaps a trait derived from primitive medicine. The Iroquois had a sort of theriac, a cure for all bodily injuries, made from the dried and pulverized skin of every known bird, beast, and fish. Erminnie A. Smith, in Powell's Second Bureau of Ethnology Report, 73.

Note 20, page 65.

"In that country [Java] but very seldome there grows a Stone in the Stomach of a Porkapine, called Pedro Porco: of whose virtue there are large discriptions: and the Hollanders are now so fond that I have seen 400 dollars of $\frac{8}{8}$ given for one no bigger than a Pidgeon's Egg. There is sophistication as well in that as in the Bezoar, Musk, &c., and every day new falsehood." Sir P. Vernatti, in Sprat's Royal Society, 171. There was exhibited in the University of Leyden "the horne of a goat in whosse ventrikle the bezar stone is found." Marmaduke Rawdon, Camden Society, 105. Compare the accounts in Monardes and Acosta and the discussion in Castrillo's Magia Natural, last chapter. Castrillo calls the bezoar "Regna de los Venenos," and says that it cured pestiferous fevers and other diseases caused by melancholy humors. Joannes Juvenis, in his essay De Medicamentis Bezoardicis, published in Antwerp in the latter part of the sixteenth century, treats the bezoar very mystically. A disease of an occult and divine origin—divinus et Secretus morbus—like the plague, exacts a medicine of a heavenly and concealed faculty, and, as he said, with a blind and hidden potency. The plague, he says, "is a mysterious disease of the heart caught by inhalation from poison dispersed in the air by a malign conjunction of the planets." It requires a bezoardic remedy. Under this head he includes alexipharmical mixtures and remedies whose supposed virtues have no rational basis, as well as amulets. He describes an amulet of gold, silver, and arsenic made into the shape of a heart and worn next that organ by Pope Adrian, and he recommends the wearing of six precious stones and some brilliant pearls in finger rings or about the neck. They are to be frequently looked on, for in them resides "the hidden bezoar" against all poisons and the plague. There is here the sense of alexipharmical in the word bezoar. Compare the citations of Adams in Paulus Ægineta, iii, 247. Beguin's Élémens de Chymie, edited by Lucas de Roy, 1632, describes seven kinds of "bezoart"—to wit, mineral, solar, lunar, martial, jovial, metallic, and solar of Harthmannus. None of these have anything to do with the bezoar stone. Paré says that it is called by the Arabians *bedezabar*. But he quotes Garcias ab Horto as saying that the goat is called *pazain*, wherefore the stone should be called *pazar*. Paré's (Parey's) works in English, book xxi, chap. xxxvi.

Note 21, page 66.

The colonists were cut off by distance from that most potent remedy for king's evil, the royal touch, by which thousands of English people were healed, and the administration of which the Church of England sanctioned by a form of prayer. See in Sparrow's Collection, 1671. In 1684 six or seven people were literally crushed to death in the mad eagerness of the crowd to secure the blessing of the royal touch. Evelyn's Diary, 571. It is remarked by Aubrey with his wonted innocency that "whether our kings were of the house of York or Lancaster" the touch "did the cure (i. e.) for the most part." Worse than all, in the time of Monmouth's rebellion, the illegitimate touch of the pretender cured some of his believing partisans. Castrillo, the Spanish Jesuit, declared in 1649 that the intercessions of Joseph of Arimathea, the first missionary to England, had secured to its monarchs "el cura de la gota." The Spanish kings, on the other hand, had the gift of exorcism. "Los reges de España tienen gracia de ahuyentor demonios por auer sus antecessores professado la propagacion de la Fé," etc. Magia Natural, folio 81. The miraculous touch of the English kings was believed to date from the Confessor. The touch of a seventh son—"a seventh son and no daughter between, and in pure wedlock"—was almost as good as the king's perhaps. Aubrey's Miscellanies, fourth edition, 124, 125. Seventh sons were to be reached in America sometimes. Faith in the virtue of their touch is not yet quite extinct in America or in England. Compare Diary of Walter Yonge, 13, note. In 1688 a man afflicted with ulcers petitioned the Governor of Massachusetts to give him a brief to solicit money in Massachusetts to defray the expense of a trip to England to crave the royal touch. Green's Medicine in Massachusetts, 48.

Note 22, page 68.

I am indebted to Miss S. F. Price, the well-known botanist of Bowling Green, Ky., for technical information regarding dittany. The authorities on dittany are too numerous for citation. Virgil perpetuated the memory of the wild goats of Candia, and old medical books continued to refer to them. See Paré's works in English, 1600, p. 41.

CHAP. II.

Note 23, page 68.

As early as 1568 André Thevet's New found World or Antarctike appeared in an English version. Although quite vague, and on many accounts untrustworthy, it probably awakened curiosity regarding the medicinal value of American plants. The far more significant and much-esteemed work of Monardes, a Spanish physician, was probably read in England on its first appearance in Spanish in 1565. Fourteen years later, in 1577, the first English edition was issued, and its influence can be traced in the account which Hariot gave of Virginia in De Bry. Through Monardes the English public first became familiar with the extraordinary medicinal virtues attributed to tobacco, and in his pages sarsaparilla and sassafras, strongholds of quackery to this day, were first made known to a public that soon became enamored of two plants which had the virtue of innocuousness. In the estimation of Monardes the "leaves, plants, herbs, roots, blossoms, gums, fruits, seeds, liquors, and stones of great medicinal virtues" which had come from America were of as much greater value than all other wealth of the New World as "bodily health is worth more than temporal good." First Spanish edition, 1565, p. 3.

Note 24, page 69.

Books of reference and most writers on Virginia confound John Clayton, author of various papers in the Transactions of the Royal Society, with Clayton the botanist, whose observations in the eighteenth century supplied the foundation for the *Flora Virginica* of Gronovius. A writer in the National Dictionary of Biography, with bibliographical detail, ascribes all the writings of John Clayton, the seventeenth century clergyman, to John Clayton the botanist in the eighteenth century, making the latter the precocious author of papers published five years before the date of his birth as given in the same work. John Clayton, the parson, was also the author of a posthumous paper in volume xli of the Transactions of the Royal Society. Neill calls him "the parson of Jamestown," but, so far as I know, without any authority.

Note 25, page 71.

I am unable to identify the little creatures found on oak leaves which proved a remedy in some diseases when worn about the neck in taffetie bags by New England women. Josselyn's Two Voyages, 63. Increase Mather gives a popular cure for ague in New England, aimed at its periodicity. Five pieces of bread having letters written on them were given into the custody of the patient, who was to write in succession on one of these each day the word kalend (ant) for five days. Toothache was cured in Boston by giving a sealed piece of paper on which was written, "In nomine Patris, Filii, et Spiritus Sancti, preserve thy servant," etc. Illustrious Providences, 185. In Queen Elizabeth's time there was a curious remedy, which is alluded to as follows:

> Gellia wore a velvet mastick-patch
> Upon her temples when no tooth did ach.
> —Hall's Satires, vi, i.

Note 26, page 72.

A belief in the value of perfumes for sickness, and especially for the plague, prevailed in Elizabeth's reign. See Bullein's Dialogue against the Fever Pestilence, *passim*, and the remark of Mulcaster on perfumes: "It is wonderful that is written and strange that we see, what is wrought thereby in nature of Physick, for the remedying of some desperate diseases." Positions, 37. I have not chanced to note anything of the sort in the seventeenth century writers, whose nostrums were far from sweet-smelling.

Note 27, page 72.

The curious reader may consult on the use of animal substances the regular pharmacopœias of the time. See also such works as Emanuel König's Regnum Animale, and in particular his chapter De Insectorum in Medecina utilitatibus. Culpepper's Commentary on the London Dispensatory, 1675, contains lists of these animal substances in undisguised English. Cotton Mather said of Wait Winthrop, the third of the family to practice medicine on his neighbors, that he turned nearly all Nature to medicine:

> Et pene omnem Naturam fecit Medicam.

Note 28, page 73.

Clayton, in the Transactions of the Royal Society for 1687, xli, 149, describes the Indian method of curing wounds by sucking them and then using the mouth as a syringe to inject a biting decoction. Instead of cupping, the savages cauterized with lighted punk.

Note 29, page 74.

The practice of surgeons was not held in high esteem in England in the sixteenth and seventeenth centuries. John Halle, in the preface to Lanfranke's Chirurgerie, 1565, says: "Whereas there is one Chirurgien that was apprentice to his arte, or one phisicien that hath trauayled in the true Studie and Exercise of Phisique, there are tenne that are presumptious Smearers, Smaterers, or Abusers of the same, yea, Smythes, Cutlers, Carters, Coblers, Copers, Coriars of lether, Carpenters, and a great rable of women, which forsake their handle Craftes and for filthy lucre

CHAP. II. abuse Phisick and Chirurgerie." After lauding the medical profession, Peacham says: "I here intend no common Chirurgians, Mountebanks, unlettered Empericks, and women-Doctors . . . whose practice is infamous, Mechanick, and base." Compleat Gentleman, 11. See in Malgaine's Introduction to Paré's works, pp. 124 and 138 ff., decrees and ordinances for the regulation of barber-surgeons in the middle ages, with an account of the struggle of the surgeons to abase the barbers. In England matters had come to such a pass in the sixteenth century that Sir H. Gilbert, in his Queen Elizabeth's Achademy, says that "Chirurgie is not now to be learned in any other place then in a Barbors Shoppe." To the practice of barbers, and surgeons little better, the colonists were usually shut up by circumstances. One early Virginia surgeon was a Dutch bond servant. A library consisting of The Surgeon's Mate or of Barrough's Method of Phisicke, rarely of several books, gave the suffering what comfort can be had from quackery that is self-reliant from mere ignorance.

Note 30, page 76. Crocus Metallorum, the favorite Virginia remedy, was an officinal preparation used in several formulæ by Sydenham at that time. The editor of the works of Sydenham (Sydenham Opera Omnia, 1844) makes it "Antimonii Sesquioxyd cum Antimon. Sequisulphur." It was emetic. See Sydenham's Epistle I, works in English, ii, 19. It was prepared according to the London Dispensatory by calcining together equal parts of antimony and saltpeter. On the use of sulphuret of antimony by the Jews, Greeks, Romans, and Arabs, see an interesting note in Adams's Paulus Ægineta, iii, 356. The curious reader may also consult Basil Valentine, p. 37, who makes antimony "one of the seven wonders of the world." The tract Von den Particular Vnd Vniversal-Tincturen, appended to the Triumph Wagen, Thölden's issue, 1624, contains a section "De Crocis Metallorum, et eorum Salibus," written in alchemical style. Venice treacle was the world-famed theriac, which, according to the English formula, contained about sixty-five ingredients, and was given as a universal antidote. Gascoin's powder was the compound powder of calcined crab's claws, so called. I do not know what it was, but not literal crab's claws. Snakeroot is the only American remedy in the list, and this had been accepted in Europe. Evidently the Virginia doctors were old-fashioned, and, according to their slender knowledge, Galenist. Medicines of the other school and simples were perhaps used in domestic and irregular practice.

CHAP. II.
Note 31, page 78.

Forsyth's Antiquary's Portfolio, i, 36, has the broad statement that in the Heptarchy and to the time of Richard II physic was in the hands of old women and the clergy. It was taught in the nunneries to girls before the Reformation as a womanly accomplishment, ibid., 238. The sense of its appropriateness to women, and the habit of prescription by accomplished women, survived in the seventeenth century and later. Clayton said of the Indians in 1687, "Every one according to his skill is a doctor (as some women are in England)." Transactions of the Royal Society, xli, 143. Tiraboschi, in his Storia della Litteratura Italiana, iii, lib. iv, sect. ii, cites from Odericus Vitalis a passage implying that the most skillful physician in the world-famous school of Salerno in 1059 was a woman. Of Rodolfo he says: "Nella medecina ancora egli era cosi versato, che in Salerno . . . non si trovo chi es uqualiasse fuor di una dotta matrona." This is supposed to refer to Trotula, some of whose writings have come down to our time. The wording of the decree of 1281 cited in Astruc's Histoire de la Faculté de Médecine de Montpellier, p. 20, is considered by Malgaigne to imply the habitual practice of medicine by women in the middle ages. In this decree Jacques "defend . . . à toutes personnes tant aux Chrétiens qu'aux Juifs," to practice without degrees. Compare Malgaigne's inference from this in his preface to Œuvres d'Ambroise Paré, but Malgaigne's reference to Astruc and his date are both slightly inaccurate. On the women professors of the school of Salerno, Henderson's pamphlet on that school and Ordronneaux's Code of Health of Salerno. As late as 1691 Cotton Mather, in "Ornaments for the Daughters of Zion," mentions "chirurgery" as an appropriate study for women. It is said that in colonial New Jersey women engrossed a considerable share of the medical art, such as it was. This is no doubt true of all the colonies.

CHAPTER THE THIRD.

MOTHER ENGLISH, FOLK-SPEECH, FOLK-LORE, AND LITERATURE.

I.

CHAP. III.

The language of the time.

AT the beginning of English emigration to America the language was the narrow speech of an island people not much given to foreign enterprise. This stay-at-home tongue was very different from the comprehensive English spoken now in many climes and antipodal countries, and heard more world-widely than any other language since speech began. It is the implement of two most powerful, adventurous, and versatile peoples. Then it was held in contempt of scholars, who preferred to use imperial Latin, which made the learned men of Europe one nation and distinguished them from the vulgar. Long after the religious unity of the Western world had ceased, the Roman Empire dominated the language of philosophy and law and religion. English was an insular speech, but it was not by any means the language of the whole island. To the Scottish Highlanders and to the Welshmen it was a foreign tongue; Cornishmen had violently opposed the Reformation mainly because they would not endure to have their service read and their Bible printed in English, to them a jargon

Note 1.

Diary of W. Yonge, Camden Soc., p. xiv.

more unintelligible than the Latin they had been wont to hear in church from childhood. Even in what may be called English England the language was everywhere cleft into dialects and subdialects. It was still a matter of discussion where standard English could be found. The rugged forms of the shires north of the Trent were accounted the purer English; there the language had absorbed a smaller number of French and Latin words than it had in the south. On the other hand, the speech of London and its environs was preferred, because it was "more courtly and more current." This courtly speech, the language of poetry and the playhouse and the forerunner of our modern English, prevailed in the region that lay within about sixty miles of London "and not much above." There were gentlemen in all the shires that could "speak good Southerne," but most of the gentlemen and men of learning—the "learned clarkes," as they were called—habitually spoke the dialects of the common people of their counties. Even the "good Southerne" of the court was not yet fixed by rule, but was in a state of flux. This gave an advantage to the writer of first-rate power; he might select from the varied and ever-varying storehouse of common speech, and even from homelier dialect sometimes, such vital words and vivid proverbial phrases as fitted his thought. He could bend the yet supple language to his purpose untrammeled by conventional restraint and without fear of the grammarian. The language has never been more

Compare also Symonds's Diary, Camden Society.

Note 2.

Puttenham's Arte of English Poesie, 1589.

Note 3.

CHAP. III.

fresh and effective than it was in the hands of the masters of the Elizabethan time. But the great body of writers, being men of mediocrity, found in it no well-worn grooves through which commonplace utterance might flow smoothly without expert guidance.

II.

The exigency of English.

On the side of poetic and imaginative expression English had been enriched before the sailing of the first Virginia emigrants, and it was further enriched in the years immediately following, chiefly through the drama and prose works in theology. But almost the only refining and enlarging influence of that time of literary activity that reached the speech of the common people, to which class most of the emigrants belonged, was the authorized translation of the Bible, which was published in 1611, and which by degrees took the place of the older and ruder versions. The language may have acquired something from the sea ventures of the time to Turkey and Russia and the Spanish main. "Secretaries Marchaunts and trauailours" were already introducing alien words, but England possessed little foreign commerce and did not yet promise to take rank as a sea power. The sudden demand upon this close-cabined island speech in the seventeenth century for means to represent the endless objects, actions, and experiences of the New World and of a widening commerce was one of the most efficient forces for developing modern English.

Puttenham's Arte of English Poesie, A. D. 1589. Arber's ed., 158.

Note 4.

III.

Misapprehensions of English.

A language carried into a new environment brings with it preconceived notions not in harmony with the surroundings; the ideas that are imbedded in our ordinary speech seem to us a part of the original constitution of the universe, and the traditional notions associated with common words serve to fortify local and national prejudice. In the wilderness of America English speech was a misfit; an Indian chief, however squalid and beggarly, was forthwith translated into a king; the stark-naked little squaw child Pocahontas, turning herself into a wheel in imitation of the boys with whom she played at Jamestown, bore in English the incongruous title of princess. We hear of an "Indian king" in New Jersey who was hired to carry a traveler's baggage; and after encountering many scrubby royalties, it is a relief to find in New England one chief who was only a duke. The early adoption into colonial speech of the discriminating Indian titles—werowance, sachem, sagamore, and cockerouse—and the application at last of the generic English word chief, helped to dissipate a swarm of erroneous notions. More specific terms were the result of fuller knowledge; the compound bark house in which an "emperor," like Powhatan, dwelt as co-tenant with numerous families of his wife's totem, ceased to be a palace and became a wigwam. It was thus that English by degrees adjusted itself to a new environment.

CHAP. III.

IV.

Naming the animals.

The settler in America, like Adam in the new-made world, was called upon to give names "to the fowl of the air and to every beast of the field." This was done in some cases most naturally by descriptive epithets, such as bluebird, mocking-bird, catbird, canvas-back duck, flying squirrel, black bear. But the newcomer was sure to think he recognized in the primitive woods the plants and birds and beasts known or half known to him in the Old World. American creatures thus got second-hand names from real or supposed resemblances. The bison became a buffalo; the plantigrade raccoon does duty in some accounts as an ape or a monkey; the puma, as the largest American cat, became a "lyon" in Virginia, a panther and a catamount in various places, while it remained a "tyger" in South Carolina for more than a hundred years. The ear of the homesick emigrant caught the melody of bird songs that reminded him of the delicious vespers of the nightingale which he was nevermore to hear. Various birds were thus brevetted with the name of the European songster. In Virginia this substitute nightingale was the voluble redbird, according to Clayton, though in earlier lists both redbird and nightingale appear. In New England there were also so-called nightingales "painted with orient colors—black, white, blew, yellow, green, and scarlet," according to Josselyn's multitudinous description.

For example, Clayton, in Miscell. Curiosa, iii, 338.

Comp. A Perfect Description of Va., 1649. Statutes of S. C., 1726. W. Bartram's Travels, 46.

Perfect Descr. of Va., 1649, and Bullock's Va., 1649, p. 6. Josselyn, iii, Mass. Hist. Coll., iii, 278. Campa-

The Delaware region had its nightingale. The brown-throated song sparrow is unhesitatingly identified with the nightingale of Europe by French Canadians to this day. With one accord English settlers north and south endowed a migratory red-breasted thrush with the name and all the traditional sentiment that belonged to the smaller and more domestic "robin redbreast" of England. The mistake did not go unsuspected, for in some northern regions there is an attempt to rectify it by calling the Baltimore bird "the old-England robin," a name that misses the mark again, but that from its form must have been set agoing in the earliest colonial time.

nius, New Sweden, p. 41.

V.

The turkey.

In popular thought at the period of American settlement every place beyond the countries of Europe was a region of outer darkness dominated by devils who were worshiped as deities. The typical infidel was the Turk, the ancient foe of Christendom ; an idol was therefore called a mawmet, that is to say, a Mahomet, from a notion that the Arabian prophet was a false god. It may have been from this general confounding of all the world that lay without Christendom that some plants and animals from the New World easily got the name of Turkey or Turkish attached to them. The fowl we call by that name was in French a *coq d Inde* or Indian cock, whence the modern French *dinde* and *dindon*. The confusion between the East and

West Indies led no doubt to the curious German name "Calcutta hen," though even in German "Indian cocks and hens" appear. In England the turkey was sometimes called the Indish peacock or the "peacock of Inde" in the sixteenth century, so that the peacock pies on which judges and others were sometimes feasted at the time may have been concocted of turkeys. If the English name of turkey did not come from a general disposition to trace all outlandish things to the home of the Eastern infidel, it perhaps was borrowed from the bustard, with which the turkey was supposed to be allied in the easy natural history of the time.

Penny-packer's Historical Sketches, 188.

Note 5.

Note 6.

VI.

Indian corn and beans.

Indian corn, an American plant in origin, cultivated throughout almost the whole western hemisphere, was early called Turkish corn by the Italians. The name seems to have been transplanted from Italian into other Continental languages, and in English speech it was also sometimes Turkish wheat. Ralph Lane, Ralegh's commander in North Carolina, calls it "Gynneye wheat." From the time of Acosta there have been those who have sought with futile ingenuity to deduce an Oriental origin for maize, founding their argument mainly on the blunder in the Italian name. This prolific mistake may have sprung from a confusion of maize with buckwheat, which on account of its Asiatic origin bore the name of Saracen corn. Maize,

Lane to Walsingham. Sainsbury's Calendar, i, 4.

Acosta, Hist. Nat., etc., l. iv, chap. xvi.

Note 7.

CHAP. III.

as another sort of coarse grain, was also called Saracen corn, but usually Turkish corn. Other nations were wont in the sixteenth century to take fashions of all sorts from Italy, and the name there given to maize became common. Even the kidney bean, which was one of the most valued contributions of the American Indians to European food products, was called the Turkish bean, for no other reason perhaps than that it twined about the so-called Turkish corn. It was mistakenly identified with the "Turkish garavance," the chick pea. The word maize did not come into use in the English colonies; a letter of the Virginia Company calls the plant "maes" and "mace"; but maize remains to-day only a book word in America. In 1651 a Virginia writer calls the plant Indian wheat, and later it appears as Virginia wheat. It gradually came to be called in all the colonies Indian corn, to distinguish it from other cereals. The natural abridgment of the word in popular use has made the generic word corn stand for a particular kind of corn unknown in England. In New England, where the phrase English corn long survived, the other end of the word was dropped, and "Indian" very early came to stand for maize even after it had been ground and cooked. Grotesque combinations like "fried Indian" have lingered in dialect to our time. The season for reaping the familiar English grains was called by the emigrants the English harvest, the later ingathering of maize was the Indian harvest. From this distinction, perhaps,

Acosta, as above. Comp. also Campanius, New Sweden.

Note 8.

MS. Bk. of Instructions, Nov. 11, 1621. Comp. E. Bland's Newe Brittaine, 1651. Rev. John Clayton to Royal Society, 1688, in Force, iii, 20.

Comp. John Hull's Diary, 221.

Note 9.

came the name Indian summer for the season of balmy weather that befalls in the autumn when a halcyon stillness pervades the hazy air and the whole landscape lies enchanted. The name was probably of merely agricultural origin, but is nowadays full of poetic associations with the delicious season and a vanished people.

VII.

The parts of maize and dishes made from it.

Indian corn became the staple food product of the colonists, and English was put to all its makeshifts to find names for its parts and products and the novel processes attending its culture and uses. Stalk, blade, and ear were easily transferred from other sorts of corn, but for the blossoms the words silk and tassel were felicitous tropes. The envelope of the ear gave trouble. Megapolensis, an early Dutch writer, calls the husks "leaves." Strachey, in speaking of "a kind of wheat" which the Indians call "poketawes," describes the ears as growing each "with a great hose or pill about it." The Virginians applied an English dialect word, "shuck," to the "hose" about the ear, the New England colonist adopted husk, and in the extreme South the infelicitous phrase "corn trash" came into use, and all three are still living. Husk, which in New England expressed the outer covering of the ear, was in the middle and in some southern regions quite as fittingly given to the bran, the covering of the grain, while in certain regions of Virginia the same word, usually pronounced

Virginia Britannia, p. 117.

"huss," meant the cob on which the grains grew; nor is this use yet obsolete. This cob was at first called "the coare of the ear," the word cob was in New England at first used for the whole ear, as it was in English dialect for ears of wheat or barley. It has at last come to mean in America the spike on which the grains stand. In all this effort of the English language to stretch its vocabulary to embrace the new plant and its parts it strangely disdained to borrow a word from the Indian tongues. But when we come to the dishes prepared from maize, the Indian words incorporated in our speech are living witnesses to the adoption of aboriginal cookery. Bread was called ponap in the dialect of the James River Indians; from this word we get "pone," variously applied in American English to several sorts of maize bread. Ustatahamen, a name for the grits or coarser parts of the crushed corn, gives us the word hominy. Samp, supawn, succotash are Indian dishes which brought their ancient names with them as a convenient mode of distinguishing them from food preparations of other cereals.

Comp. Mather's Illustrious Providences, 113, ed. 1850.

Smith's Oxford Tract of 1612.

Compare Sot-weed Factor, 1708. Shea's reprint, 5.

Note 10.

VIII.

American animals.

The animals were not easily fitted with English titles; their skins and flesh were objects of trade between the two races, and many kept a semblance of their ancient names. The Virginia mussascus of Captain Smith is the

Tract of 1612.

> Civet-scented musquash smelling ever,

of New England poetry, and his skin appears by

CHAP. III.

Wood's Prospect.

Claypole's MS. Letters. Penn Hist. Society. British Empire, i, 187.

Purchase, 945.

Perfect Description of Va.

Clayton to Royal Society.

Compare Smith's Tract of 1612.

this title in the dull prose of English customs returns. A Pennsylvania form, "musquasses," appears to be midway between the Virginia and the New England names. With a gravitation toward English forms the word is musquagh in Oldmixon, but it changed more swiftly in America; it was sometimes muscat, a name given to the civet, and as early as 1649 it was "a muske Rat so-called for his great sweetnesse and shape," as though the Indian original had been forgotten. As early as 1688 Clayton called it mush-rat, a form still generally used in rustic speech. Other Indian words put on bits of English toggery; matchcore was a word in Algonkin dialects meaning a deerskin. When the Indian accepted a colored blanket from the white man in exchange for his matchcore, he gave the same name to his blanket. The colonial trader was impelled to put a semblance of sense into the word by calling it matchcoat, and the word in this form was widely used by the colonists. Copyists of old handwriting, not suspecting that it was only a blanket, have made it watch-coat, and in this misleading form it will puzzle posterity in Irving's prose. The general repulsion to the use of aboriginal words was no doubt increased by the polysyllabic prolixity of the agglutinated vocables that gave stateliness to the intervals of utterance with which a savage broke the monotony of his native taciturnity.

Note 11.

Indian words were unhandy vehicles for the ideas of a colloquial and gossiping race. Ustatahamen had to be reduced to hominy to match the corresponding English word furmity, applied at first to corn. Pawscohicora was split through the middle to get the English word hickory, and the last syllable of isquontersquash was all that could be transplanted into New England English. Chechinquamen was a hard nut in English mouths until the Virginians made it chinkapin. Wampumpeak, the Indian name for white shell beads used for money, was divided; wampum passed current in one region, and peak or peague in another. The New York Dutch called the shell money sewant from another Indian word, while Virginia shell beads were known as roenoke from the Indian rawrenock. In the course of traffic and friendship between the two races a sort of pidgin English was formed as a medium, a half-breed speech only partly intelligible nowadays. Certain words of greeting, like "netop," friend, came into temporary use among the colonists along with honorary titles of leadership, such as the "cockerouse" of Maryland and Virginia, and the "mugwump" of parts of New England. Much of it was local and temporary, and the residuum is small. To-day the English language, with the tolerance of a cosmopolitan, begs or borrows from barbarous sources the world over, but the home-bred speech of the period of American settlement seems to have cherished fastidious prejudices against foreign words without Latin ancestry to back them.

Note 12.

Wood's N. E. Prospect, 58.

Smith's Tract, 1612.

See example in Ames's Almanac, 1730.

E. g., Sotweed Factor, 19.

Note 13.

CHAP. III.

IX.

English dialects.

The absence of a well-established standard for English speech in the early Stuart period produced confusion in the colonies. Travel was not frequent between the several parts of England, and local feeling had the intensity of patriotism. Selden tells us that societies of men from a particular shire were formed in London. The men from a given county might thus allay the homesickness of their exile by meeting those who held to the same customs and sauced their speech with the same local words and accents. When an American region, larger or smaller, was settled by a body of emigrants from the same English neighborhood, many of the words and much of the twang of their ancient dialect would survive for generations. We have here a probable explanation of a marked difference of speech between two adjacent communities. John Lyon Gardiner recorded, in 1798, that on Long Island an Easthampton man might be known from a Southampton man "as well as a native of Kent may be distinguished from a Yorkshire man." The two towns adjoin and the two communities had been living side by side for more than a hundred and fifty years when this wide difference of speech was found still persisting. In Dorchester, Massachusetts, the land measures retained a local English trait; one finds the old Dorsetshire measure of a goad in the early records. In Groton there are heard to this day "some little expressions

Table-talk, 161.

Doc. Hist. of N. Y., i, 678.

Dorch. Records, 1633, p. 3.

Private letter from Dr. S. A. Green.

and quaint uses of words" not known twenty-five miles away. In yet another Massachusetts town such unusual survivals as "dafter" for daughter have been noted in recent years. In some regions the English dialects must have been neutralized by interference; there were many colonial families in which the mother tongue varied from the father's speech. In a single Virginia parish register between 1660 and 1670 emigrants from Yorkshire, on the one hand, and from Kent and Surrey, on the other, rub shoulders with men and women from the midland of England. Now and then the word "native" against a name in the marriage register marks the young Virginian bred in this babellian confusion of English diversities. It is hard to say how his speech would be affected by the varieties of vocabulary and the contrarieties of pronunciation about him. The peculiarities known in his descendants of to-day as Americanisms, or localisms, he might readily have borrowed from both ends of England without leaving his parish, possibly without leaving his own doorstone.

Note 14.

Register of Christ's Ch. Parish, Middlesex Co., Va.

X.

American dialect.

American rustic lingoes show innumerable expressions detached from the ancient dialects and rearranged not by hazard, but as the result of influences too obscure to be traced. There have been natural selection, modification by intermingling, and changes of use produced by environment; no

Note 15.

CHAP. III.

English dialect has bodily survived removal. But the English origin of our rustic words and accents is generally evident. For example, the twang longest associated with America by dialect writers is the distortion of certain words imperfectly represented in the spelling of heouse, teown, and keow, for house, town, and cow. Franklin long ago set down in Poor Richard's Almanac his observation that the residents of Connecticut and Cape May called a cow a keow "by a certain involuntary twist at the root of the tongue." This crescendo vowel is the recognized tag of the burlesque Yankee of the stage and comic literature. Its feline drawl may yet be caught in a state of nature in some of the mountain districts of New England, but it also exists far to the southward. There are London small shopkeepers who, along with a mock Latin "dies" for days, have an unmistakable mew in "heouse" and "teown" and "abeout." There is nothing in English dialect more evidently ancient, for it was a trait of the archaic patois of a portion of County Wexford, in Ireland, which was settled by a colony of English people who crossed St. George's Channel in the middle ages under Strongbow, full two hundred years before Chaucer's Canterbury Tales were written. These mediæval emigrants took out of England with them in A. D. 1169 and a little later such Yankee forms as "greoune" for ground, "pleough" for plow, and "teown" for town. They had other words found in American rustic dialects so widely distributed

Poole's Dialect of Forth and Bargy.

as not to be local, such as "kotch" for caught, "kiver" for cover, "man" for husband. These and other words were transplanted from England to America four or five hundred years after the species had taken root in Ireland. Take another of the many examples of tough survival. The farmer in some parts of northern New York and elsewhere calls a fraction of a wagon load a jag. The word was colonial; in a diary of 1763 a New England parson takes pains to set down among the small doings of his farm that he had "gott in 2 jaggs of Rowens." This and other bits of American dialect can be explained only by going to the mother country. In Yorkshire some primitive modes of transportation still survive. The pack horse that climbs the steep moor side laden with coals for the limekilns in the mountains that overlook the Dale of the Wharfe is known as the jagging horse and the burden under which he reels is a jag. The American settlers used the jagging or pack horse on narrow forest trails throughout the colonial period. When wheels in summer and sleds in winter took the place of packing or "jagging," a small load of hay or wheat or rowen, suitable for a horse's back or to be drawn by a single horse, was still called a jag.

Note 16.

MS. in my possession.

XI.

Negro speech.

Negro speech in the early colonies was of as many varieties perhaps as there were tribes, and

CHAP. III.

this may be one reason why there remains no considerable admixture of African words. Broken English, some grotesque examples of which are recorded, succeeded to the African tongues, and as there were large bodies of new negroes it is likely that some habitual distortions persisted in negro speech. Now and then an African word survived for a while. There was "quaqua," an instrument of music or of noise, but the word and the thing went down together. Buckra, a name for the white man on the African coast, reappeared in the West Indies and in the Carolinas. Perhaps the only old negro word surviving now is "juba," to which no definable sense attaches. The negro "hit" was court English in Elizabeth's time; the supposed negro words "den," "dey," "dat," for them, they, that, appear in verses written in the modern dialect of Surrey. African speech has left hardly a trace even upon dialect in the United States. Slave speech caught its first accents from the bond servants and convicts who worked alongside the negro and from illiterate overseers. It probably preserved much that was worst in the English of the seventeenth century.

Note 17.

XII.

Social conditions.

Social conditions in America affected speech; the environment produced practical changes. The old labels applied but imperfectly to new classifications. In England a gentleman did not object to the title of servant, which in some cases was even an honorable distinction. But the large number of bond people sold into America to pay their passage, or as a penalty for petty crimes, seem to have gradually brought the word servant into disrepute. The bondage of a redemptioner, who might be sold from owner to owner, was degrading and his treatment was sometimes oppressive. Those who were employed not bound were at pains to be known by a distinctive term; hence the frequent recurrence of the words "hired servant." When negro slaves were added in large numbers to the servile class, the name of servant was naturally rendered more odious by English race pride and Christian detestation of the heathen. As early as 1651 the phrase "any servant or other helpe in the family" occurs in the Massachusetts Records. "Hired man," "hand," and "hired girl" have come into use later from the same disposition to avoid the word servant. This dislike, which seems to have been half latent in the colonies, was greatly helped perhaps by that strange and widespread irruption of democratic sentiment which occurred in the later colonial and Revolutionary times. The distinction between a "Goodman" and a "Mr." or gentleman had not disappeared in the seventeenth century; it was in general use at Salem in the time of the witchcraft.

Note 18.

Ruggles's Hist. of Guilford, Conn., quoted in Judd's Hadley, 252.

Note 19.

CHAP. III.

XIII.

Proverbs and proverbial lore.

Along with words the early emigrant ships brought a supply of proverbs, the accepted coin of popular wisdom and almost as long-enduring as words. A writer for children in 1583 has phrases which are familiar to Americans often in a somewhat changed form. He says to his reader "looke before thou leape" and "thinke or you speake," and he says "A byrd in hand as some men say is worth ten flye at large." He says "not worth a pin" at a time when a hand-made pin was worth much more than one of those ground out now in myriads. The modern phrase "as plain as a pikestaff" appears in its older form in Hall's Satires as "pack-staff plaine," the allusion being perhaps to the rough stick which a pedestrian traveler laid over his shoulders to hang his pack upon. Lord Hunsdon writes to Cecil in 1596 that "beggars may be no chusers," and two years later he remarks that a "burnt child dreads the fire." "Down with his dust" in the modern sense is used by Fuller, the quaint church historian. When the birth of a young prince who became Louis XIV took the world by surprise twenty years after the marriage of his parents, an English letter writer alluded to the overthrow of the hopes of the displaced heir by saying, "Monsieurs cake is dough." "Thereby lies a tale" is older than Shakespeare, who gave the phrase a punning form. In a simple life with little literature sen-

Hugh Rode's Boke of Nurture, E. E. T. S., lines 420, 545, 577, 625.

Hist. MSS. Comm., Hatfield House, *passim.*

Royal Hist. MSS. Comm., Hatfield House, pt. v, p. 201, 1595.

tentious proverbs abound, and the English of the period of settlement had many more of such allusions than have survived. An Cotton, in her account of Bacon's rebellion in Virginia, compares the soldiers besieging a camp from which Indians had already escaped to Scoggin's wife "brooding the eggs which the fox had sucked," an allusion to a "merry song" of that time. "Fair play from foule gamesters" is another of her phrases. When she says that certain events put Bacon "and those with him shrodly to their trumps believing that a few such deals or shufles . . . might quickly ring both cards and game out of his hands," she shows us familiar games and popular phrases in primitive forms. "Like the corn, light between the stones which might grind him to powder," reminds one of the current phrase "between the upper and the nether millstone." "Resolving with the Persians to go and worship the rising sun," is an everyday acquaintance very slightly changed more than two centuries after this clever woman wrote in the racy colonial English. Almost all our most current proverbial philosophy has come down to us from the period when people liked to shape their thoughts into epigrams, and lacking light literature were fain to spice their speech with quaint allusions. Proverbs abounded for other reasons in communities where utterance was trammeled and phrases with quaint outshinings were sent from man to man to carry denunciation in enigmas. "No bullets can pierce beaver skins" was short and crisp and ambiguous if reported to the authorities, but the angry Virginians expressed in these words their estimate of Berkeley's motives in not making war on the murdering Indians lest the fur trade from which he levied an enormous personal tribute should be interrupted. Believing at last that their oppressions were made heavier in order to incite them to rebellion, another proverb with a more sinister meaning went like a courier of discontent up and down the river settlements. "Rebel's forfeitures will be loyal inheritances" was the prophetic phrase repeated from one indignant planter to his next neighbor. Such proverbs do not become folk-lore, they express political passion smothered but ready to burst into flame. There is another sort of ready-made traditional speech that is neither proverb nor politics. Friday was of old a marked day among the credulous vulgar as it is now, but the ancient notion had to do with weather. They called it either king or worling (worlding) "bicause it is either the fairest or foulest of the seauen." "Oisters," says Harrison, in 1577, "are generallie foreborne in the foure hot moneths of the yeare, . . . which are void of the letter R." This rule for oysters must have been much older and prevalent beyond England. The Dutch over their tankards had a humorous variant of it, to the effect that water was to be taken only in months without an r. The familiar mnemonic jingle that begins with "thirty days hath September," in its older form

Harrison in Holinshed, i, 378.

Harl. Miscell., viii, 338.

"hath November," was recited in the days of Elizabeth; its pedigree runs far back to an ancient Latin calendar verse about ideas and nones. Trivial as these instances seem, they enable us to imagine the motley assortment of antique mental furniture with which the emigrants were outfitted for homely thinking and everyday talking in a new hemisphere.

Harrison, i, 409, 410.

XIV.

Folk-superstitions.

Cotton Mather accounts the visitation of witches in 1692 a retribution for the little sorceries of the young people who "would often cure hurts and spells and practice detestable conjurations with sieves and keys and peas and nails and horse-shoes to learn things for which they had a forbidden and impious curiosity." Such minor "conjurations" are still known in by-places, and this mode of pretending to satisfy "an impious curiosity" must have been very ancient. That a knife, fork, or a pair of scissors which sticks in the floor is lucky was an article of folk-faith in the good old colony time, and for how long before no one knows. Certain texts of Scripture were in use for divination in colonial New Jersey, perhaps by the same kind of charm that has been used down to our own time, to tell whom the rustic swain or the curious kitchen maid will marry. The very ancient European tradition that the horned cattle uttered audible prayers at midnight on each return of the anniversary of Christ's birth in a stable was still handed

Journal of Sarah Eve.

Barber's New Jersey Collection, 149.

CHAP. III.

down to children in the up-country and elsewhere in the first half of the nineteenth century. The American back-country man, finding his horse's mane almost hopelessly tangled in the morning, remarks as he tries to extricate it that the "witches" have done it. This faded relic of a picturesque superstition that came down through a long line of English ancestors from the middle ages Shakespeare touched into poetry:

Romeo and Juliet, i, 4. Comp. Douce, Illustrations of Shaks., ii, 180.

> . . . The very Mab
> That plats the manes of horses in the night,
> And bakes the elf-locks into foul sluttish hairs,
> Which once untangled much misfortune bodes.

The same ancient belief in small deviltries is embalmed in the name "feather-bed witches" yet applied to the knotted feathers in a bed. Countless other bits of folk-wisdom were transported to American shores as part of the intellectual kit of uncritical people. To call such surviving mediæval and ancient beliefs quite useless would be rash; they at least supplied material to the imagination and rudely served as substitutes for literature.

XV.

Folk-literature.

The higher forms of folk-lore may be called folk-literature. The rustic classic of other days was carried in the memory as folk-tale and ballad and transmitted orally from generation to generation. Legends of place and fairy myths, the achievement of giant-killing Jack, and the romantic tale of lucky Cinderella, now relegated to the nursery, delighted men and women for thousands of years. For ages in one form and another innocent simplicity, wearing a red riding hood, and crafty ferocity in the form of a wolf, afforded a needed excitement in the long wintry evenings. Ballads of love and bloody ballads of slaughter were sung while the flicker of failing firelight on the wide hearth peopled the remote corners of the room with grotesque shadows in motion. Chevy Chase and other ballads, the heritage of the English generations, were chanted to young people, keeping alive British tradition and feeling in the American woods. The merry mirth-provoking old English songs of primitive humor reappear in Virginia. One of these, the Song of Scoggin, is preserved to us by title only in a proscription of it by the eminent and godly Mr. Perkins. As the ideas and feelings embodied in the old unwritten ballads brought over the sea grew dim and remote, these same ballads absorbed by degrees, and with no more change than was necessary, a flavor of America. The highly interesting Scottish-English ballad of Young Beichan, or Lord Bateman, for example, the versions of which in Great Britain are many, became American when repeated by generations who had forgotten the crusades. Susan Pye, the Saracen girl, became Suky Fry, an American, who, having cared for an English nobleman in prison, goes to England to have the same incredible adventure that befalls the heroine of the older

Compare Child's Version L,

CHAP. III.

and see note *a*.

ballad, and she wears the same jewels and is described in almost the same lines. Other ballads and songs, manifestly of English origin, were current with slight changes in the older States until recent times. But American events sometimes gave birth to American rhymes: Bacon's rebellion was versified in Virginia, and Lovewell's gallant but disastrous fight in Maine gave rise to a gory ballad that put Chevy Chase out of countenance, and became "the most beloved of all" in New England. Very curious and perhaps very antique forms of English folk-tales were brought to America. For example, there was in New England a version of the world-old tale of Cinderella known as Rose, Pink, and Piney (or Peony), a version apparently unknown to collectors of English folk-lore, and yet other traditional tales were long preserved in ancient forms that have been lost in the mother country.

Note 20.

XVI.

Literature in the colonies.

Some collections of books were brought to the colonies at the outset that might be called large libraries in a time when entire libraries of average size were often kept in a single chest. Elder Brewster, of Plymouth, who had been a printer in Holland, left some hundreds of books. John Eliot, the Indian apostle, if one may trust family tradition, brought twenty-three barrels of literature with him. "Worshipful Mr. Winthrop," of Connecticut, had the most princely library of the time

Stiles MS., Itinerary, Yale College.

The remains of Winthrop's library in N. Y. Society Library.

in the colonies, though it contained but about a thousand volumes. He prized alchemical, astrological, and other esoteric trumpery; some of his books of this character that yet remain are bound in sheets of ancient black-letter with illuminated initials and in bits of manuscript missals in color. Antiques were thus sacrificed as superstitious, perhaps, and used to wrap up favorite essays on the philosopher's stone and potable gold, superstitions dear to the heart of the learned fellow of the Royal Society. Winthrop had also many unpractical works on practical themes—books on agriculture and medicine by followers of Pliny and Paracelsus. John Harvard had a library which was a part of his gift to Harvard College. There were a considerable number of books in the colonies, but in the first period there was very little literature in the strict sense of the word. Theology dominated in every collection. If George Sandys, the traveler and poet, consoled his lonely hours in Virginia with a few books of English literature we have no record of it, but he brought with him a copy of "the sweet-tong'd Ovid," which he rendered into English verse in Jamestown "by that imperfect light which was snatcht from the hours of night and repose," while the unhappy colony of which he was an officer was agitated by the alarms of Indian war and pestilence. Most of the books read in the colonies were far removed from the "never-discontinued rhymes" of Ovid. There is ever a literature below literature that has to do with the hopes and fears, the beliefs and aspirations of uncritical people. In 1619 many little sub-colonies were fitting out for Virginia. With one of these there were sent by the shareholders, along with arms and armor, axes and beetle rings and provisions, certain necessary books. The original list is preserved. There were two church Bibles and two books of common prayer. The literary outfit was completed by "2 books of the practice of piety, 3 books of the playne man's pathway," and "halfe a reme of paper." Bishop Bayly's "Practice of Piety directing a Christian how to walke that he may please God" is at once half mediæval and wholly Puritan in tone. Its popularity and its almost divine authority with the men of that age is a remarkable literary phenomenon. It turns up in almost every Virginia probate inventory, and is found far into the eighteenth century, often associated with its running mate, Dent's "Plaine Man's Pathway to Heaven wherein every man may clearly see whether he shall be saved or damned." At the urgent request of the eminent Robert Boyle, the Practice of Piety was translated into the Indian tongue of Massachusetts. In a Virginia library of five volumes, in 1648, the inevitable Practice of Piety has for companions "Mr. Calvin's Institutions"—that is, Calvin's Institutes—"the true watch," "Christ's combat with Satan," and "effectual Calling." A Virginia clergyman three years earlier left "thirty great books in folio, most of them old authors,"

Smith of Nibley MSS., N. Y. Pub. Library.

Note 21.

Note 22.

and "about fifty books in quarto, most of them being lattin books." We have here two typical libraries—the cumbrous folios and the handy square small quartos, mostly Latin, of the scholar, on the one hand, and the half dozen more or less guide books to piety, sound doctrine, and paradise which gave a sense of security to a reputable family. It was not until the latter half of the century that one finds among the richer planters those encyclopedic books on various subjects that gave their owners an air of general information, and it is only in the last quarter of the century that we can trace in the houses of a few educated Virginians such masterpieces of real literature as Ralegh's History of the World and Bacon's Advancement of Learning. There were also the Essays of Montaigne, who figures in the inventories as "Michael, Lord Montague," and the Religio Medici. In an inventory of 1699 a copy of Macbeth turns up opportunely to give notice that the slowly widening fame of Shakespeare had reached the New World before the century closed.

Note 23.

XVII.

American literature.

Nothing that can properly be called American literature was produced in the colonies in the early seventeenth century—nothing worthy of the name in its later time. Narratives of American travel were written by Captain John Smith and others. George Sandys, an English poet, translated Ovid while sojourning in Virginia; and Anne Bradstreet,

CHAP. III.

whose birth and education were wholly English, wrote in Massachusetts some clever verses in imitation of Sylvester's translation of Du Bartas—"divine Du Bartas," as he was called, translated by "silver-tongued Sylvester," admiration for whom was the literary vogue in England in the seventeenth century. But all such productions in the first generation belong to English letters; they have no relation of any kind to American literature; and all have gone into an oblivion as profound as that which has enveloped the admired Du Bartas himself. Vigorous works of polemical theology were produced by the great lights of English Puritanism exiled to New England, but they were addressed to an English audience, and were mostly printed in the mother country, where they were part of the current debates on church government and theology. Notwithstanding the ability of their authors, these books have no permanent value except as documents of historical reference.

Note 24.

XVIII.

The Day of Doom, and other poems.

Nor can much be said for the writings of the period following, when the valetudinarian Wigglesworth produced his Day of Doom, in which the Christ is alternately a country judge and a fierce Moloch, and where the pious reader confronts such scenes as the damnation of non-elect infants for the guilt of Adam's sin, though they are assigned to "the easiest room in hell." The poem is done in the characteristic doggerel of the Bay Psalm Book, without taste or humor. Its hideous descriptions, irresistibly comic to a modern reader, were suited to the temper of the time; they seemed realistic forecasts of the almost imminent final catastrophe, and edition after edition was sold. Only ten years before the outbreak of the American Revolution a Boston paper could speak of Michael Wigglesworth's "divine poems." Versification was an unreproved amusement in all the colonies, but most of the wooden rhymes of the time rested in manuscript. In New England the habitual use of the printing press gave opportunity for prolific facility to win something like distinction. Benjamin Tompson was a later and less lugubrious writer than Wigglesworth, and he achieved fame enough to have it graven on his tombstone that he was the "renowned poet of New England." The histories of the Indian wars of New England, the political tractates, and the accounts of Bacon's rebellion in Virginia and the poems about it, the indigestible tales with which Increase Mather filled his books on illustrious providences and ominous comets, the Quaker and anti-Quaker diatribes of gall and wormwood, as indeed all the writings in all the colonies during the seventeenth century, are almost without exception utterly non-luminous. Their lack of any inspiration is witness to the truth that notwithstanding intellectual activity artistic creation is impossible in an unsympathetic environment. Life was too material,

Notice appended to funeral discourse of Wigglesworth's son, Dr. E. Wigglesworth.

Dr. S. A. Green in Mass. Hist. Soc. Proc., June, 1895.

human energy and thought were spent in the battle with circumstances and the more bootless struggle of petty religious and theological debate. There were no detached minds, there could be no production of true literature. The odds would have been against Shakespeare himself.

XIX.

The anti-naturalistic sentiment of the time.

Compare Hakewill's Declaration of the Providence of God, 1627, *passim, et al.*

Howell's Letters.

The age was partly responsible. If there had been any love of Nature in the seventeenth century, American settlers would have shown some appreciation of its aspects in a new world. But the prevailing sentiment of the time was that Nature had long been steadily deteriorating, and that the everlasting frame of the universe was in a state of rack and decay. For the sublime in external Nature there was no taste. An accomplished English traveler in 1621 describes the "hideous" Alps, which he had crossed, as "uncouth, huge, monstrous excrescences of Nature." This, we may suppose, represents the sentiment of English settlers toward the grand primeval wilderness about them. "Uncouth" is Captain John Smith's only epithet for the picturesque wilderness trails through which he marched; and George Sandys, though a poet, never seems to look upon the wilderness except as an obstruction and an enemy. The colonial verse writer does not suffer any intrusion into his meditations of the over-awing effects of Nature, primitive and unsubdued, as he encountered it. What contemplation there is in the books and letters of the time expends itself on the supernatural or revels in the merely grewsome.

XX.

Men of the woods.

This "uncouth, huge, monstrous" wilderness puts its thumb mark on the character of the people otherwise than by contemplation. They grew up in the earlier generations woodsmen. Distinctively English characteristics fell away from them. The exigencies of a new country made them quick-witted and shifty. The dignity and repose of bearing that belong to a fixed position in an older civilization were lost, for the time at least. The American was pushing, aggressive, inquisitive. He was also more open-minded than his ancestors; a change of circumstances broke up the conservative crust of centuries of English life. The "go" of a new country came into the new life and a hundred years after the early settlement of the colonies an English clergyman in Virginia sketches the American as we have known him—nimble-witted, but less patient and profound than the Englishman.

Hugh Jones, Present State of Virginia, pt. ii, chap. v.

XXI.

The old books.

The survivors of seventeenth century libraries let us know what the old books were like. They varied greatly in size. There was the princely tome in folio, sometimes at least stoutly corded

CHAP. III.

and honestly bound in good leather, now and then it was gilded and richly tooled. Then there were small quartos thick and small quartos thin, some bound and tooled, but many stitched and home-bound by the owner in parchment sewed through and through by strings of sheepskin or clad in scraps of old missals or merely covered with leaves of old books. Below this the sizes and shapes are too various and often too nondescript to be set down, running all the way to twenty-fourmos or something of the sort. Regularity in size or shape was not important in libraries that usually were not shelved but stored in chests. If there were Latin works, there would be many in parchment cover, or if from the Rhine country some would be elaborately stamped in pigskin and held together by ockumy clasps. A few manuscripts one would be pretty sure to find—a diary or a journal of travel, or a controversial tract, or some poems innocent of print. From college the owner brought in his own handwriting a carefully copied digest of logic, metaphysics, divinity, with arithmetic, or geometry. He may have added some rules and diagrams for land surveying. Many of the manuscripts were transcripts of printed books not easily come by in those days. Some professional men of the time saved money and learned their texts by transcribing from books borrowed from others; and lawyers bound later laws in manuscript in the same volume with printed statutes. Works on alchemy, with some on the art of war, have come

Note 25.

to us in transcripts. The elegance of the old decorative "secretary's hand," learned by patient application under a writing master or his usher, shames the slovenliness of modern scribbling, and sometimes excels in beauty the fine old typography which carried over the traditional taste and painstaking of the mediæval copyist into a rare mechanical art.

ELUCIDATIONS.

Note 1, page 96.

James Laing, a Scottish writer of the Reformation period, expresses this contempt for vulgar tongues as proper only to barbarians and heretics: "Tres sunt linguæ elegantes et ingenuæ, Hebraica, Greca, et Latina quæ nobilibus principibus sunt dignæ:—Ceteras linguas cum sint barbaræ barbaris et hæreticis tanquam propriis relinquæ." Quoted in McCrie's Life of Knox, 472.

Note 2, page 97.

Puttenham's Arte of English Poesie, published in 1589, is a principal authority, but the condition of the language may be mainly deduced from the literature of the period. One of the sources of corruption noticed and lamented is "the peevish affectation of words out of primative languages" by "schollers." Many "inkhorne termes" were brought in by preachers and schoolmasters. The words "penetrate," "penetrable," and "indignitie" are examples of these fresh intruders. Arber's Puttenham, 156–159. In Alexander Gill's grammar of 1619, quoted in Masson's Milton, i, 55, is a denunciation of the intrusion of words of Latin origin, such as "common, vices, envy, malice" and "virtue, study, justice, pity, mercy, compassion, profit, commodity, color, grave, favor, acceptance." "But whither pray," demands Gill, "in all the world have you banished those words which our forefathers used for these new fangled ones? Are our words to be exiled like our citizens?" The enriching of the language with Latin and French terms was inevitable; the three languages had been in juxtaposition in England for centuries, and they were sometimes jumbled together unconsciously. In Brayley and Britton's History of Hertfordshire is an example of a three-ply interweaving of the languages in an old Description of the Manor and

Chap. III. Manor House of Rye: "Item granarum, 16 equi et vaccæ, cum le storehous mercandizarum 2000 marcae, Item le byldyng de le inner court edificat cum bryke," etc. Many such triple macaroni passages could be accumulated.

Note 3, page 97. "And certaynly our langage now vsed varyeth ferre from that whiche was vsed and spoken whan I was borne. For we englysshe men ben borne vnder the domynacon of the mone which is neuer stedfaste. . . . And that comyn englysshe that is spoken in one shyre varyeth from a nother." Caxton's Prologue to the Eneydos, A. D. 1490. The changes in speech in the sixteenth and early seventeenth centuries were nearly as rapid as in the time of Caxton. Take this intimation from Evelyn's Diary in the year 1654: "Here [at Beverly] a very old woman shew'd us the monuments, and being above one hundred years old spake the language of Queen Marie's daies, in whose time she was born."

Note 4, page 98. "Victories, plantations, frontieres, staples of commerce," etc., are enumerated by John Evelyn as "reasons both of additions and corruptions, of the English Language." All changes of usage were accounted corruptions, and stay-at-home men have grieved for three centuries over the "corruptions" introduced into the tongue from the various offshoots of the mother country.

Note 5, page 102. The word "turkish" had perhaps come to signify "foreign" or "outlandish" in European tongues. It is to be noted that a third German name for the turkey was *wälsches huhn*, the foreign fowl. This may indeed be sufficient reason for "turkish corn" in several languages, as *wälsch-korn* or foreign corn is one of the designations of maize in German.

Note 6, page 102. John Clayton, the parson, says in a letter to the Royal Society in the seventeenth century about Virginia: "There's a great sort of ravenous Bird that feeds apon Carrion as big very nigh as an Eagle, which they call a Turkey Bustard, . . . whence its name; it is nothing of the same sort of Bird as our Turkey Bustard." Johnson's Dictionary of 1755 defines "bustard" by "a wild turkey." We may not conclude from Clayton's term that the great vulture was called a turkey bustard before he became a buzzard, for a dozen years earlier in these Transactions, xi, 631, Glover writes "Turkie Buzzard," and very much earlier yet, in 1614, Hamor has "Turkie Bussards." The author of the True Declaration of Virginia, 1610, does not know either name; he calls the birds "cormerants." One might suspect that the name is a corruption of "bastard turkey" (compare "bastard plover" in the regulations of Henry VIII's household, Forsyth's Antiquary's Portfolio, i, 187), or that it has some relation to the French *dindon batard*, but there is no evidence in favor of such a conjecture. The vulture was often mistaken for the turkey. Castiglioni Viaggio negli Stati Uniti, i, 225. We have indeed a tangle of the names of two large European birds, the buzzard and the bustard, with the American turkey and turkey buzzard. It is with pleasure that I pass the puzzle to philologists. Apropos of the possible confusion one way or the other between *dindon bastard* and turkey bustard or buzzard, there is in Le Page du Pratz, Histoire de la Louisiane, 1738, ii, 418, a curious distortion of another English name of this same vulture, which he calls "Carencro" [that is, carrion crow], "qui est aussi noir qu'un Merle & aussi gros qu'un Dindon."

Note 7, page 102.

The suggestion of Acosta is that since the Italians call maize grano turco, Pliny's description of millet may have been intended for maize, and that the plant may have been known to the ancients. It was as hard to believe in that day that there was anything of value unknown to Pliny as that there could be any truth of philosophy not deducible from Aristotle. The confusion between buckwheat, or "saracen wheat" as it was called, and the newer maize, though not heretofore suspected, is almost beyond doubt. Lescarbot, in La Conversion des Savvages, 1610, gives a list of plants cultivated by the Iroquois. In it there appears "du blé mahis (ou Sarazin)." In the Burrows reprint of the Jesuit Relations, i, 85, this passage is Englished by "maize wheat (or Buckwheat)." If this rendering were correct, it would still show the confusion of the two, but Lescarbot did not suppose any grain but maize to exist among the Indians. "Sarazin" is here but another name for maize, in explanation of the less familiar "blé mahis," or more properly "mays." The name in French or Italian was conferred, no doubt, when it was yet not well distinguished from buckwheat, and it was probably used at first interchangeably with blé de turquie, the notion of origin conveyed being identical in the two names. "Grano saraceno" appears to be still applied in Italian to both maize and buckwheat. Baretti's Italian-English Dictionary, edition of 1854, has no other definition of "grano saraceno" than maize, while it defines maize by "fromentone, grano saraceno, grano turco." Yet Castiglioni adheres to "frumento saraceno" or "grano saraceno" for buckwheat, and "grano turco" for maize. Viaggio negli Stati Uniti (1785, 1787), i, 36; ii, 7, and *passim*.

CHAP. III.

Note 8, page 103.

Strachey, in his account of Virginia in the "yearely daies" of the colony, to imitate his expression, says of the beans of the Indians, "Their beanes . . . are the same which the Turks call garvances," an identification as wide of the mark as most of those on which names of American plants are founded. In 1633 De Vries, the Dutch explorer, was making his way up the Delaware to secure some of the "Boonen van de Wilde," or Indian beans, and these on the next page he calls "Turchse Boonen"—that is, Turkish beans. Korte Historael, etc., 101, 102. In the English version of Acrelius "Turkish beans" and "large beans" appear as two of the garden vegetables cultivated in New Sweden. The original Swedish at p. 167 has "Turskska Bönor" and "störa Bonor," which in our common speech would be Turkish beans and pole beans, indicating that the so-called Turkish beans were not grown on poles, but, as we know, twined themselves about the growing corn stalks. In the papers reviewing and, it might be said, enriching De Candolle's Origin of Cultivated Plants, the learned authors, Gray and Trumbull, have missed the passage above in De Vries, which would have shown the error in Van der Donck that they suspect. See American Journal of Science for August, 1883, p. 134. Van der Donck is so far misled by the name "Turkish" as to suppose the Indian bean to have been introduced by the Dutch. The name gallivance is applied to some plant in Pennsylvania soon after Penn's settlement, and in a Complete Discovery of the state of Carolina, 1682, the name appears as "Callavance," from which we need not infer the presence of the garabanzo as cultivated in Spain, Mexico, etc., but merely a confusion of very different plants by people who had not seen both.

Note 9, page 103.

The New England "rye and Indian" was known in the eighteenth century, and perhaps earlier; it figures strangely in Castiglioni's Italian as "grano turco misto con segale formano delle crescenze senza lievito." The phrases "English grain" and "English grass" appear to have survived in New England until the American Revolution abolished all things English, in name at least. In a manuscript diary of Rev. Justus Forward, of Belchertown, Mass,, in my possession, it is set down, under date of June 15, 1763, that "grass and English grain look extraordinary well"; and on the preceding May 11th the diarist notes that there is "considerable feed in English pasture."

Note 10, page 105.

The use of husk for the bran or covering of the grain was in accordance with English usage at the time. A Virginia writer, in the Transactions of the Royal Society for 1666, uses the verb "un-husk" in speaking of rice and barley. Clayton, the clergyman, in writing of Virginia in the Philosophical Transactions, speaks of husks of the kermes or little galls on oak trees. The application of the word to the bran of the corn, the skin or husk of the grain, was thus very natural. In some doggerel by Davy Crockett when a boy these lines occur:

> She sifted the meal, she give me the huss;
> She baked the bread, she give me the crus.

This use of husk I found still extant in Charleston, S. C., in 1884. "Nubbin," used in English provincial dialects for the stump of a tree, came into general use in America for a dwarfed ear of corn, and I suspect that some analogous use of the word existed in colloquial English at the time. Roasting ears, an early name for green corn in the Chesapeake and middle colonies, is yet applied to green corn however cooked, and whether cooked or not, over a large part of the United States. Compare Beverley's Virginia, book iii, 15, and Rush's letter in Castiglioni, Viaggio negli Stati Uniti, ii, 44. Acosta speaks of a large round variety of corn that the Spaniards ate roasted "as a delicious food, more savory than roast beans or peas." Livre iv, chap. xvi.

Note 11, page 106.

The aroughcun of John Smith goes through innumerable forms. There is raconne very early in Morton's New English Canaan, p. 79, and in the perfect Description of Virginia of 1649; ratoons in Wilson's Account of Carolina, 1682; and roacoans in the State of England, 1683, p. 63. Barrett's maps, of about 1775, have three forms—"Aroughena, a sort of badger," and "roscones," in the same Virginia list; in the New England list the animal is "rackoon."

Note 12, page 107.

It is pohickory in some early writings, as in Baltimore's "Relation" of 1634, where it is said to be a "wild sweet wall-nut." The hickory nut is still called a walnut in parts of New England and New York; it is the white walnut in contradistinction to the black. But Gronovius's Flora Virginica, 150, calls the butternut white walnut thus: "Juglans alba . . . Anglice white walnut, Clayton"—that is, on the authority of Clayton, the Virginia botanist. It is still usually so called in communities of Virginia derivation.

Note 13, page 107.

Barbecue is generally accounted a West Indian word, but it was in general use in the colonies, and may have been known to

CHAP. III.

some of the Indians of the mainland. Beverley, in his history of Virginia, 1705, says that the Virginia Indians have a second way of "broyling . . . by laying it upon Sticks raised upon Forks at some distance above the live Coals, which heats more gently . . . this they, and we also from them, call Barbacueing." The word is elsewhere among the colonists "barbecute," and is applied to the roasting of venison wrapped in leaves in the ashes. Compare also Bossu's Nouveaux Voyages, 1777, where barbecue is traced to an Indian word, barboka, which signified the wickerwork—"les claies"—on which the meat was laid. Page 178 and foot-note.

Note 14, page 109.

Compare this word dafter, for daughter, with the old pronunciation "oft," for ought. In the Order of Orthography, by Joseph Prat, London, 1622, the word ought is thus given "oft." Prat lays it down as a rule that where "s" precedes the terminal "tion," the sound shun must not be given, by which rule the accepted form of such words in good speech would be, for example, combus-ti-on. Honor and honour, favor and favour, are "indifferently written," says Prat. The word mile is unchanged in the plural, as "one mile, twenty mile." As an example of the "barbarous speech of the common people," he has "yerbs" for herbs, "dater" for daughter, "twonty" for twenty, "feale" and "finegar" for "veale and vineger."

Note 15, page 109.

This mixing of variant forms of rustic English was kept up by fresh arrivals from England, and in the eighteenth century it was complicated by the great exodus of people to some of the colonies from the north of Ireland. Manifest traces of this Scotch-Irish admixture may be found in Pennsylvania, in the Ohio Valley and westward, and along another line of emigration in the Appalachian valleys and the table-lands of Virginia and the Carolinas.

Note 16, page 111.

"Gom," in this dialect of the Forth and Bargy, means a simpleton; in other local English it is, as in America, "gump." "Goss" in various dialects means gorse or furze. As gorse is not known in the United States the word has no popular meaning, but it has survived in the single dialect phrase often heard in certain places, "Give him goss!"—that is, a chastisement as with gorse or furze.

Note 17, page 112.

The following nonsensical verse was remembered by my father as sung by the Virginia slaves in his boyhood—that is to say, in the first quarter of the nineteenth century:

Juba dis an' juba dat,
An' juba roun' de kittle o' fat;
Juba heah, an' juba dah,
An' juba, juba ebry whah.

In the coast region of South Carolina, where the negroes are much the larger part of the population, and where "new negroes" were run in from Africa at a late period, the corrupt speech is called the Gullah dialect, from the Gullah or Angola negroes. The vocabulary has few words that are not evidently English in origin, The effect is somewhat that of English badly spoken by a foreigner, who ignores the natural quantity of the vowels. There is a French nasal in the sound of final n—fine, for example, takes the sound of the French fin.

Note 18, page 113.

In Smyth's Tour, i, 235, he remarks on the unwillingness to be called a servant by the frontiersman of the late colonial period. The use of the word servant was evidently narrower in the colonies than in England, though Mr. Albert Matthews has furnished me with several references to "hired servant" and "hired servant man" in the first half of the eighteenth century. As some of these were in advertisements of runaways, the hired servant must have been bound by contract for a year, according to the custom at that time. Even in such advertisements for runaways in New Jersey, Mr. Matthews notes the term "an Irish hired man," and he has furnished me with a number of instances of the modern use of the word "help" in England for a person employed in a capacity a little above that of a domestic servant. Under date of Philadelphia, December 6, 1748, Kalm says that a distinction was made by the English inhabitants of Pennsylvania between a servant and a "serving or bond servant" for a term of years. As the phrase does not occur in any advertisement of runaways or elsewhere, so far as I know, its use must have been local. Servant was applied to a slave, and thus the depth of infamy was reached.

Note 19, page 113.

In Halliwell's English Dialects, 28, there is a Lovers' Dialogue, a Wiltshire piece. "Hold not so breach now," says the maiden to her wooer. The word is in the exact sense of the popular American word "brash," and sheds some light on its derivation, regarding which both the Oxford Dictionary and the Century Dictionary grope a little for want of this instance. In a fifteenth century Essex poem in Halliwell—

Be thou never to smert
To her mennys consayle—

is an older form of an Americanism—"too smart to take advice."

CHAP. III.

Chief-Justice Morris, of New York, in 1737 said in the Zenger trial, "An ingenious man has smartly enough observed," etc. In the couplet—

> Tharefore y wylle me holly halde
> To that language that Englisch ys calde—

quoted in Halliwell's Dialects, p. 7, from a MS., the word "holly," for wholly, suggests the "New England umlaut," as it has been called. In Hearne's works there is an extract from a version of Pierce the Ploughman's Crede which closes with the words—

> And in the heighe holy gost holly I beleue,

where the difference between the words "holy" and "wholly" appears to be that which one often hears in New England, even among educated people. I have pointed out in a previous note, on the authority of Franklin, the early existence in parts of Pennsylvania of what are now deemed New England peculiarities. John Bartram, the Pennsylvania botanist, probably used the umlaut pronunciation like a Vermonter. In his Observations he writes, "We rod over middling land," p. 66. "To get shut of," for to get rid of, appears in various English and American dialects. "Bail" for the handle of a pail or kettle is still used in dialect in England. It appears in a will of 1463, where the English editor finds it needful to explain it. Compare Bury Wills, 23, 242. It is in general use in the southern and western parts of the United States, and accounted a preferable word. "My woman" appears more than once in Braithwayt's Drunken Barnaby, 124, 171, as a respectful equivalent for my wife, with "uxor" on the opposite page as the Latin. This is precisely the usage of the rustic people in New England; farther south the farmer says "my old woman," though his wife be never so young. "Party" for person, which modern purists account recent and reprehensible slang, was in abundant use in older times. Increase Mather has the "sick party recovered," Providences, 192, and one even hears of dear parties. The Camden Miscellany, vol. iii, quotes from MS.:

> The partie nowe is gone and closelie clade in clay.

In northern regions of the United States a sick person is said by the country people to be "handled" by his disease. In Howard's Collection of Letters, 273, the Duke of Norfolk writes to Henry VIII, "I have ben so sore handeled with myne old Disease," and there are other examples. "Fall" for autumn is now mainly American, but there are English precedents enough for it, and it would be a pity to lose from literary use so good a word.

There are instances of its early use in the colonies sometimes in the full form, as "this last fall of the leafe." Virginia Calendar, 1688. (But what is "the fall of the leafe" directed to be taken out in drawing a fowl in the Compleat Cook of 1658?) Parson Clayton, writing of Virginia, says, "When they go a Shooting or Hunting, as they call it," etc. He marks here an early difference of usage that has persisted. It has been asserted that "rooster" is a word produced by American mock modesty. But "roost-fowl," at least, was a form that appeared as early as 1701, Sewall's Diary, vi, 33, and I have seen "roost-cock" in English use earlier than the beginning of colony planting. "Toat railes" appears in the Remonstrance of Gloucester County, Virginia, as early as 1677. State Paper Office, Virginia Papers, 62. Tote must have been of English origin. It appears in a Boston paper before the Revolution, and is found in the old "tote roads" of Maine. But there are words of distinctly colonial origin. "Gum" for beehive in some local dialects, came from the use of a section of a hollow gum tree for hiving bees and other purposes. Compare "a large cask or gum" in Virginia Gazette, June 21, 1744, and the Western pioneer's proverbial boast that he was cradled in a "bee-gum." The number of illustrative instances that might be given from my own notes alone would require a volume. See two papers in Century Magazine, April and October, 1894.

Note 20, page 120.

For Sukey Fry and other ballads I am indebted to my daughter, Mrs. Elizabeth Eggleston Seelye. They were taken from the lips of an old lady of New England birth and lineage who may have been the last person treasuring these bits of colonial folklore. She could remember only a few verses of Sukey Fry, supplying the rest by narrative. "A young nobleman coming to America met a young girl, Sukey Fry, and they fell in love. He was put into prison, and she visited him and carried him things to eat. He agreed, when released, to wait for her seven years unmarried. He returned to England:

"Seven years passed away,
And seven years more followed on.

He at length married some one else. The scene is at the wedding. The servant at the door says:

"'At your gate, sir, stands the fairest creature
That ever my two eyes did see;
On every finger she has a diamond,
And on her breast plates one, two, three.

. . . .

CHAP. III.

> The golden ringlets on her shoulders,
> Are worth more than you and your bride too.'
>
> "Lord Bateman smote his hand upon the table,
> And split the leaf in pieces three,
> 'I'll stake my life and all my living
> That Sukey Fry has crossed the sea!'

The father of the bride says:

> "'Oh, cursed be that Sukey Fry,
> I wish she had on the ocean died!'

Lord Bateman replies:

> "'I married your daughter to-day 'tis true,
> I'm sure she's none the worse for me;
> She rode here on my horse and saddle,
> She may go home in her coaches free.'"

See the many versions of the ballad in Child's Scottish and English Ballads, and especially Child's learned treatment of its variations in the quarto edition, part ii, 454–483. One can not but regret that Professor Child did not have the pleasure of knowing that the "Isbel," "Dame Essels," "Susy Pye," and "Sophia," of other versions had emigrated with the colonists and assumed the name of Sukey Fry. Many comparisons with the Scottish and the English versions suggest themselves, but they must be left for folk-lorists. But is it on account of the name "Susy Pye" in the ballad, or perhaps on account of the sense of colored or painted in the word "pie," or "pye" that this seems to have been a name for a Moor? In the Records of Massachusetts Colony, 1638, p. 239, "George Pye, a Moor," appears. Rose, Pink, and Piney is among the tales collected by Mrs. Seelye. Piney is the most frequent pronunciation of peony in rustic speech. There is an allied story in the little collection referred to called Pussy Catskin. It is substantially the same story as that given in Catskin's Garland in Child's Ballads, but the American version is in prose and much more antique than the ballad as Child gives it. The word trencher is preserved in it, though the meaning of the word must have been very obscure to those who recited it last. The tale is known in many tongues. See Child's English and Scottish Ballads, viii, 172 ff. See also Marian Roalfe Cox's Cinderella.

Note 21, page 122.

In 1697 All Faith's Parish received a library from "the Honorable Kenellem Chiseldene." It was composed as follows: "foure Bibles, one booke called the whole duty of man, three bookes in defence of the Common prayer, three Catekisme, and one lecton booke"—that is, a "lecture" book as it is elsewhere called, perhaps a book of homilies. Vestry Book of All Faith's, Manuscript in Maryland Historical Society. We have here, and in the instance cited in the text, traces of the ancient custom of keeping certain books in the churches, sometimes chained. Compare Marsden's early Puritans, 236. See the seventeen books provided for the use of the first clergyman in New Netherlands, O'Callaghan's History of New Netherlands, i, 454.

Note 22, page 122.

After much seeking I found a copy of the Practice of Piety where it was least to be expected, in the Graham Library at the Century Club, New York. It owes its preservation from the destruction that has befallen a myriad other copies to the chance that Samuel Butler once owned it and wrote some lines in it.

Note 23, page 123.

Prof. C. E. Norton, in his Life of Anne Bradstreet prefixed to a modern edition of her poems, says, "There is, I believe, no evidence that there was a copy of Shakespeare's plays in Massachusetts during the seventeenth century." Apropos of a line of Mrs. Bradstreet's which resembles the line in Hamlet, v, ii, 337, 388, this remark is made. But, as Mrs. Bradstreet was an inmate of the family of the Earl of Lincoln in her youth, and a late and reluctant adherent to New England Puritanism, she may have seen Hamlet on the stage in England. Shakespeare was never mentioned or quoted by any American writer in the seventeenth century, so far as I know. Even in England his fame was of slow growth. Peacham's Compleat Gentleman, 1660, calls George Buchanan, whose fame rests on his Latin poems, "the prince of poets of our time," and he does not think Shakespeare worth naming at all. The bare word "Macbeth" in the Virginia inventory of Captain Arthur Spicer, 1699, is the first allusion to his work from an American source that I know. Another Virginian, Edmund Berkeley, who died in 1718, had Shakespeare's works. William and Mary Quarterly, ii, 134, 250, and *passim*.

Note 24, page 124.

Nathaniel Ward, a contemporary, says of Anne Bradstreet that she is "a right Du Bartas girle." A single verse of hers will serve to illustrate her method and her admiration for her model:

> But when my wondering eyes and curious heart
> Great Bartas sugared lines do but read o'er,
> Fool do I grudge the muses did not part
> Twix him and me the overfluent store.

The reader who cares to see what the so-called American literature of this time was, may consult Mr. Tyler's History of

CHAP. III.

American Literature, or Mr. Stedman's Library of American Literature.

Note 25, page 125.

The custom of making a library by transcription prevailed among the lawyers in Edward I's day, according to Lord Campbell. Lives of the Chancellors, i, chap. xi, cited in Allibone's Dictionary, p. 1993. The Reverend Edward Taylor, of Westfield, Mass., in the last quarter of the seventeenth and the early eighteenth century, copied more than a hundred borrowed books. Nearly all his professional books were copied by himself, and "his manuscripts were all handsomely bound by himself in parchment." Sibley's Harvard Graduates, ii, 410. There are volumes of old Virginia statutes in the Library of Congress partly manuscript. As late as 1715 (chap. xxv) Maryland enacted that all acts passed should be transcribed on parchment and sent to each county, to be lodged with the clerk after they had been "published and proclaimed in court." A like usage prevailed in other colonies. The Mennonites in Pennsylvania were advised from Europe to transcribe the colossal Martyr Book for their own edification. Many examples of books written which were never destined for print might be given. President Stiles's manuscripts and those by William Byrd, of Westover, are notable examples. In my own collection are manuscripts some of which seem to be sixteenth century copies of books probably in print, others are manuscripts of the seventeenth century not intended for print. There are also manuscript books on various studies, especially geometry and surveying, that appear to have belonged to old New York families. The custom of college students making manuscripts came with the first settlers. Massachusetts Historical Society Collections, vi, 102, 103.

CHAPTER THE FOURTH.

WEIGHTS AND MEASURES OF CONDUCT.

I.

In recent times the preconception that gives its color to moral judgment is the belief in an equality of rights for all. To do justice to the weak, to defend the helpless, to free the enthralled—this, in a nutshell, is the moral passion of the present age; a passion which sometimes obscures other phases of human duty. But when English settlers first broke ground in the New World the prevalent notions of life and obligation were everywhere monarchical and aristocratic. Primary duties were to those above you—to God, to the king, to the magistrate, to the social superior. Special privileges and exemptions rightfully belonged to the man of high birth and official position; worship and authority were theirs by divine right. "Noble or Gentle-men," says the author of The Compleat Gentleman, "ought to be prefered in Fees, Honors, Offices, and other dignities of command and government, before the common people." This was the voice of the age, which even thought that rank exempted its possessor from challenge when he cheated or bore false witness. "We ought to give credit to a Noble or Gentle-man before any

The aristocratic conception in morals.

Comp., for example, Cotton's Abstract of Laws, 1641, i, 1, and iv, 3.

Peacham's Compleat Gentleman, ed. 1661, pp. 14, 15.

of the inferior sort. He must not be arrested or pleaded against on Cosenage." The intrusions of gentlefolk with hawk or hound into the fields of poor men were not to be resisted, however ruinous they might be. "They ought to take their recreations of hunting and hawking, etc., freely without controul in all places." This rather abject reverence for superiors extended to domestic life. The shining virtue of a wife was obedience; resistance to a husband was rebellion against God. The son served his parents in menial subjection; in some houses he was required to attend them at table as a servant. He was often sent to play serving man to some greater kinsman, in order to learn the etiquette of subjection to superiors. When the well-trained lad encountered his father or mother he did them reverence and said, "Sir," or "Madam, I crave your blessing." In such an age it was easy for New England lawgivers to revert to the severity of the Mosaic law against disobedient children. Harsh penalties were denounced against "child or servant convict of any stubborne or rebellious caridge against their parents or governors," and incorrigibleness was "adiudged to be a sin of death" by Puritan lawmakers.

Comp. The Husband's Authority Unvailed, 1650, p. 77.

Conn. Records, i, 72, 1642. Comp. p. 80 and Mass. Rec., *passim*.

II.

Reverence for rank.

Not only reverence for parents and masters, but the sentiment of reverence for rank was brought to America, and cherished as an inseparable element of piety. Subordination to social superiors was accounted the only basis of order. Distinctions were nicely marked; it has been estimated that of the emigrants to New England before 1649, about one in fourteen was entitled to the prefix of "Mr.," the rest were called simply "Goodman So-and-so." Harvard students took their place in the catalogue according to the social position of their parents as appraised by the academic authorities, and the lad of humbler birth yielded the baluster side of the stairs to one conventionally his superior. The seats in New England meeting-houses were formally "dignified," a process by which their relative value as a mark of rank was fixed, and it was then decided by carefully weighing against one another the various offices in town and church and trainband, as well as by comparison of estates, who should sit in the places of honor. Social aspirants seeking to advance themselves by intruding into seats higher than those assigned to them, created disturbance in the meeting-house, and their ambitions had to be repressed by fines. In the Chesapeake colonies emblems of rank were sometimes attached to the pew of a governor or other officer, and the great families of the parish—those from whom justices of the peace and vestrymen were chosen—were wont to lend the countenance of good society to divine worship from exclusive pews perched high in the gallery under the roof, like swallows' nests, or placed at some point of conspicuity on the floor below. For

Judd's Hadley, 251.

CHAP. IV.

humble people to dress "above their degree" was clearly sinful, because "they that wear soft clothing are in kings' houses," according to Scripture. So declared the New England Synod of 1679, which stigmatized the rising of a democratic spirit at that time as "a refusing to be subject to order, according to Divine Appointment." It was even in accordance with the notions of the time that the scales of justice should slant a little toward a plaintiff or defendant of dignity, and a high-born felon did not lose the benefit of his birth. In Maryland, for example, the criminal of quality was to be beheaded according to English precedent, and not hanged like a vulgar rogue, while Massachusetts politely refused to send "any true gentleman" to the whipping-post.

Results of Three Synods, 96, 97. Comp. Perkins, Cases of Conscience, 139, 140.

Note 1.

Maryland Archives, i, 71.

Mass. Liberties, 43.

In the colonies generally the dignity of a ruler was guarded like the ark of the Lord, and a spectacular show of reverence was made to judges and governors by means of escorts of gentlemen or sergeants with halberds. Criticism of magistrates in the early colonial period was little less than blasphemy. Pitiful was the case of a Mrs. Oliver, whose opinions were too large for a narrow time. Publicly whipped for reproaching the Massachusetts magistrates, this brave woman of rare gifts bore her cruel chastisement without binding. Years afterward her animadversions on the clergy were cleverly refuted by pinching her tongue for half an hour between the forks of a cleft stick. A poor devil of a servant, who ventured to reproach

Savage's Winthrop's Journal, i, 232, 233.

Clap's Memoir.

the magistrates in 1631, had his plebeian ears cropped. "I saw it done," says Roger Clap with righteous exultation. If Cotton's scheme had been adopted in 1641, all unpleasant criticisms of God's appointed would have been strangled outright by the hangman's rope.

CHAP. IV. Cotton's Abstract, vii, 13, 14. Mass. Hist. Coll., vol. i. Comp. Code of Mass., 1649, 143.

III.

Theocratic ethics.

This upward trend of moral obligation was associated with a more fundamental notion. The age summed up its body of ethical doctrine in the compact statement that "the chief end of man is to glorify God." This doctrine, lisped by babes and sucklings, found its counterpart in the declaration of the famous Westminster Assembly, that the only living and true God "works all things according to the Counsell of his owne . . . Will for his owne glory." Men were taught to be good, not from any aspiration for honesty or goodness, nor out of any regard for the rights and welfare of others, but solely with reference to the will and pleasure of God. "This Good Pleasure or Will of God is the rule of Righteousness," says John Norton, the Massachusetts Calvin. The moral law was made moral by divine command; theft would not have been wrong had there been no commandment. "That the moral law should be a constant rule of manners," says Norton, "is from the Meer Will of God."

Note 2.

The Humble Advice of the Assembly of Divines concerning a Confession of Faith, chap. iv.

Note 3.

IV.

Submission to the king.

We have intruded here into the region where "reason builds beyond Nature, but into emptiness

CHAP. IV.

only," as Schiller has it. But many practical consequences were deduced from the speculative notion of God as a despot who was the arbitrary source of right and wrong and who sought nothing but his own glory. It was the period of emblemism in theology, the period of the doctrine of correspondences in philosophy and of signaturism in medicine. To the mind of the time a clever metaphor was more convincing than an argument, and an analogy was almost irrefutable. Passive obedience to the reigning sovereign was fortified by the prevailing conception of right and wrong as dependent solely on the pleasure of the Deity. But the great leaders of Puritanism, finding their plans opposed by royal authority, cleverly succeeded in making the rule work the other way. From the notion of God's relation to morals they evolved an ideal of theocracy. Divine sovereignty became a cover for latent disobedience to the king. "The allegiance we owe to our dread sovereign lord King Charles" is the courtly phrase of Cotton, but while he thus doffs his hat to the king with his right hand, he furtively opens a back door of escape with the left, by adding the ambiguous saving clause, "whilst he is pleased to protect us as his loyal subjects."

Compare T. B.'s Royal Charter granted unto Kings by God Himself, 1649.

V.

The state secondary to the Church.

Puritan theory was strangely akin to ultramontanism in one regard. It made the state secondary and subordinate to the Church. Cartwright, the great Puritan of Elizabeth's reign, had embodied this in the maxim, "No man fashioneth his house to his hangings, but his hangings to his house"; and Hooker, the founder of Connecticut, was fond of repeating the proverb. When he shaped the Constitution of that colony in 1638 he made the government an humble auxiliary of the churches. Cotton found in the Scriptures a complete and infallible platform of politics, and of half a dozen other things besides. By what picking and snipping of texts he succeeded in getting whatever was desirable from the Bible we may see in his proposed code, to many of the provisions of which he appended Scripture references. That a court of law should have a clerk seems clear enough without a proof text, but Cotton must needs bolster this obvious expedient of common sense by citing the fact that there was a scribe's chamber in the court of the king's house in the time of the prophet Jeremiah.

Note 4.

Note 5.

Abstract of Laws, i, 6. Jeremiah, xxxvi, 10, 12.

VI.

The analogy between monarchy and divinity was so strongly felt that one is not surprised to find in the last will of Hooker, the founder of Connecticut, that God is called "His Majestie," and the same term occurs in more than one local record of the time in England. It was to conciliate this dread potentate that blasphemy was suppressed in laws and military orders, and the prevailing notion of the austere despotism of God had much to do

Defense of divine dignity.

Conn. Rec., i, 500. Royal Hist. MSS. Com. Reports.

with the unrelenting persecution of heretics as his sworn foes. This cringing attitude toward a jealous God appears in the fine-spun inhibitions of constructive idolatry. The success of difficult enterprises was thought to be secured by the suppression of heresy and blasphemy. Captain John Smith undertook to abolish swearing even among the rude and calamity-smitten Jamestown emigrants; but he did it not by Puritan severities, but in a jolly, rough-and-ready way by pouring cold water into the sleeve of the swearer. Varying penalties were denounced against swearing in New England; the profane man was fined and set in the stocks. One Connecticut blasphemer was to have his second whipping in the January following his first, "except the governor judges the weather unseasonable." In early Virginia records the fines for swearing are from one to three shillings, and in one case, in 1634, the parson is the prosecutor. A Harvard student, who had spoken words regarding the Holy Ghost which were thought blasphemous, was publicly solemnly beaten; the punishment was preceded and followed by prayer, a kind of grace before and after. The student's offense lay probably in the expression of unorthodox opinions, the most atrocious kind of blasphemy. He was subjected to other indignities after the beating, either to convince him of error or to propitiate an offended Deity. It was an accepted theory with ardent religionists, whether Catholic or Protestant, that heretical opinions regarding God

Note 6.

Conn. Rec., 1640, 1649.

MS. Records Accomac Co., Virginia.

Sewall's Diary, i, 4.

should be punished with death. A denial of the divinity of Christ was a capital offense under the early law of Catholic Maryland, and in later Protestant Maryland any objection offered to the doctrine of the Trinity was to be punished by boring the objector's tongue; for a second offense the Unitarian was branded on the forehead with B for blasphemy; the third time he was to be put to silence forever by the last resort of the law. New York, in its first year under English authority, denounced death against him who should deny "the true God and his attributes." Inhumanity and injustice were not absent from the colonial codes, but the "rights, immunities, and privileges" of Almighty God were always guarded.

CHAP. IV.

Bacon's Laws of Md., 1726, xvi, i.

Duke of York's Laws, so called, 1664.

Note 7.

VII.

This apparent excess of reverence has ever a basis of self-interest, quite cold-blooded and undisguised. The very buccaneers of that age went to prayer and confessed their sins whenever a rich prize hove in sight; and early Virginians sent expeditions against the Indians with general orders which usually began with a prohibition of profanity, or some other precaution for securing the favor of Heaven. The Virginia Company thought the Indian massacre of 1622 due to the "sins of drunkenness and excess of apparell" in the colony. The Massachusetts Company in London wrote to Endecott, in charge of their pioneer settlement, to "make good laws for the punishing of swearers"

Self-interest in morals.

Comp. Hist. des Filibustiers, pp. 45, 54, 55.

Randolph MSS. in Va. Hist. Society.

Young's Chronicles of Mass., 189. Compare

CHAP. IV.

Vaughan's Directions for Health, 1602. E. E. T. Society, v, 251. Letter in Bradford's Plymouth, 277.

and other offenders "if you ever expect a comfort or blessing of God upon our plantation." The first church was organized in Massachusetts during an epidemic, "to pacify the Lord's wrath." Winthrop, in his journal, is able to point out the particular sin that provoked almost every calamity of fire, illness, death, and financial loss that befell any individual. One man, for example, ventured to work too late on Saturday evening, the beginning of the Puritan Sabbath, and his child forthwith fell into a cistern on Sunday night and was drowned. In the time of King Philip's Indian war the obliteration of a town by firebrand and tomahawk was traced, not to the lack of a blockhouse and a vigilant garrison, but to the doomed town's neglect to secure "an able, faithfull dispenser of the word of God." The blight of 1665 that extinguished all hope of wealth from the growth of wheat in Massachusetts was attributed by the common people to the execution of the Quaker martyrs, and the Indian wars of 1676 and 1677 were thought a punishment for persecuting laws. But the conservative party proceeded in the latter year to make the laws against Quakers more stringent. Archdale, the tolerant Quaker Governor of South Carolina, thought that a pestilential fever in that colony was due to the persecution of dissenters.

Plymouth Rec., v, 177.

Mass. Rec., v, 59. Archdale's Carolina, 30.

VIII.

Scruples about idolatry.

In the seventeenth century there was much fear of lapsing into idolatry by inadvertence. Lord

Bacon recommends the pouring of wine into newly dug earth for the remedial effect of the vapor, but he adds the caution "that it be not taken for a heathen sacrifice or libation to the earth." The clause in the Massachusetts Body of Liberties of 1641 which made it a capital offense to have "any other god but the Lord God," could have had no practical aim unless it was the suppression of constructive idolatry. Many members of the train-bands in that colony regarded the English ensign as a gross idol, and refused to march behind it, because it had a cross in it. Endecott, the New England Jehu, thinking three fourths of a cross no cross at all, cut off one arm of it in the Salem colors. Hooker wrote a paper to prove the ensign harmless; but the rising zeal against idolatry obliterated the cross of St. George from the colors of the train-bands in 1635. After this reformation the red flag had only a white field in the upper corner for a union. For similar reasons the early Puritan settlers omitted the prefix "Saint" from familiar geographical names. For long generations Englishmen had paid rents and wages on the penultimate day of September, when the harvest was fully in hand. For such purposes it had been the habit for ages to count the year from Michaelmas to Michaelmas, and the term could hardly be spared. In Connecticut it was Protestantized into Miheltide, so that neither mass nor archangel might get any good of it. In the first half of the seventeenth century, and later, there were scruples

Winthrop's Journal, i, 186, 189, note, 224, 225. Mass. Records, 224 and elsewhere. Stoughton's letter in Mass. Hist. Soc. Proc., 1861, 135.

Sewall's Diary, ii, 12. Danker's Journal, L. I. Hist. Soc., i, 393.

Conn. Rec., i, 182, 1649. Comp. Ben Jonson's Alchemist, iii, 2.

CHAP. IV.

Winthrop's Journal and others.

Sewall's Diary, 1696, i, 428.

Mather's Ratio Disciplinæ.

Bozman's Maryland, ii, 403, 404.

against using the ordinary names of months and days of the week on account of their pagan derivation. Ordinal numbers were introduced instead to avoid etymological idolatry. "In Boston," said the royal commissioners of Charles II, "neither days, months, seasons, churches, nor inns are known by their English names." The practice of numbering the days gradually passed out of fashion, after it became a badge of Quakerism. Efforts to revive it in the last years of the century were vain. The pinch of the inconvenient scruple was got over by a trick of words: the names of the days were purified from idolatry by being called "planetary names"; but colonial New England continued to refuse to speak of "the Lord's Day" as Sunday. Puritan refugees from Protestant persecution in Virginia refused to take an oath of fidelity to the government of Maryland, because the officers of Maryland had sworn not to molest Roman Catholics, and what was that but swearing to countenance and uphold Anti-Christ? And so by many links, through their oaths to the government and Church and through the governors and their oaths, and through the unmolested Catholics with their saints and images, these tender consciences would at last be drawn into a long-distance paganism.

Not only was there danger in those perilous times that the individual might fall into damnable idolatry without knowing it, but the Puritan governments were ever on the alert to keep the land from being polluted by heathenism. Soon after the earliest settlement of Massachusetts, Governor Endecott cut down one false god, the maypole at Merrymount. A few years later, in 1633, the Massachusetts General Court went further and prohibited the natives from practicing their ancient custom of powwowing in the land of their forefathers. Weird dances, accompanied by gourd rattles and punctuated with grunts and inarticulate cries, were naturally taken for worship of a false god or of a devil. The Virginia Company had much earlier proposed to capture the Indian medicine men and thus put an end to such heathen mysteries. The ancient maxim that "dominion hath its foundation in grace" was accepted in the earliest colonies, and hence Christians dominated pagans by right divine. One writer intimates that some of the Virginia planters, about the middle of the century, carried their Christianity so far as to believe that a pagan had no right to property for which a Christian might have use.

Gatford's Public Good without Private Interest, 1657. Comp. Young's Chron. of Mass., 387.

IX.

The sense of moral proportion was obscured and confused in a reverent dread of offending God. The prevalent English custom of drinking healths was deemed "an abominable practice," and put under ban in New England, and later in Pennsylvania, not for the promotion of temperance alone, but mainly because it was a profane mixing

Trifling offenses magnified.

Note 8.

CHAP. IV.

of prayer and drinking and "a vain custom." It was also "an occation of the wasting of the good creature" at which the Creator might take umbrage. In 1643 the Virginia law made the evil of "the loathsome sinne of drunkennesse" to consist partly "in the abuse of God's good creatures," and this pious phrase has left its trace down to our time in a cant name for strong drink, "the creature." In modern times the objections urged against gaming turn upon the supposed danger of falling into the vice of gambling. The Puritans were at much pains to explain that the chief sin in games of chance was one of profanity. The lot was "an appeal unto God," and games of chance were therefore declared by the Connecticut General Court to be "altogether unlawful in the very nature of them," since in cards and dice "that great and sollemne ordinance of a Lott is expressly and directly abused and prophaned." Cotton even unlimbered his scholastic logic to prove that the merry nonsense of choosing mates on Valentine's day by drawing papers from a hat was an appeal to God's "immediate providence for dispensing these ludicra," and hence "a taking God's name in vain." To check "the great dishonor of God" that was wrought by games, the Massachusetts Legislature, in 1670, excluded cards and dice from the colony as things pernicious in their very nature. The observing of Christmas was objectionable because it was an occasion for the profanity of playing games. But Christmas observance

Hening, i, 240.

Conn. Rec., i, 289.

Hutchinson Pprs., 182, 183. Code of 1672, 37, 38. Comp. Mass. Rec., 1631, p. 184, and Judd's Hadley, 98.

was iniquitous on its own account, for all honoring of times and seasons other than the Sabbath seemed to the finespun Puritan mind a masked idolatry. It was ordained in Massachusetts, in 1670, that the mere abstaining from labor on the 25th of December should be a penal offense. By this system of far-fetched deduction innocent acts were made technically superstitious, while intolerance and superstition, with consequent cruelty to "heretics" and "witches," walked abroad unabashed in garments of sanctity.

Note 9.

X.

Sunday in pioneer Virginia.

When the early English settlements were made in America, the observance of a strict Sabbath was a newly discovered virtue brought to light in the later Reformation period. Never before was a new obligation so swiftly and widely accepted as was strict Sabbath keeping in England and Scotland. Several things had prepared for this acceptance; nothing had done more than the recoil of religious people from the coarse and brutal amusements that made the English Sunday of Elizabeth's reign a school of frivolity and cruelty. From morris dancing, from intolerably coarse interludes, and from the pitiless baiting of bulls and bears, the reaction to severe restraint was natural. Like all other novelties of the new century Sabbath keeping was impatiently exported to be tried in the virgin communities of the New World. A severe

Note 10.

Note 11.

See The Beginners of a Nation, book ii, chap. i, sec. xx.

CHAP. IV.

Sabbath was imposed on the infant Virginia colony in the relentless military code under which De la Warr, Gates, Dale, and Argall ruled. Argall, though a tyrant, a semi-pirate, and a finished despoiler of other men's estates, was religious none the less; the combination was not uncommon in that time. Under this versatile master of rapine the colonists were required to be religious willy nilly. He who did not go to church on Sunday must "lye neck and heels"—that is, with chin and knees drawn close together—"on the corps du gard" the following night and be reduced to slavery for a week. If this did not take the atheism out of the culprit, a harsher penalty was visited on succeeding offenses. The sub-colony sent to Virginia in 1619 by the estimable Smith of Nibley and his associates was provided with instructions which required that "vain sports bee refrained" on the Lord's Day, which was to be observed with "divine exercises according to the common prayer." James I had tried to check the tide of Sabbatarianism, but his so-called Book of Sports had precisely as much effect as the memorable command of his remote predecessor Knut against the incoming sea. He never learned that great lesson of statesmanship that once Humpty Dumpty is down the king himself can not replace him. James tried to compel Englishmen to amuse themselves on Sunday as in former times, but we find this company of good churchmen spurning his "vain sports" in their general orders, and sending copies of the

Stith's Virginia, 148.

1618.

Smith of Nibley MSS., folio 61.

Note 12.

"Practice of Piety" along with the prayer book to teach the emigrant subjects of the king an opposite doctrine. Bishop Bayly's Practice of Piety was much read in Virginia during the seventeenth century, and it gives seventy-five pages of its small bulk to enforcing the duty of sanctifying the first day of the week. Beside the forbidding of all business and burden carrying, it is particularly severe on the "trimming, painting, and pampering" of one's self on Sunday, which is "doing the divel's work vpon God's Day." Bayly also forbids "Studying any Bookes of Science but the holy Scripture and Divinitie," and "all recreations and Sports which at other times are lawful," with "all grosse feeding" and "all talking about worldly things." This view of duty was enforced by arraying the very same horrible examples that had served in Bownd's famous treatise on the Sabbath. Did not the scaffolding fall like the tower in Siloam and kill the people at a Sunday bear baiting in London? And this not at all on account of their inhumanity to the bear, but solely because they were enjoying "carnall Sports on the Lord's Day." Dr. Bownd's nobleman whose hunting on Sunday caused his child to come into the world with a dog's face reappears in Bayly. A disastrous conflagration in Stratford-on-Avon and a peculiar combustibility in other towns with Sunday fairs were also edifying examples of the danger of obeying King James in this regard. But whatever effect such dire examples may have had on the seri-

Twenty-fifth edition Delft, p. 303 ff.

See Beginners of a Nation, pp. 124–133.

ous minds of pious men and women, the great majority of early Virginians took their Sundays without fear of divine judgments and without regard to the Sabbath law of the colony passed in 1643. Many of them spent the day in gregarious and demoralizing idleness.

XI.

Secular culture in Virginia.

Here we come upon those forces that made the culture of Virginia as distinctively secular as that of New England was dominantly theological. There were physical difficulties obstructing religious observance in the Chesapeake region, where habitations were thinly strung out along the estuaries, rivers, and tributary creeks—mere sinuous lines of water side settlement with only forest behind. There were plantations that had never an entrance or exit by land. Some parishes were thirty miles and more in shore length, and when the web-footed pioneers would attend church they must commonly do it by sailing in their sloops or by laborious paddling in dugouts. After the passing of Hunt and Whittaker and other brave missionaries of the first generation there came a different race of clergymen, "such as wore Black Coats, and could babble in a Pulpet, roar in a Tavern, . . . and rather, by their dissolutenesse, destroy then feed their Flocks." The church was far away, the parson contemptible, but no doubt some of the isolated settlers resorted to service to meet their neighbors and relieve the tedium of loneliness.

Hammond's Leah and Rachel, 1656.

But many of the younger Virginians, and those of the rougher class, generally preferred to spend the idle day of the week at the nearest Indian village in rude amusements and intercourse with the barbarians. There was a considerable betterment of manners in the times of the English Commonwealth, when exiled Cavaliers brought in a more dignified way of living and a better regulated Sunday. Throughout the colonial period the Virginia Sunday was never a rigorous Sabbath, but mainly a day of leisure, of sport, and of social enjoyment, with resort to the Church service when convenient. The typical country squire of the Chesapeake region treated religion as a mere propriety, by no means to be taken too seriously; there were many in the eighteenth century who rejected it altogether. It came to pass, thus, that the Virginia mind was coolly secular and unspeculative—an intellect trained to affairs, and above all to politics and social intercourse. Virginia's early contribution to the intellectual life of the country was naturally a political one. The difference between the outcome of colonial Virginia and that of colonial New England might almost be anticipated by observing the wide difference between the early Virginia Sunday and the Puritan Sabbath. New England was cradled in religious enthusiasms that gave tone to life in the whole northern belt of the United States. If Virginia and the States of her planting have lacked that reformatory zeal which has made New England so generally serviceable,

CHAP. IV.

Note 13.

and sometimes so tedious, it is probably because Virginia was almost untouched by any strong religious sentiment, until it was at length stirred by the evangelical movement in the middle of the eighteenth century.

XII.

The New England Sabbath.

Note 14.

Mass. Records, 1653, vol. iii, 316.

Although the keeping of Sunday with sabbatical strictness began soon after the Reformation in some parts of England, the doctrine made no great stir until Dr. Bownd's elaborate work on the Sabbath of the Old and New Testament burst upon an astonished public in 1595, and by its boldness brought down upon itself condemnation to the flames and the prohibition of further issue. Ecclesiastical and governmental interference helped to make a painfully rigorous repose on Sunday a distinctive badge of Puritanism. The Sabbath in the superlative degree crossed the high seas with the Puritan migration. In New England it was argued that, as the Sabbath was the principal outward means of honoring God, it stood for the whole duty of man toward God. And a right divine reverence was paid to it. Contrary to English custom, the greatest Puritan divines, Cotton and Hooker, maintained with consistent literalness that the consecrated time began at sunset on Saturday evening, because the Jewish Sabbath began on Friday, and the evening and the morning made a day in the first chapter of Genesis. Judaism sat hard on the Puritan conscience in many ways;

even the Jewish preparation for the Sabbath was imposed on the people in the first years of New England. "All that inhabit the Plantation" were ordered, in 1629, to "surcease their labors every Saturday throughout the year at three o'clock." The rest of the day was given to catechising and other painful preparations of the soul for the irksome austerities of the Sabbath. In mediæval times mortifications of the flesh were sometimes savagely severe, but they were voluntary and affected only the individual inflicting them upon himself. Puritan austerities were imposed by family authority on servants and little children, and enforced with ruthless severity on a whole community by the magistrate. On the Sabbath cattle might not be pastured in the common field where they would have to be watched, food must not be prepared, nor must one pay a visit or walk in the streets or the fields except to meeting, nor might one stay at home from meeting without danger of fine or whipping-post. In New Haven, and probably elsewhere, indulgence in eating an apple or cracking a nut was accounted reprehensible. In solemn awe of the Sabbath the innocent gambols of the children were repressed as something particularly heinous. "We should rest from labor, much more from play," says Cotton in a catechism ludicrously entitled Milk for Babes. The aged Increase Mather, as late as 1712, urged that children must not be suffered to play on the Lord's Day. Of rest the Puritan mind had no

Instructions to Endecott in Young's Chron. Mass., 163, with note and authorities there cited.

Lambert's New Haven, 188 and elsewhere.

Milk for Babes, in Prince Library, Boston.

Mather's Meditations on the Sanctification of the Lord's Day.

CHAP. IV.

conception; it was a technical term that included the attending to public prayers, stretching sometimes to a full hour in length, and to sermons of yet greater prolixity, interspersed with home exercises to fill up the time and banish repose. The leaders were generally sincere enthusiasts bent on pleasing God and not even comprehending what a huge burden of unbearable Pharisaism they were binding on the backs of men. Probably nothing else in Puritanism, not even its hatred of heretics and its horror of witches, caused so much human unhappiness in the aggregate as did its effort to transform the Christian Sunday into a punctilious Hebrew Sabbath. For the attainment of this end almost every sort of outrage on personal liberty was perpetrated by the magistrates and by domestic authority. Even foreigners presumably ignorant of the law were liable to arrest and other indignities, if caught strolling in the streets of Boston on Saturday evening after sunset. Ambassadors from a French Catholic colony were shut into Winthrop's house the entire Sunday for fear of collision with public opinion and the constables. This polite incarceration was mitigated by "the liberty of a private walk in the garden." In New Haven, in 1647, a young man was sent to the whipping-post on Monday for not going to meeting on Sunday, and two brothers were beaten by their father for visiting young women on Saturday after sunset. They lived unmarried to their deaths from mortification. Much of the

Cal. Col. Papers, State Paper Office, 1660–'68, No. 51.

Lambert's New Haven, 193, note.

torture proceeding from the Puritan Sabbath was self-inflicted. There is a pitiful story of Wigglesworth, the author of the popular Day of Doom, sitting long on a windy Sunday in an agony of scrupulous uncertainty, unable to decide whether he might with a good conscience venture to go and shut a neighbor's swinging stable door and so save it from wreck. He ended by leaving the door to its fate for the Lord's sake.

Sibley's Harvard Graduates, i, 268, 269.

The yoke of bondage enforced by law galled the necks of those who were less religious or who held to the easier habits of the Church of England. There were many in the first generation who "accounted it their happiness to live in the wast howling wilderness" to escape this unblinking supervision, giving up many advantages to preserve that liberty so dear to men not broken by oppression. Later in the century there was a party that denied the right of the colonial government to enforce the Sabbath and prescribe modes of worship. An election sermon was leveled at this uprising, and the Synod of 1679 even shakes at it the old superstition used by Dr. Bownd in 1595, and later in the Practice of Piety, that conflagrations are intimately connected with lax Sabbath observance. And indeed the New England Sabbath, though almost too much for flesh and blood, had by this time become a fixed tradition, good for yet more than a hundred years of survival before it should begin to show signs of decline. In 1740 we find it still the custom to shut the gates of the Boston peninsula and to put

Chauncey's Commencement Sermon, Cambridge, 1655.

James Allen's Election Sermon, 1679.

Results of Three Synods, 100.

Note 15.

CHAP. IV.

Bennett MS. in Mass. Hist. Soc. Proc., 1861, 115.

a guard at the ferry, that no one might go forth on Sunday. And the traveler who gives us this account of the state of siege in which Boston put itself once a week adds that if "they could escape out of the town, it wouldn't answer their end; for the same care is taken, all the country over, to prevent travelling on Sundays . . . They will not suffer any one to walk down to the water side, though some of the houses are adjoining to the several wharfs, nor even in the hottest days of summer will they admit any one to take the air on the Common. . . . The justices, attended with a posse of constables, go about every week to compel obedience to this law." Even a group of two or three might not talk together in the street on Sunday. Thus uneasily with wearisome diligence and infinite watchfulness did the New England metropolis take its rest. There is a reverse to this picture of strait-laced government that is more agreeable. The traveler just quoted tells us "it is a rare thing to meet with any drunken people, or to hear an oath sworn, in their streets."

XIII.

Sunday in Maryland.

Md. Archives, i, 83, 1639.

In Maryland the early law regarding Sunday was Catholic in tone; work was forbidden on "the Lord's Day or other holy days." This modest prohibition may have been tolerably well observed, for the roistering settlers were ready enough to abstain from work on any day of the week when excitement could be found. But the law probably bound them little; certainly they freely disregarded the act passed at the same time against "drinking to a notable perturbation of any organ of sense or motion." There were pious Catholics who spent their Sundays becomingly, no doubt, and there were many Puritans in Maryland whose Sabbaths were characteristically strict.

Note 16.

In the Dutch colony.

In the Dutch colony of New Netherlands many laws were made regulating the sale of liquor on Sunday, and in 1663 a bill was passed in favor of a strict Sabbath, but against this New Amsterdam protested, and refused to proclaim the law, as contrary to the freedoms of Holland. It would have been impossible to enforce a strict Sabbath on the mixed population of residents and the yet more varied comers and goers in New Amsterdam. The Dutch, says Sir George Mackenzie, have "few Merchants and Tradesmen who do not sell and work freely on the Sunday."

Dutch Manuscripts, vol. x, pt. iii, 119. O'Callaghan's Laws of N. N., 448. Moral Hist. of Frugality, 1690, p. 20.

XIV.

Zeal without pity.

Religious zeal was abundant in the seventeenth century among devout people of all creeds, but it lacked that touch of generous pity that in more recent times would fain convert men for their own benefit. It was a zeal for church, for party, for faction—a zeal for sound doctrine as each sect understood sound doctrine. There was a disinterested zeal for the glory of God, or, as the devoted Catho-

CHAP. IV.

lic missionaries of Maryland phrased it, "for the glory of the Blood of our Redeemer." But men of all shades of opinion took pleasure in the disasters of obstinate opponents and unbelievers. Roger Clap does not conceal the pleasure it gives him that one of the gainsayers of the Massachusetts theocracy had probably been roasted alive by the Indians; and the same religious but ruthless spirit crops out in all churches and parties of the time in England and America. It was not Laud, but his predecessor and opponent, Archbishop Abbot, who took pains to secure the burning of two heretics by packing the court with judges already pledged to decide against the accused. The undertone of philanthropy that we confidently expect to find in religious feeling in recent times was lacking in the fiercer and, if we must say so, more religious spirit of that day.

Abbot's Letters in Egerton Pprs., 447, 448.

XV.

The religious societies.

In order better to mark the distinction between that age and this later time, let us digress to trace, along one of several more or less obscure lines of cause and effect, the evolution of altruistic zeal. When that tide of frivolity and scoffing profligacy that overflowed English life at the fall of the Commonwealth and the return of Charles II to the throne had swelled to the full, there sprang up in some London parishes, about 1679, "religious societies." By whose agency the first were planted, or whence came the seed-thought, we shall prob-

Woodward's Rise of the

ably never know. Intended only to promote devoutness of spirit and seriousness of life in individuals, these little groups of brethren pledged to one another, and, solemnly taking the communion together in their own parishes, offered a warm and sheltered soil in which germinated those ideas that formed the religious life of the eighteenth century. By a gradual modification some of these associations appeared in 1691 as the famous societies for the reformation of manners by appeal to the law. Their most effective work was done in Queen Anne's time. This tendency to do by means of societies what the half-palsied English Church of that time could not do, resulted in 1699 and the following years in the establishment of societies for religious propagandism—both by printed publications and the sending of missionaries—a device by which Protestantism has sought to supply the loss of the mediæval religious orders. The outgrowth of the devout societies did not weaken their organizations. One of these nurseries of pietism at a much later time bore the nickname of the Holy Club of Oxford, and out of it issued the Wesley-Whitefield revival—a revival that primarily sought not to build up any Church or sect, but to benefit the brutal and neglected by means of religious influences. Thus a zeal for pity's sake took the place of the old stern and pitiless passion for what was thought to promote the glory of God. White-hot agitations that assume wide proportions are gradually changed by the resistance they encounter, and

Religious Societies, 3d ed., 1701.

A Short Acct. of Several Kinds of Societies, 1700. White-Kennett Library, London.

Acct. of Foundation of Soc. for Prop. Gospel, Appx. to the sermon of 1706.

CHAP. IV.

are modified by cross-forces, until their momentum spends itself in achieving what the first promoters did not have in mind. Religious movements in this way become at length political and social forces. The "Great Awakening" in the eighteenth century was presently metamorphosed, in part, at least, into philanthropic and reformatory agitations. The wish to save men's souls became an aspiration to deliver them from oppression, to educate them, and free them from the hardships of poverty. This outcome of the religious movement coincided with the philosophical and political tendency toward democracy, that played so conspicuous a part in the transformation of ideas that took place in the wonderful eighteenth century.

Note 17.

Note 18.

XVI.

Plan of salvation in the Practice of Piety.

We shall not understand the age of colonization unless we look into its schemes of salvation which are in some sort an index of moral stress. Bishop Bayly's now forgotten Practice of Piety, "Directing a Christian how to walke that he may please God," shall inform us, as it instructed nearly all men in that time. Its teaching regarding the Sabbath we have already noted. Editions of this guide to godliness tumbled headlong from the press in a succession so rapid that the booksellers of the time became confused in attempting to number them. A minister complained in 1656 that the "generality of the Plebeians" held its authority to

Comp. sect. ix above.

Wood's Athen. Oxon., i, 567.

be "equal with that of the Scripture." Bunyan's watchdog conscience was awakened by it and Ben Jonson's mocking humor laughs at the veneration for it. Colonists frequently carried it to Virginia and elsewhere, sometimes in company with the Bible, the prayer book, and Barrough's Method of Phisicke, and throughout the seventeenth century it turns up frequently among heirlooms left to descendants by deceased planters, and in New England it was even translated into the Indian tongue by the apostle Eliot. A Virginian of the early period, while wrestling with the unsubdued wilderness for bread and meat, and trying to decide whether or not his malarial fever was to be treated as an "intermitting tertian" or "a continuing quotidian," or whether it was both of these combined according to the systematic Barrough, must also pick out in the intervals of business and the pauses between ague fits the proper way of saving his soul. The Practice of Piety explained it in such a fashion that no wayfaring man, be he ever so wise, could by any chance understand it. It was also complicated by a folding diagram. In order to please God the plain man must know "the essence of God in respect of the divers manner of being therein," and also the "attributes which are either Nominall or Real." That is to say, he must appreciate the "absoluteness," "simpleness," and "infiniteness" of Divine existence, and then must know five "relative attributes" besides. If the acclimating fever has not haply carried him off while he is mastering these

Jonson's Gypsies, quoted in Int. to Braithwaite's Barnaby, 1818, p. 77.

Edition "Printed at Delft-haven for the good of Great Britain."

CHAP. IV.

Note 19.

complexities and perplexities, he finds that he must likewise "competently know and necessarily beleeve" other scholastic propositions, finespun to invisibility all of them, regarding the nature of God. He is also required to know himself—not himself actually, but only himself as John Doe in certain theological relations and in a wholly impersonal way. Having now glorified God by knowing him analytically, he comes to the second branch, which is to glorify God by serving him. One looks for a treatise on moral duties, but we are in the seventeenth century. This service of God begins and ends in acts of devotion performed "privately," "domestically," and "publicly," with remembrance of feasts and a yet more scrupulous observance of fasts. Religious etiquette all! For closing so futile a life there are directions for dying with proper devoutness. Duties to one's fellows, such as fill the Sermon on the Mount, find no place in the outspread diagram of duties with which the book begins, and it is with difficulty that they find standing room in a few subsidiary parts of the work. The mediæval virtue of almsgiving, with an eye to the welfare of the giver in the next world, appears in traditional form with a Protestant tag to it: "Liberalitie in alms-deeds is our surest foundation that we shall obtaine in eternall life a liberall reward through the Mercie and Merits of Christ." It was with this end in view no doubt that well-to-do Virginians kept up a custom of leaving exactly ten pounds to the poor of the par-

Early MS. Records of Virginia Vestries.

ish, and this was the only bequest that was in every case described not in colonial currency or tobacco, but in sterling money. If we inquire into the reason for the marvelous popularity of Bishop Bayly's Practice of Piety we shall find it in the fact that the book was the fullest expression of the religious sentiment of the people in an age of transition. It was, besides, written with considerable vigor. So much was it esteemed in England that in some instances at least it was read aloud by those who watched witches as a counter sorcery to confound the devil. A change in the sense of moral proportion, the waning of a belief in diabolism, with a growing notion that the heavens are not wholly unpropitious even to men who do not understand all about divine existence and attributes, and keep fasts, have caused this once utterly popular book to fall into a fathomless oblivion. When with difficulty, after tedious searching of public libraries, one finds by good luck a copy of the Practice of Piety that has escaped the waste-basket, it is worn and torn by seventeenth century thumbing.

Gentleman's Magazine, 1830, p. 26.

XVII.

"Effectual Calling."

"We han't glorified God as God," laments the preacher of the Massachusetts Election Sermon in 1704. In the effort to please an austere God wholly intent on securing his own glory, the age lost in some measure what it could ill spare, the propulsion of religious sentiment in the putting forward

CHAP. IV.

of civilization and the uplifting of the individual. Puritan writers made holiness merely relative, the result of a mysterious transaction between God and the soul, in which transaction the soul had little part. This holiness, according to Cotton, was so persistent that it might survive much base living. He instances Solomon. On the other hand, uprightness of life, not preceded by "effectual calling," was mere sin. Wigglesworth in his Day of Doom marshals at the bar of God a company of

Cotton's Holiness of Church Members, 1650.

> . . . civil honest men,
> That loved true Dealing and hated Stealing,
> Ne'er wronged their Brethren.

Day of Doom, strophe 92.

But these worthy men, whose like is none too common, are summoned only to be scorned and damned. "The Ninevites and Sodomites," they are told, had no such sin as theirs. "Their righteousness is sin," the Judge tells them, "whereas the same deserveth Shame and meriteth Damnation." Thus the ideal of morality itself is abrogated in order to "glorify God as God" in the damnation of civil honest men. Fortunately for the world, theories that controvert fundamental intuitions are likely to be only speculatively believed. Neither Cotton nor Wigglesworth could have been as bad as his theory; in practice they probably respected honest men and detested scoundrels regardless of theological considerations. But such speculations when they reached weaker natures would serve as pretexts for immorality.

Note 20.

XVIII.

The God of that age.

"Take heed," wrote Herbert of Cherbury to a friend, in 1617, "of superstition and blasphemy, and above all that you make not a worse God than yourself." In these words he touched the weakness of the age: moral judgments were off their center when men adored a God worse than the worshipers. It seems like a paradox, yet it is true, that the more intensely religious a people were in that time the worse was their representation of the Deity. The great and long-continued popularity of Wigglesworth's Day of Doom in New England makes it good evidence in this case. His damnation scene is mediævally horrible:

> They cry, they roar, for anguish sore
>   and gnash their Tongues for horror:
> But get away without delay,
>   Christ pities not your cry,
> Depart to Hell, there you may yell
>   and roar eternally.

There are passages more ghastly than this, but why disfigure white paper with them? God is made the direct ruthless agent of physical torture everlasting, kept up for no conceivable end but his own glory. . . . "God's direful wrath, their bodies hath forever immortal made . . . And live they must while God is just, that he may Plague them so." A popular versifier like Wigglesworth, and he bred up among pioneers and Puritans, may be thought to hold views more extreme than those of his age. But Archdeacon Hakewill, much esteemed

CHAP. IV.

Apologie, etc., 1627, p. 572.

for learning and philosophy, could write the same thing with more dignity of expression: "Our fire hath neede to be fed continually with wood and fewell. . . . that burneth eternally without feed . . . for that the breath of the Lords owne mouth doth blow and nourish it." The monarchical idea dominates the thought of the time. Hakewill does not shrink from comparing the ingeniously cruel torments which vengeful kings had inflicted on their foes to God's punishment of sinners, and says that "so terrible is the judge to his enemies that he hath devised a wonderful way how to torment them," and that his "invention that way is as farre beyond the reach of all mortall wits as his power." Words of piety these, rank blasphemy none the less.

The same, 513. Comp. also Tymme's Silver Watch Bell, 1625, pp. 90, 91, and many others.

XIX.

Damnation of unbaptized infants.

Irresponsible infants were condemned to perdition by the ruthlessly systematic theology of the seventeenth century, and this also for the glory of the God who made them. The mediæval churchly doctrine that none could be saved without the sacrament of baptism had carried with it the harsh corollary that many infants were damned, some of them lost through mere accident or inadvertence. Cranmer's Catechism of 1548 declares that the children of heathen parents will be "damned everlastingly" for want of baptism, and in this he follows the Lutherans of the same period. In the next century Archbishop Laud, while affirming that baptism

Note 21.

CHAP. IV.

is necessary to salvation, declines to bind God to the sacrament, probably from his habitual dislike of constitutional limitations to sovereign power. But the popular belief remained, after the Reformation as before, that a child dying unbaptized was doomed. In the dark ages of Virginia and Maryland the parishes were very long-suffering in their dealings with tavern-haunting, brawling, and sometimes almost criminal parsons, apparently from fear of having their children grow up nameless heathens or die heirs of perdition for want of baptism. North Carolina had few clergymen even in the eighteenth century, and one finds the settlers plodding many rough miles, each with his covey of offspring, to intercept a wayfaring parson at some wayside spring and thus secure a chance of salvation for the young natives. Governor Eden of that colony wrote to the Propagation Society lamenting especially that "above fourscore" infants had perished unbaptized in the massacre by the Tuscaroras in 1712. This view of the massacre is rendered more picturesque when we remember that Eden was the governor who sheltered Blackbeard the pirate, and almost certainly shared his plunder.

Laud's Conference with Fisher, ed. 1673, p. 36.

Byrd's Dividing Line, 1728, *passim.*

XX.

Damnation of non-elect infants.

The Church of England divines feared that unbaptized infants might be damned because of some one else's fault, but the Calvinistic portion of the religious world was certain of the damna-

CHAP. IV.

tion of non-elect infants, baptized or unbaptized. Even John Robinson, of Leyden, the sweet-hearted pastor of the Pilgrims, could not escape this horrible conclusion, though he seems to accept it with a sore heart and averted face. It was the misery of religion in that day that good men worshiped a God less just and merciful than themselves. As late as 1690 "the ministers of the Gospel in Boston" published a defense of infant damnation in reply to a Quaker who disliked the doctrine. The Boston ministers did not, as the Anglicans did, leave a narrow fringe of uncertainty. They averred, as others of their school of thought had done long before, that an obscure phrase in St. Paul's most obscure epistle rendered it certain that some infants had already been damned for eating the forbidden fruit by proxy before they were born. On the other hand, Wigglesworth, the doggerel Dante of pioneer New England, reserved the damnation of unlucky babes to make an effective scene at the day of doom. The widespread circulation of his verses must have sown broadcast notions out of which every bereaved mother could build a tabernacle of perdition for her desolate soul. Minds so simply serious failed to see the *bouffe* grotesqueness of the speeches put into the mouth of the Divine Judge, whom Wigglesworth makes a little lower than a pettifogging country justice. The foredoomed infants argue their case rather cleverly, and, from a modern point of view, they get the best of it. But Christ, the Judge, has

Note 22.

The Principles of the Protestant Religion maintained agt. Geo. Keith.

Note 23.

Note 24.

the last word, and when they remind him that while Adam is saved they are damned for Adam's sin—

> Then answered the Judge most dread,
> God doth such doom forbid,
> That men should die Eternally
> for what they never did ;
> But what you call Old Adam's Fall
> and only his Trespass,
> You call amiss to call it his,
> both his and yours it was.

Note 25.

This is followed by a disquisition on original sin, delivered by the Judge for the edification of the lost infants or to clear the minds of the assembled universe. The infants are assured that they are sinners, and can expect only a sinner's share, "for I do save none but mine own elect." The colloquy, evidently growing embarrassing, is cut short by a verdict which reverts to the Judge's only reliance—the sin of Adam:

Strophe 165.

> A crime it is, therefore in bliss
> you may not hope to dwell:
> But unto you I shall allow
> the easiest room in hell.

Strophe 181.

Note 26.

XXI.

Harsh devotion.

Beautiful and merciful lives have blossomed and borne fruit under the shadow of harsh and repulsive beliefs. It would be easy to fall into the error of exaggerating the evil effects of creeds of iron. At a certain stage of social development the severity of a dominant creed sometimes serves a useful purpose of repression where repression is needed. The seventeenth century had inherited most of its harsh doctrines in some shape from the schoolmen or the Church fathers, and it set itself to forge them into formal creeds for its own enthrallment. The welding of doctrines into elaborate and systematic confessions and the writing of concise expressions of the quintessence of dogmatic theology in innumerable catechisms were regarded as a sort of heavenly vocation. Antique doctrines tinged with the barbarism of older ages, when thus formally propounded and authoritatively imposed, served to blur the ideal of even-handed justice and arrest the growth of humane sentiments. The gentler side of Scripture teaching was more or less obscured in an age when master teachers insisted on giving a perpetual divine authority to the sternest laws of the early Hebrews. It was an age that embittered its devotions by singing unsoftened the imprecatory psalms. It was a matter of obligation to sing all the psalms, even such vindictive verses as these in the New England Bay Psalm Book of 1640:

Note 27.

> And let the prayer that he doth make
> be turned into sinne;
>
> . . . .
>
> His children let be fatherless
> and's wife a widow make.
> Let's children still be vagabonds,
> begge they their bread also;
> Out of their places desolate
> let them a seeking go.

Ps. cix.

The primitive ferocity of such prayers is not chargeable to Puritanism; the versifiers of the Bay Psalm Book had heard the Sternhold and

Hopkins version sung in English churches from infancy, and had probably used it for their primary reading book in school. It had accustomed them to such lines as these:

> Yea blessed shall that man be cald
> that takes thy children yong
> To dash their bones against hard stones
> that lye the streets among.

Thus sang the Virginia and the Maryland churchmen, and thus also the New York and Carolina churchmen. The metrical version made by the poet George Sandys, once Secretary of the Virginia Colony, was far more elegant and was "set to new tunes for private devotion." But even Sandys will have the Christian in his closet pronounce a blessing on the men

> That dash thy children's brains against the stones
> And without pity hear their dying groans.

This non-Christian commingling of revenge and religion gave force to the hatred for heretics and embittered persecution and religious contests. Hear the bitter words of Ward, a New England minister, against the Irish rebels: "Cursed be he that holdeth back his sword from blood, yea cursed be he that maketh not his sword starke drunk with Irish blood," and so on breathlessly to the end. These words of Nathaniel Ward were printed in London in 1647; two years later Cromwell translated them into ghastly fact by the pitiless slaughters of Drogheda and Wexford.

XXII.

Brutality in sports.

Note 28.

The dash of fanaticism in the religion of the time and the narrow and literal adherence to the precedents found in the most ancient Hebrew Scriptures had something to do with the lack of humaneness in the law and its administration. For this reason ecclesiastics of all schools were often more ruthless than laymen; they carried their pitiless severity up to the credit of their piety. Massachusetts clergymen protested in 1635 against Winthrop for a leniency that to the modern man seems severe. In the controversy with the Gortonists the Massachusetts clergy advised that men not properly subject to the colony should be hanged for constructive blasphemy, but the magistrates were wiser or less zealous. The clerical profession, by its very nature, is more dominated by ideal considerations than others, and the severity of clergymen in governmental affairs is not necessarily from harshness of spirit, but rather from devotion to an ideal of conduct. The pressure of religious feeling in former ages was often distinctly opposed to the sentiment of humanity. But the seventeenth century needed no religious persuasion to severity; it was not at all a humane age. Traces of mediæval barbarism are found in the laws, in the customs, and in the brutal sports of the people, as well as in the sermons and other ecclesiastical deliverances. For generations the thoughtless populace had taken a savage delight in seeing bulls and bears baited to the death with fierce dogs; in an exceptional case a horse was turned over to be torn by mastiffs for the delight of the people. Bear baiting was the favorite way of spending the Sunday afternoon in Elizabeth's reign. One finds in a view of London in 1574 two buildings on the Bankside, "The Bowll Baytinge" and "The Bear Baytinge," carefully indicated as places of chief interest. After the scaffolding fell with fatal results at the bear baiting on Sunday in 1583 the people became superstitiously afraid of such sports on Sunday, but they were enjoyed on week days without suspicion of wrongdoing. Some of the later Puritans argued that as the animosity of animals to one another was the result of man's sin, men ought not to make sport out of it. The suffering of the animal is rarely alluded to in these debates; theology did not care for bulls and bears. Cockfighting had been for ages a reputable sport, highly praised by such men as Ascham, the tender-hearted school reformer, and it was practiced (annually or oftener) in schoolrooms apparently as a part of education. Against this also some later Puritans protested. As late as 1737 an English traveler says that Continental people were accustomed to complain of the cruelty of "the sports of our vulgar"—the very charge Anglo-Saxons are wont to make against the Spaniards to-day. Bull baiting and the tormenting of tame bears were not imported to America; bulls were too scarce and valuable, and bears were too plentiful and fierce. But the relish for inhumane

Beschreibung und Contrefacture der Vornehmster Statt der Welte, 1574.

Compare the opinion of Mr. Perkins and Mr. Bolton . . . concerning . . . cockfighting, 1660. Harl. Miscell., vol. vi, 122.

Note 29.

Note 30.

sports remained. Entrapped wolves were made to sell their lives in a bloody fray with mastiffs, or were tied to the tail of a wild horse to be kicked and dragged to death. Josselyn speaks of some large New England bird, which he calls a "cormorant," as making rare sport when wounded and turned loose to be badgered by dogs. Animals appear to have been preferably put to death by dogs. One finds Archbishop Sandys in Elizabeth's time trying to recover a "brinded dog," and complaining that he had never a dog with which to kill some bucks that had lately been given him. Puritanism was reformatory, though it could never go far beyond its age, and did not break the tether by which the great Cartwright in the sixteenth century had tied it to the temporal laws of the Jews. Massachusetts had gone to the limit by its creditable and ungrammatical law of 1641 against "Crueltie to any bruite creature which are usuallie kept for man's use." The wild creatures were left without the pale for want of Mosaic precedent, no doubt. In Virginia and Maryland cockfighting was a gentlemanly and Christian amusement throughout the colonial time. The laws of the Puritan colonies show that the reformatory spirit in Puritanism had begun to soften a little the harsh cruelty of law and its administration at the time, but notwithstanding prohibitions against cruel and unusual punishments, burning to death took place in Boston and Cambridge and pressing to death was resorted to in the witchcraft trials in Salem.

Liberty, 92. Comp. also 93.

Paige, Hist. of Cambridge, 217.

Punishments more barbarous, if possible, were inflicted in other colonies. Legal torture to produce confession was in use in New Netherlands under Dutch rule. In Pennsylvania a gradual translation of Quaker theories of non-resistance into milder laws took place, and the administration of the law was less severe than the law.

XXIII.

Obligation of worship.

The obligation of worship, as we have seen, was thought to be infinitely greater than moral duty. "The languishing and improsperous condition" of the Virginians after the Restoration was not attributed to the strangling of their commerce by the enforcement of the Navigation Act, but to the neglect of the people, mainly on account of physical impediments, to render to God with regularity "that publicke Worship and Service which is a Homage due to his great name." For this "sacriledge" the people were believed to be under a curse. In 1677 the Bishop of London took Virginia in hand and set about reforming a colony that by all accounts needed attention. He proposed that the thinly settled planters should be compelled to renounce the "profane custom of burying in their gardens and orchards," and forced to give up their habit of accepting such marriage as they could get from men not ordained, in a land where men in orders were exceedingly few, often dissolute, and frequently so far away as to be

Virginia's Cure, 1662, p. 4. Force, iii.

Cal. Col. Pprs., Nos. 337-339. Comp. 123.

reached only by a tedious sloop voyage, down one river and up another. There were things in the colony infinitely worse than the Virginia graveyard at the back of the garden to preserve it from prowling wolves, and the conservation of social order by marriage at the hands of clerks and lay readers, failing a better. But to Bishop Compton, as to others in that antique world, ecclesiastical impropriety, even when well-nigh unavoidable, was a sin more heinous than the oppression of bondsmen and unregulated morals.

Comp. Gatford's Public Good without Private Int., 1657. Morgan Godwyn's Negro's and Indian's Advocate, 1680 and many others.

Virginia had been settled when no hard-and-fast line had yet been drawn between Puritan and non-Puritan churchmen, and its church cherished both, retaining down to the Revolution the party-color of the transition period in which it was planted. Its clergy wore no surplices for more than a hundred years after the settlement, and in some parishes the eucharist was taken in a sitting posture. In New England the sacraments were hard to come by; in some parts of Virginia they could not be refused. One Virginian, in 1645, was threatened for refusing to go to communion in his parish church and required to bring to the next session of the court a certificate that he had reformed in this particular. In New England the baptism of babes was not always to be had for the asking; Virginians who declined baptism for their children were sometimes dealt with.

Hugh Jones, Present State of Va., 1724, pp. 68, 69.

MS. Records York Co., Va., p. 61, Va. State Library.

XXIV.

Eccentricities of Church government.

In the Puritan attempt to reconstruct the Church on a scriptural model, all sorts of scruples had an opportunity to crystallize. The coupling of pastors and teachers in Paul's writings was a source of trouble and debate. The notion that the pastoral office was dual appeared in the ferments among the excited English Protestants at Frankfort before the accession of Elizabeth, it was a trait of the Dutch church life in the seventeenth century, and it was elaborated among the English Separatists before 1582. In New England each church undertook to sustain two ministers in the hard conditions of pioneer life where the burden of one might have been thought too much. A ruling elder and several deacons shared authority with the "pastor" and the "teacher"; to complete the hierarchy, "ancient widows" were concluded to be church officers from their position in the Pauline epistles. This system in five tiers, originally separatist, was brought to America, in theory at least, by the Pilgrims, and, after discussion, came to be adopted by most of the Massachusetts churches. No plan could well have suited less with frontier conditions. The support of two ministers was an irksome financial burden; a double leadership promoted factions; ministers in the second generation were scarce; and the dual system, unsuited to the environment, went into swift obsolescence in spite of the lament of ideal-

Note 31.

CHAP. IV.

ists and the futile efforts of the Synod of 1679 to restore the double pastorate of the founders. The unnecessary ruling elder went out more gradually, and the proposed ecclesiastical widows were found impossible from the first, in a new country where every woman not decrepit was sure to be sought in marriage.

Winthrop's Journal. vol. i, 38, note.

Note 32.

XXV.

Scruples about psalm singing.

John Cotton says Satan has "mightily bestirred himself" in suggesting doubts about psalm singing. It was a question whether psalm singing was to be allowed at all. It was held that Scripture psalms were not to be sung, but only songs "indited by some personall spirituall gift of some officer or member of the church." Then there were other scruple-breeders who thought that one should sing and all the rest content themselves with saying "Amen." It was a question whether women should be suffered to sing, and it was proposed to confine vocal music to godly men regardless of their voices, not allowing "carnall men and Pagans" to join in public singing. There were other propositions of the sort, but as Cotton opposed them and attributed them to Satan, we need not drag them out of their centuries of oblivion. One that Cotton does not mention was that of the saintly Separatist and master scruple-monger, Smyth, of Amsterdam, who regarded it as "unlawful to have the book before the eye in the time of singing a psalm." The Pilgrims of Leyden, on the

Cotton's Singing of Psalms a Gospel Ordinance. Compare Gospel Musick or the singing of David's Psalms, 1644, with Preface to New England Psalm Book and Wm. Ames's A Sound out of Zion and others.

Barclay's Inner Life, 106.

other hand, would not read the psalm line by line as sung, until at length they adopted the common mode of the time out of regard for a brother who could not read. To such extremes did anti-ritualism go. A scruple against using music books in service time caused musical notation to be forgotten almost throughout New England in the seventeenth century. The number of tunes in general use was about eight or ten, and in certain congregations but half that number. In some places the worship was without singing, failing any one who could "take the run of the tune," as the phrase was. Familiar tunes were corrupted in oral transmission; the same tune varied essentially in congregations a few miles apart; in some places the name of an old tune was all that could be recognized, the music having been "miserably tortured and twisted and quavered into a horrible medley of confused and disorderly noises." A writer of 1721 declares that the music was so "dragged" that it was necessary sometimes to take breath twice in one note. Psalm singing in the other colonies was probably not better than that in New England. In the Anglican churches, as in Puritan worship, the psalm to be sung was read off line by line before the several lines were sung. One of the reforms advocated by Commissary Bray during his brief dash into Maryland in 1700 was the teaching of catechumens to sing the psalm "artificially." Even at the beginning of the Revolution Boucher declares that the psalmody was everywhere "ordinary and mean."

Note 33.

CHAP. IV.

There were not six organs in Maryland and Virginia, and there were churches in which there was no singing at all. Scruples aside, the obsolescence of music in New England was probably inevitable. But when soon after 1700 efforts were made to introduce music books into Puritan meeting-houses a sol-fa controversy arose, the conservative mind imagining that devotion itself would perish if written music displaced the barbarous discord that harmonized with bare and square architecture. In the preface to the New England Psalm Book the versifiers wind their logic through a sinuous argument to prove that the use of instrumental music in Jewish worship was "ceremoniall," while the psalm singing itself was "morall" and of perpetual obligation. The preface makes a merit of the rough-hewn literalness of the version urging that "God's altar needs not our pollietys." Beneath this ostensible argument lay an element of all austere systems of morality, a notion that pleasure had something reprehensible about it. People opposed church music on this ground, accusing it of "bewitching the mind with syrenes sound." But colonial psalm singing could hardly be charged with such perilous seductions.

Conn. Valley Hist. Society Collections, 42. N. E. Chronicle, *passim.*

Preface to New England version of the Psalms, 1640. The so-called "Bay Psalm Book."

Mulcaster's Positions, 38.

XXVI.

The multitude of scruples.

New England did not stop with forbidding music books; in spite of Cotton's judgment to the contrary, the Bible itself was excluded from the service for fear of ritualism, except where the reading was for immediate exposition. In 1699, when Puritanism was fast losing its vigor, the new Brattle Street Church in Boston took the bold step of having passages from the Bible read as a part of public worship. Colman, the Brattle Street pastor, was so bold a ritualist as to repeat the Lord's Prayer after his own. Very slowly these new decencies of worship made their way. A church organ was too "ceremonial" even for the innovating Brattle Street Church, which refused a proffered gift of one. Not only must music be sung by rote and prayers not be read, but sermons must be given without notes. Warham, the first to use notes in the pulpit, was "much faulted for it." Puritanism habitually regarded religion and beauty as antagonists. Its leaders in England condemned the use of rhetorical ornaments, particularly those drawn from heathen sources. The bare hardness of expression and the absence of anything like style in early New England sermons was probably voluntary at first. Little conventional decorums, like the ring in marriage and marriage by a minister, and receiving the eucharist without gloves on, were the butt of scruples. At their first coming the New-Englanders called their places of worship churches, but here was a fine opening for scrupulosity. In order not to ascribe sacredness to a building, the merely descriptive term meeting-house was substituted, that being wholly free from any pleasant or decorous associa-

Mather's Ratio Discipl., 65. Lewis's Lynn, 106. Turell's Life of Coleman, pp. 42, 178. Compare Sewall's Diary, ii, 394.

Magnalia, iii, 121, folio ed. Nugæ Antiq., *passim.*

Lewis's Lynn, 108. Sewall, iii, 279. Prince's Annals under Oct. 15, 1629.

CHAP. IV.

tion. A minister might not pray over a new-made grave; it would grow into prayer for the dead. As there was no axe or hammer heard in the Jewish temple work, the Plymouth Pilgrims refused to take the negative in asking the assent of the church to a conclusion of the elders, and perhaps for the same reason the early Massachusetts churches formally confirmed the choice of a pastor by "silent votes" of some sort in the presence of the magistrates. Strangest of all was the scruple generally accepted at first that obliged women to wear veils during public worship. After Cotton's arrival and opposition, it was only in Salem, where Endecott was the chief upholder of the practice, that all the women went to meeting veiled, as if to deprive public worship of its last element of extraneous interest.

1 Mass. Hist. Soc. Col., iv, 138.

Note 34.

XXVII.

Minor scruples.

Many scruples of that age must pass unnoticed; a few others we may select for their bric-a-brac interest. The giving to children pious and significant names was not primarily a Puritan notion; Bishop Jewell has a whole page of black letter in favor of it, and he derives it from Chrysostom, the Church father. Cartwright, the Puritan leader of Elizabeth's time, also opposed the giving of pagan names to children. The scruple was too congenial to the Puritan mind not to find a place in New England, and the early Latin canons, already quoted, forbade the giving of "barbarous and superstitious names," and recommended those that are "expressed in sacred letters." New England accordingly blossomed, not only with Hebrew names whose frequent incongruity with Saxon surnames was not then felt, but also with nouns, verbs, and participles, such as Love, Hope, Unite, Increase, Seaborn, Preserved, Wrastle, Humility, Supply, Hopestill, Waitstill, and other significant and hortatory words, some of them given indifferently to either sex. But the practice did not take deep root, and it was one of the first peculiarities to disappear with the relaxing of Puritanism when New England life began to line up again with English traditions in the second half of the century. The scruple against taking interest on money prevailed widely among religious people generally, and the matter was much debated, but New England seems to have escaped thralldom to a precept so illogical. In a new country where capital is lacking and opportunities for its profitable use are many, the reasonableness of an interest charge is evident, and a scruple about usury is too expensive to be afforded. Under the circumstances, the law forbidding the Jews to lend on interest to one another became ceremonial, on what ground does not appear.

Note 35.

Note 36.

Another instance of this narrow scripturism is found in the aversion to a census. In 1634, when the population of Massachusetts was estimated at four thousand, the magistrates did not dare enumerate them on account of "David's example," and

Winthrop's letter to Sir N. Rich.

it is probably owing to this fear that we are without trustworthy information regarding the growth of population in the colonies. In 1712 Hunter, Governor of New York, proposed to ignore David's example, but the fear of the people defeated his attempt to secure a census of that colony, there having been an epidemic after an earlier count. By numbering the freemen not in the militia, and adding in the already known number of militiamen, he learned the number of men. The women and children were afterward taken separately, and the inquisitive governor found means of counting, probably from tax lists, the white and black bondsmen. Simple addition did the rest, and there was no pestilence. The inhabitants of New Jersey, "being generally of New England extraction, and thereby enthusiasts," as Governor Hunter said, "were more difficult to count." In a later census of New York, females above sixty years of age were omitted. This bit of chicane practiced against Omniscience allayed the pious fears of the people. New-Englanders were not the only enthusiasts on this subject. Even after the Revolution, Pennsylvanians attributed an epidemic of yellow fever to the first United States census.

Docs. rel. to N. Y., v, 339, 459.

Smith's Hist. N. Y., 302.

XXVIII.

The supremacy of conscience.

Puritanism made one great contribution to human culture. More emphatically than any other movement of modern times, it taught the supremacy of conscience. There were instances of men who slew their natural affections in a sublime devotion to duty as they understood it. A minister felt bound to report the seditious speeches of his son, and a magistrate sentenced his own daughter to the whipping-post. Conscience could not long remain at high tide, the ebb was inevitable. The last half of the seventeenth century saw a swift declension from primitive Puritan ideals. But through such temporary and aberrant exercises the moral nature of the race is developed; by such efforts to attain a visionary and impossible excellence is the sense of right and wrong made strenuous enough to refuse the bribes of sensuality and of worldly ambition. The successors of those who exercised their consciences on frivolous judgments about apparel, psalm singing, and imaginary idolatries in the names of islands and days, may put their hereditary strenuousness or their traditional preference for ethical considerations into the promotion of substantial social betterments. The ferment may not be pleasant, but the brew is good at the last. The weakness of Puritanism was the weakness of its age. The Virginia justice, like the New England magistrate, toiled at the task of reformation by punishing with fines, and stocks, and branks, and ducking stool, and whipping-post, offenders for lying, swearing, scolding, drunkenness, and other sins. Such was the English method in the Stuart period. Neither among Puritans nor among Anglicans was there any clear vision of the spiritual advantage of

Winthrop's Journal, i, 158; ii, 114.

Comp. Nichol's Eng. Poor Law, i, 219.

morality. It was the outside of the cup and platter that got all this rubbing. But Pharisaism is a stage in human progress. More objectionable than the externalism was the absence of humanity. The pitiless penalties, the punishments inflicted on mere children and on half-insane women for hysterical words and acts, the ruthless creeds, the ferocious pursuit of the weak and defenseless accused of witchcraft or heresy, the unreproved delight of the mob in seeing brutes torn to pieces by dogs, provoke something like execration. But condemnation dies upon the lips when we reflect that ages to come may find many things damnable in the civilization of a more modern time.

ELUCIDATIONS.

Note 1, page 144.

Down to the Revolution class distinctions were sharply marked, especially in New York and Virginia. Compare Castiglioni, Viaggi negli Stati Uniti, *passim*, Pictet's Tableau des États Unis, ii, 181, and the remarks in Virginia Calender, i, p. ix, with many other well-known authorities. The maintenance of social distinctions in the assignment of seats in church was of course English. There is an instance of elaborate classification according to the rank in the Assembly Books of the Borough of Eye in 1650, in the Tenth Report of the Royal Historical MSS. Commission, part iv, p. 534, where both the northern and southern colonial ways are exemplified. The twenty-four common councilmen of Eye sat together, as the burgesses did at Annapolis in the eighteenth century. On the effect of the aristocratic preconception in law, compare Cotton's proposed laws of 1641, where three punishments are prescribed for slander. The third is, "By stripes if the slander be gross, or odious against such persons whom a man ought to honor and cherish, whether they be his superiors or in some degree of equality with himself or his wife." Ward, who wrote the code preferred to Cotton's, did not like the referendum by which his code was sent to be considered in the several towns. "I question," he writes, "whether it be of God to interest the inferior sort in that which should be reserved inter optimates penes quos est sancire leges." Whitmore's Introduction to Code of 1660, p. 19. There have been in every age those who demanded justice for the lowly in the name of religion. In an Anglo-Saxon manuscript of the tenth century a bishop is enjoined not to suffer "any Christian man too greatly to injure another; nor the powerful the weak, nor the higher the lower, . . . not even his thralls, because they and those that are free are equally dear to God." Institutes Civil and Ecclesiastical, published by the Record Commission.

Note 2, page 145.

The notion expressed in this beginning of the Assembly's Catechism was perhaps suggested by the first question and answer in Calvin's Catechism:

M. Quis humanæ vitæ præcipuus est finis?
P. Ut Deum, a quo conditi sunt homines ipsi noverint.

Note 3, page 145.

Compare the Select Cases of Conscience, by Shephard, of Cambridge, Mass., p. 14, and his Treatise on the Sabbath. A more moral theism than that of the Westminster Assembly was held in that time by Sir Kenelm Digby, who says, "Man is governed by God alwaies for the good of Man himself."

Note 4, page 147.

By the Constitution of 1638 the several plantations in Connecticut agreed to "conjoyne our selves to be one Publike State or Comonwelth," and entered into "Combination and Confederation together, to mayntayne and presearve the liberty and the purity of the Gospell of our Lord Jesus which we now professe, as also the disciplyne of the churches which, according to the truth of the said gospell, is now practiced amoungst vs." Connecticut Records, i, 20. On this subordination of the State compare Cotton's Abstract of Laws, iv, 4.

Note 5, page 147.

Cotton appeals to the favorite casuist of the Puritans, Dr. Perkins, who held that the Scripture contains a "platforme, not onely of theology, but also of other sacred sciences (as he calls them), . . . ethiks, oeconomicks, politicks, church government, prophecy, academy." It was characteristic of the age that this conclusion was not deduced from the subject-matter of the Bible, but from the fitness of things. "It is very suitable to God's all-sufficient wisdome," argues Cotton. Letter written in 1636 to Lord Say and Seal in Hutchinson's Massachusetts, i, 497. In the same letter Cotton writes: "Democracy, I do not conceyve that ever God did

CHAP. IV.

ordeyne as a fitt government eyther for church or commonwealth. If the people be governors, who shall be governed? As for monarchy and aristocracy, they are both of them clearly approoved, and directed in scripture, yet so as referreth the soveraigntie to himselfe, and setteth up Theocracy in both, as the best form of government in the commonwealth, as well as in the church."

Note 6, page 148.

About the same period Samuel Danforth, a student, afterward a well-known minister and one of the earliest mathematicians in New England, refused to recite the praises of the gods in heathen poetry, but saved the point by amending his classics as he proceeded, to the disgust of his tutor. Cotton Mather adds a marvelous ending to this anecdote, to the effect that the tutor was smitten with convulsions for reproving the lad; but we may in turn take the liberty to revise Mather before believing. Magnalia iv, c. iii, 2.

Note 7, page 149.

Punishment for blaspheming was derived from the mediæval codes. Antonius Matthæus the second, in his De Criminibus, published in 1644, p. 643, says that in Holland the old rubric against blaspheming "the Mother of God, the saints or saintesses" (Moeder Gods, oft den sancten, of sanctinnen), was changed at the Reformation to a law against blasphemy of Almighty God or his holy word. But Matthæus quotes Plato's Minos that it is an indignity to the Deity to speak evil of a "man like himself"—that is, any good man.

Note 8, page 153.

There were those apparently who evaded the law against health drinking by merely drinking to one another. This is condemned in a Massachusetts act of September, 1639, Records, i, 271. Compare the Pennsylvania law of 1682 and that of 1705 "Against Health Drinking," in which the tendency to intemperance is made the ostensible reason. See also Winthrop's Journal in various places. Practical reasons, such as the danger of excess, probably lay below all the objections to health drinking, but it was characteristic of the age that the religious reasons were sent to the fore, especially by the earlier objectors. In the "Great Evil of Health Drinking," published in 1684, the profaneness of the practice and its danger are both urged. Retrospective Review, xii, 322. Health drinking was thought to have been introduced into England at the time of Sir John Norris's expedition to the Netherlands—that is, after 1585.

Note 9, page 155.

"Every shred of Gold drawn out of a wedge of Gold is as much Gold as the whole lumpe and wedge. Whatever is drawn out of the scripture by just consequence and deduction is as well the word of God as that which is an expresse Commandment." Cotton's Grounds and Ends of the Baptisme of the Children, p. 4.

Note 10, page 155.

Ninth Report of Royal Commission on Hist. MSS., part i, appendix, p. 155, Records of City of Canterbury, 1554–5: "Rec[d] of Rich. Orchardson, Shomaker, for openyng his wyndowes on a Sonday in servyce tyme, and for that his chymney was on fyre by nyght, and for that he was very poore he was forgevyn payment for the whole." This is said to be the first record of indictment for Sabbath breaking.

Note 11, page 155.

Archdeacon Hakewill says in 1627: "Common swearing, simple fornication, prophaning the Lord's Day and the like, in former times were scarce knowne to be sinnes; but being now by the light of the Gospell discovered to be such, and that in a high degree, as they are straitly forbidden by God's Law, so is the edge of our Lawes turned against them." Apologie, 466.

Note 12. page 156.

"Our pleasure likewise is, that the bishop of that diocesse take the like straight order with all the Puritans and Precisians within the same, either constraining them to conform themselves, or to leave the countrey according to the lawes of the kingdome and canons of our church, and so to strike equally on both hands against the contemners of our authority and adversaries of our church. And as for our good people's lawfull recreation, our pleasure likewise is, that, after the end of divine service, our good people be not disturbed, letted or discouraged from any lawful recreation, such as dancing, either men or women, archerie, for men, leaping, vaulting or any other harmless recreation, nor from having May games, Whitson ales, and Morris dances, and the setting of May-poles and other sports therewith used, so as the same be had in due and convenient time, without impediment or neglect of divine service; and that women shall have leave to carry rushes to the church for the decoring of it, according to their old custom." The King's Majesties Declaration to his Subjects concerning lawful Sports to be used.

Note 13, page 160.

The allusions to the early Virginia life in the text are based on the whole literature relating to colonial Virginia in print and manuscript, and the authorities are too numerous for specification. The multitude of documents of all sorts relating to Virginia life in the eighteenth century throw a strong backward light on the earlier and ruder period, but there is no lack of seventeenth

CHAP. IV.

century writings from which to make up a picture of the times. The period has usually been misapprehended. It is necessary to remember that until the last fifteen years of the seventeenth century negro slavery was an insignificant element of Virginia life. This is one of the great points of difference from the later period.

Note 14, page 160.

The reader is referred to my tracing of this early rise of Sabbathism in The Beginners of a Nation. To the authorities there cited I here add Cranmer's Catechism, so called, which I had not seen when that work appeared. Its date is about 1548. "And therefore that this Christian libertie maye be kepte and mainteyned, we now kepe no more the saboth on Saturday as the Jews do, but we observe the Sondaye and certayne other daies as the maistrates do iudge it convenient." This catechism was rendered from a Latin version made by Justus Jonas of a German catechism. The Lutheran catechism adds "the pastors of the churches" to the magistrates in the passage quoted above. In both catechisms these Sabbaths and holy days of human appointment are to be rather strictly devoted to religious duties and not to idleness and "ungodly works." Compare Catechism of Thomas Becon, chaplain to Cranmer, pp. 82, 83, where the ground is substantially the same.

Note 15, page 163.

Laxity in Sabbath keeping brought "Wrath Fires and other judgments upon a professing people," declared the Synod of 1679. There are traces of this association of fires with neglect of the Sabbath or divine worship in several places. Compare Plymouth Records, v, 177. Penhallow, writing in 1725 of the eastern Indian wars, says very ambiguously, "It is remarkably observable that among all the settlements and towns of figure and distinction, not one of them have been utterly destroyed wherever a church was gathered." Perhaps churches were rarely "gathered" in pioneer towns. Compare the "nede and povertie" anciently believed to befall Sabbath breakers, as in Cranmer's Catechism of 1548 on the "thirde precepte," Oxford edition, 1829, p. 43, and the corresponding Latin of Justus Jonas, 1539, in the same volume, p. 33.

Note 16, page 165.

During Puritan domination in Maryland a man was arrested in 1656, the charge being "that hee shott and kild a turkey upon Sunday Contrairie to the said Act" of Assembly, but he was allowed to go free on declaring himself "sorie for his Offense." Hanson's Old Kent, 212.

Chap. IV.

Note 17, page 168.

Something like the principle I have formulated, though not quite the same, may be traced in Beccaria, when in his Dei Delitti e delle Pene, he says that strong emotions, born of enthusiasm, when they become enfeebled and wasted by time, gradually become the wisdom of the age and a useful instrument in strong and expert hands. "Le passioni forti, figle del fanatismo e del entusiasmo indebolite e rose, diro cosi, dal tempo, che riduce tutti i fenomeni fisici e morali all' equilibrio diventano, a poco a poco, la prudenza del secolo, e lo stromento utile in mano forte e dell' accorto."

Note 18, page 168.

Earlier than the change of evangelicalism to philanthropy came the outgrowth of a similar altruism from the enthusiasm of the early Quakers. I have reserved the treatment of this development of the reformatory spirit for a future volume of this series, in which there will be occasion to study the origins and results of Quakerism in examining the rise of the West Jersey and Pennsylvania colonies.

Note 19, page 170.

On pp. 4 and 5 of the Practice of Piety some of the things that must be known are thus set forth for a hair-splitting generation: "In the Vnity of the Godhead there is a *plurality* which is not *accidentall* (for God is a most pure *act* and admits no accidents) nor essentiall (for God is one Essence only) but personall." There are pages of this ethereal verbalism. In the Select Cases of Conscience, by Shephard, of Cambridge, Mass., there is an abstruse disquisition "Of Conceiving aright of the Holy Trinity," and another "Of Ordering the thoughts aright in Civil Employments." From one on "Sinful Distractions" this example of the absence of a discriminating sense of proportion will serve: "You do not onely deserve, but are under the sentence of death and curse of God, immediately after the least hairs-breadth swarving from the Law by the smallest Sinne, and most involuntary accidentall infirmity," "the least sinne being (ex parte objecti), in respect of God against whom it is committed, as horrible and as great as the greatest." There were those who maintained that ringing chimes on Sunday was as great an offense as parricide, any sin being, in Shephard's phrase, "the dishonoring of infinite Majesty," pp. 13, 14.

Note 20, page 172.

The Westminster Assembly, in trying to avoid the incongruity of condemning a man for good works, takes the dilemma by both horns. "Works done by unregenerate men although for the matter of them . . . they are sinful, . . . yet their neglect

Chap. IV.

of them is more sinful and displeasing with God." The Humble Advice of the Assembly of Divines, etc.

Note 21, page 174.

Cranmer's Catechism of 1548, edition of 1829, p. 51, says, "If we should have heathen parents and dye without baptisme, we should be damned everlastingly." Cranmer here follows closely the Lutheran version, which reads: "Quando autem Ethnicos et impios parentes haberemus, et sine baptisme moreremur, in æternum damnaremur." The phrases of the catechism of Nowell, such as "digni æterna damnative," as applied to the unbaptized, have the inclusiveness of the church catechism, of which Nowell was probably the author. Thomas Becon, chaplain to Cranmer, in his elaborate catechism, vehemently repudiates the notion that Christian children dying without baptism are damned, but his arguments leave no room for the salvation of the infants of heathen parents. Parker Society edition, p. 22 and following. Bishop Jewell admits the possible salvation of men without the sacrament, and cites the penitent thief, but such cases he treats as exceptional. Works, 1611, p. 261 and following. Anglican theologians in the seventeenth century generally content themselves with ascribing saving virtue to baptism, but they seem to shrink from the converse, that all children unbaptized will be damned, which was yet the general belief. Jeremy Taylor, in his Life of the Holy Jesus, section ix, discourse vi, pt. ii, 24, does not follow the "hard father of the children," Augustine, in denying salvation to unbaptized infants, but he can not escape from the prevailing ambiguity of his class. He says "well may we lament the death of poor babes" unbaptized, because if it is due to the parents' neglect "we may weep as those that have no hope." He throws the matter on God's goodness, but with much dubiety. This narrow admission of unauthorized hope made the Anglican by so much more modern and humane than such fathers as Ambrose and Augustine on the one hand, and the Calvinist divines of the time on the other. The value attached to baptism by the people is very evident. There is somewhere an anecdote of two scapegrace parsons from Virginia, who paid the expenses of a junketing tour in North Carolina by fees for baptism. Story, the Quaker preacher, in 1699, heard a woman publicly reproach Lillingston, the incumbent of a Maryland parish, with having demanded a hogshead of tobacco for baptizing each of her five children. Story's Journal, 229. It was believed in Virginia that a son of a chief of the Doegs, who had been "pawewawd" or bewitched, was disenchanted and healed by the administration of baptism, and this miracle "was taken for a convincing proof against infidelity." T. M.'s Beginning, etc., of Bacon's Rebellion, in Force, i, 9. Traditional notions about the saving efficacy of baptism were not wholly eradicated from the minds of the first generation of New Englanders. "The people begin to complain," writes Lechford about a dozen years after Winthrop's migration, that "their children for the most part remain unbaptized: and so have little more priviledge than Heathens." Plaine Dealing, 89. The exclusion from baptism of the children of parents not in covenant with the church led to much correspondence between New England divines and Puritans in England, and tractates appeared on both sides. An Apologie of the Church in New England, . . . sent over in answer to Mr. Barnard in the year 1639, I saw in the White-Kennett Library in London, and there now lies before me Church Government and Church Covenant Discussed, etc., 1643. This is Richard Mather's reply to thirty-two questions sent him by ministers known to him in Lancashire and Cheshire. There is also before me a little volume dated 1643, with a long title beginning, "A Letter of Many Ministers in Old England." It contains two letters from England and two from New England, the dates running from 1637 to 1640. The sore question of the exclusion of many children from baptism is treated in all these publications and in others of the same period, notably Cotton's Way of Churches, 1645, and Hooker's Summe of Church Discipline, 1648. While Cotton and Hooker lived, New England made no concession to the clamor of those whose children were excluded, and the United Colonies, Plymouth reserving its opinion, demanded that "Baptisme, the seale of the Covenant, be administered only" to covenant members of the churches "and their ymediate seed." Hazard State Papers, ii, 73, 74. The Cambridge Platform, adopted in 1648, did not relax this proscription. But the younger generation was by this time coming to the lead, the example of Puritans in England was on the side of inclusion, and Quakers and Baptists were a little later making inroads. Puritanism in New England also felt the recoil of the Restoration in 1660. The fifth proposition, adopted in 1662, indicates a sweeping change in policy. Of the two old leaders still surviving, Richard Mather favored the change and John Norton was temporarily absent in England. Compare the Platform of 1648, largely the work of Norton, in Results of Three Synods (1725), pp. 1–49, with the deliverance of 1662 in the same, 74–88. On certain conditions baptized persons were, after 1662,

CHAP. IV.

allowed to bring their children to the font. This was known as the halfway covenant. Having served its purpose for two or three generations, this "halfway covenant plan" went to pieces in the religious excitement under Whitefield and others after 1740. Perhaps its disappearance was favored by the gradual decay of the old English notion of the indispensability of baptism to salvation.

Note 22, page 176.

"I desire if such were the will of God, and so could gladly believe if the scriptures taught it, that all [infants] were saved." It is with these words that Robinson qualifies his acceptance of the doctrine of infant damnation. Works, iii, 233.

Note 23, page 176.

John Cotton, whose first thought was of the integrity of his theological system, maintained in his Grounds and Ends of the Baptisme of the Children of the Faithfull, that elect infants have faith given to them and are saved by faith. But the commoner opinion was perhaps expressed by Wigglesworth, that they were sanctified "by ways unknown to men." Day of Doom, xxv. One gets the notion that in the unwritten creed of New England the elect infants were to be found among the baptized children of the faithful. A young man of Connecticut told Story, the Quaker, that unbaptized infants were all lost, but he did not think that all baptized infants would be saved, and this was perhaps the popular feeling. Story's Journal, 308. Cotton attached so much importance to baptism that in the work cited above he expresses the opinion that a house was burned on account of the owner's honest scruples regarding infant baptism. The Confession of Dort, the most authoritative of Calvinist creeds, perhaps, declares that the children of the faithful are holy by the free benefit of the covenant in which they are included with their parents, and says that pious parents ought not to doubt concerning the salvation of their children taken away in infancy—"pii parentes de Electione et Salute suorum liberorum, quos Deus in infantia ex hac vita evocat, dubitare non debent." I Doctrinæ, caput xvii, in Sylloge Confessionum sub tempus Reformandæ Ecclesiæ, p. 376. This giving a kind of certainty in the case of the children of religious parents, took the place of the old dependence on baptism.

Note 24, page 176.

Of Wigglesworth's Day of Doom, Sibley says: "This work represented the theology of the day, and for a century, with the exception perhaps of the Bible, was more popular throughout New England than any other that can be named. It passed through several editions in book form, and was also printed on broadsides and hawked about the country. As late as the early part of the present (nineteenth) century many persons could repeat the whole or large portions of it." Harvard Graduates, i, 272.

Note 25, page 177.

Cotton Mather recounts an incident of a New England minister exhorting a criminal condemned to death to repent of Adam's sin—"the guilt of the First Sin committed by Adam was justly charged upon" him. Magnalia, book vi, p. 44, original edition. On this tendency of the time to give a merely legal character to sin, compare in Fuller's Good Thoughts for Bad Times, p. 277, "Imprimis, the sin of his conception."

Note 26, page 177.

So much of the mediæval limbo survived in New England Calvinism. Compare Wigglesworth's "the easiest room in hell" with Dante's "primo cerchio che l'abisso cigne," that circle lying round the abyss, in which are heard no lamentations save sighs that made the eternal air to palpitate, and where were a great throng "of infants, of women, and mature men," who had not sinned, but had missed of heaven for want of baptism.

> . . . e s'elli hanno mercedi,
> Non basta, perch'ei non ebber battesmo
> Ch'e', porta.

This notion of baptism as "the gate" survived in the Anglican colonies, and no doubt the limbo, or "easiest room in hell," was also a popular survival elsewhere than in New England. It is noteworthy that Quakerism, having no system to complete, refused to admit the damnation of infants, or to impute "the sin of Adam to all the little children, so as to effect their Eternal State." Story's Journal, 1699, pp. 218, 219. Compare p. 308. This milder theology and the doctrine of non-resistance seem to have affected the administration of law in the Quaker colony. See Colonial Records of Pennsylvania, iii, 45, and elsewhere for instances.

Note 27, page 178.

The preface to the New England Psalm Book of 1640 maintains that it is a moral and perpetual duty to sing every sort of David's psalms. And "the book of psalms is so compleat a system of psalms which the . . . infinite wisdome hath made to suit all the conditions, necessityes, affections, etc., of men in all ages," as to "stoppe all men's mouths and mindes" from writing or singing any other psalms or hymns.

Note 28, page 180.

Cotton held that because the "temple should be filled with smoke" at a certain period described in the Apocalypse, there

CHAP. IV.

could be no general conversion of the Indians. Of the apostle Eliot Sewall records this: "Mr. Eliot in his first attempt to make them [the Indians] Christian was much concerned to find out some Promise in the Scriptures relating to them. . . . But afterward he concluded that the Thirty-seventh chapter of Ezekiel was written principally for their sakes." Phenomena quædam Apocalyptica, Dedicatory Letter.

Note 29, page 181.

In the little summary of opinions against cockfighting published in 1660 by Edmond Ellis and to be found in the Harleian Miscellany, as cited in the margin of the text, one reads, "The baiting of the bull hath its use, and therefore is commended of civil authority." Was there ever any sport so reprehensible that this defense of utility was not set up in its favor? From Perkins's Cases of Conscience, 1632, Ellis quotes: "The antipathy and cruelty, which one beast showeth to another, is the fruit of our rebellion against God, and should rather move us to mourn than to rejoice." He quotes a similar argument from Bolton's General Directions for a comfortable walking with God. From Dod and Cleaver he quotes a direct appeal to humane feeling against cruel sports, which uses the theological argument only subordinately. "This proceedeth not of a tender heart. . . . Have our sins in Adam brought such calamities upon them and shall we add unto them by cruelty in our own persons."

Note 30, page 181.

But the colony of East Jersey, predominantly Puritan, forbade bull baiting and cockfighting as sports "which excite people to rudeness, cruelty, looseness, and irreligion." Barber's Historical Collections of New Jersey, 36, under "Early Moral Laws," said to be for the most part extracted from a series of articles published in the Newark Daily Advertiser. The date of the act is not given, but others in the same section range from 1675 to 1697. Bull baiting was probably mentioned only to guard against its introduction.

Note 31, page 185.

Quatuor potissimum Ministerii ordines Ministrii, Doctores, Seniores, Diaconi. Nor do these words take either side of the controversy of the time on the position of apostolic teachers, whether they were ministers or not. Evidently there was a division on the question. The section concerning them is frankly inconclusive—De Doctoribus nondum visum est aliquid constituere. The Barrowist system prevailed generally, but not universally, in New England. Compare Lechford's Plaine Dealing, pp. 4 and 15, and The Temple Measured, by James Noyes, teacher of the church at Newbury, in New England (White-Kennett Library, West Indies, M), with various allusions in other works implying the presence of one or more churches, Presbyterian in form. The early records of the Dedham Church define church officers to be "Pastours, Teachers, rulers, Deacons, and widdowes." On the difficulty of getting widows old enough and vigorous enough, see a passage in Cotton's Way of the Churches, 1645. See also the Cambridge Platform of 1648, chap. viii, sec. 7, where the duties of "ancient widows" are defined. The New England Synod of 1679 sought to restore the twofold pastorate, already hopelessly gone to decay. Question II. "Plebeian ordination" by the laying on of the hands of the people was practiced at first, but went out after the Synod of 1648. Dexter's Congregationalism, 482, citing Magnalia, v. John Hull, in his Diary, 189, considers that the birth of a living male child of a woman who had joined the church, though her parents were Quakers, and whose other children had been still-born, was evidence that she "owned church order."

Note 32, page 186.

The system was full-fledged among Separatists in 1582. Barclay's Inner Life of the sects of the Commonwealth cites A true Discription out of the Word of God of the visible Church. No doubt Barrow, the Separatist, who was executed at Tyburn, was the propounder of the completed scheme, though parts of it had appeared earlier among the exiles at Frankfort. John Robinson's Catechism, printed in 1642, but of course written much earlier, elaborates this subject carefully. I am indebted to Barclay as above, p. 104, note, for this reference. On the double pastorate in Holland, see The Dutch Drawne to the Life, 1664, chap. iii. What I take to be the earliest New England church constitution is the Latin paper in the State Paper Office, with Laud's indorsement dated 3 March, 1634—that is, 1635 N. S. The authorship, origin, and date of this paper are obscure, but internal evidence shows that its origin probably preceded the arrival of Cotton in 1633. After Cotton's ascendency began there was no general requirement that women should wear veils at public worship, as in this paper. The Latin is in places incorrect and badly spelled, and the paper could not have come from New England after such good Latinists as Norton and others arrived. In this early document ancient widows are not mentioned among the servants of the church, but they are not excluded by its phraseology.

CHAP. IV.

Note 33, page 187.

"It is a custom generally used in most, if not in all parish churches of this kingdom, as well as among Presbyterians and others, that the Clerk alone reads aloud every verse, one after another, of the Psalm that is sung before and after the Sermon, and that all the people sing it after him." A View of the Government and Public Worship . . . in the Reformed Churches, etc., by John Durell, 1662. In New England this custom persisted generally in 1726, though some churches by this time had books, and sang without waiting for the hymn to be "deaconed." Compare Cotton Mather's Ratio Disciplinæ, 52. Of the disappearance of the custom in the Anglican churches I can give no account.

Note 34, page 190.

The last two points are on the authority of the important Latin Canons and Constitutions, indorsed, as stated heretofore, 3 March, 1634. This is no doubt the date of Laud's reception of them. The title is Canones Regiminis Ecclesiastici constituti et in reformatis Ecclesiis Novo-Anglicanus observati, breviter in ordinem digesti. I have made no attempt to control the errors in the original paper. On the silent vote the words of this document are: "Sistatur coram Magistratu et tota ecclesia, ut intra dies quatuor decim tacitis fidelium suffragis comprobetur." On the wearing of veils in meeting: "Ne quæ Mulier prœsumat sacris cœtibus adesse nisi capite Velamine tecto." See, further, Winthrop's Life and Letters, ii, 109, Winthrop's Journal, i, 149; and Hubbard's Massachusetts, 204, 205.

Note 35, page 191.

"Infantibus non sunt danda nomina barbara vel superstitiosa, sed in sacris literis expressa." Latin Canons as above.

Note 36, page 191.

D'Ewes attributes his father's loss of property to his having been guilty of the "controversial sin" of taking interest on money. Autobiography i, 43, 44. Comp. Knight's Questio Quodlibetica, whether lawful to take use for money, 1657, and others.

CHAPTER THE FIFTH.

THE TRADITION OF EDUCATION.

I.

CHAP. V.

Continuity of education.

THE history of human life and institutions is inwrought of two principles running crisscross to one another. Athwart the warp of traditional continuity there is woven the woof of variation; the pattern changes by degrees, but the web is without break or seam. Our system of education is sometimes supposed to come from some fountain head in America, or at most to be a Protestant device dating from the Reformation. But the schools that sprang up after the change of religion in England marked the persistence of an ancient tradition that even such an upheaval could not destroy. To find a logical point of beginning we must ascend to the early Christian centuries, when the work of religious teaching and proselytism marched abreast. Education was carried on in primitive monasteries and in cathedral chapters of a monastic type. These far-back monastic schools for teaching religion only are connected by an unbroken pedigree with our complicated modern systems of child training. We may account the ancient missionary schools a place of beginning because it would tax patience to little purpose to

Comp. Rept. of Royal Cath. Com., p. iv.

CHAP. V.

grope uncertainly in the gray dawn of tradition for a connection with sources yet higher up.

II.

Early Christian schools.

The instruction given in places of resort for the study of early Christian doctrine and observance seems to be whole millenniums away from the modern conception of education. There were schools or at least throngs of scholars about popular Christian teachers in England in the fifth century. Later than that the English youth even of the nobility were crossing the channel to the renowned monasteries of Ireland "for the sake of divine studies and a more continent life, . . . going about from one master's cell to another," as Bede tells us. By this voyage to a foreign land these young Englishmen learned the Latin of the service book and church song, and they acquired also the elements of the wisdom of that age, such as the excellence of celibacy and the purifying effect of self-imposed hunger, which was efficient even to the sanctifying of the polluted ground on which crimes had been committed. They learned the keeping of three Lents a year, and they were taught that it was an act of superior devotion in seasons of fasting to eat daily only a little bread and milk after sunset, the milk being carefully skimmed. The proper order of singing the psalter and a method of fixing the true date of Easter were also taught, along with the doctrine of the damnation of infants unbaptized,

Bede's Eccl. Hist., b. iii, ch. xxvii and elsewhere.

Compare Collier's Eccl. Hist., Lathbury's ed., i, 110, 111.

Note 1.

and much other lore now at last happily obsolete. These early schools with their skimmed-milk asceticism at least show the human soul in insurrection against the sordidness of barbarism, but they interest us here because from them is plainly traceable across the ages for nearly fifteen hundred years the long line of a tradition and habit of education. There have been variation and evolution, but there has been no break. The monastery school became a cathedral school in some cases, and the semi-monastic free school grew up alongside them both. The rudimentary school in the house of the detached priest got its impulse and direction from the higher schools in the cathedrals, and by slow changes the local priest's school became the parish school, and in prosaic modern times, by a series of transformations, the American district school, which last retains few traces of its remote ecclesiastical ancestry.

Note 2.

III.

Founding of Latin schools.

Before the Reformation the main reliance for education was on the convent schools. Young women were sent to the nunneries to learn to "work and reade." Sometimes girls were given a little Latin also. Boys learned Latin in their horn-books and other "abcees." English in black-letter characters came after. The barbarous mediæval Latin, often grotesquely macaronied with the vulgar speech, was widely used in records and account books of the time. When the monasteries were suppressed by Henry VIII most of the higher schools went down into the abyss with the religious houses, and the English nation was faced by the ugly fact that it had pretty nearly abolished the education of the times, such as it was. For remedy the old cathedral schools were supplied with lay teachers, and new cathedral trusts with provisions for educating choristers and other boys for holy orders were established. Now that all the religious houses with their schools had been ingulfed, efforts were made to found free grammar schools in addition to those that had survived. Sixteen such schools were established in the time of Edward VI in as many months. But the reign of the boy king was brief; the hungry courtiers had tasted the savory spoils of the monasteries, and they grudged every morsel of it that was given to the new free schools. The reactionary rule of Mary followed, and soon after the accession of Elizabeth the Speaker of the Commons reminded the young queen of the disastrous decay of learning in her kingdom. A general zeal was aroused, not for the primary and popular education so much in favor in later times, but for the founding of free Latin schools. Mulcaster, a schoolmaster of the time, relates that the schools established in Elizabeth's reign were more "than all the rest be that were before her time in the whole Realme." Another writer of 1577 says that "there are not manie corporat townes now vnder the queens dominion that hain not one Grammar Schoole at the least." The tide wave of zeal

Note 3.

Positions, chap. xl.

Harrison's Description of Britaine in Holinshed, i, 254.

for founding new Latin schools reached its flood about the time that emigration to America began, and the impulse was felt in all the early colonies.

IV.

Rudimentary teaching.

Much of the primary teaching was done at home. There was a great temptation to put this burden on the grammar schools, and one finds many complaints in England and America regarding the disposition of parents to be rid of their little children, "whereby the usher is overburdened." Efforts were made from time to time to repel from the Latin school children who were stumbling through "the Horne Booke, the A. B. C., and the Primer." In New Haven the children who "bothered the master by spelling in English" were to be forthwith sent home. To supply the place of home instruction in the rudiments the dame school had grown up. This gatehouse of learning was kept sometimes by a busy housewife, sometimes by a young woman a little better taught than other women. Schoolmasters' daughters were purposely fitted to keep such schools in which the alphabet, spelling, and primary reading were taught along with the catechism, and in which girls learned to sew. "Mary goes to Mrs. Thair's to learn to Read and Knit" is a significant entry in a Boston diary. In Holland at this period there were dame schools in the care of women who were themselves unable to read, but who taught the children the catechism

An order touchinge the Free School in Kendall, 1641. MSS. Commission, x, iv, 316.

Sewall's Diary, 1696, i, 436.

Oud Hollandsch Huisgezin.

CHAP. V.

only, and that orally. Nothing so bad as this is recorded of English schools of the sort, but the dame was, no doubt, sometimes poorly qualified even to give instruction as far as the primer.

V.

First books.

Quoted in New English Dict.

Tuer's History of the Hornbook, *passim*.

E. g., MS. Invoice in Mass. Archives, 1690.

In the middle ages education was begun with the rudiments written probably on parchment, which was for security nailed to a wooden board, or, as an old poem puts it, "Naylyd on a brede of tre." Perhaps when paper, a much more perishable substance than parchment, came into use, the sheet thus attached to "a board of tree" was thought to require an overlay of a thin bit of horn to protect it from the destructive fumbling of the child. Such hornbooks seem to have become more common in the seventeenth century than before, and there was a disposition to make them pleasing to the eye. Both plain hornbooks and gilt ones were imported into the colonies in the seventeenth century. The hornbook contained the alphabet in capitals and in lower-case letters, with those easy syllables in two letters known at least in later days as the "a b abs." The alphabet had been from remote times preceded by a cross, from which the first line had come to be called the crisscross (or Christ's cross) row. The advent of Protestantism did not drive out all Catholic usages; some English children still commended their beds to "Matthew, Mark, Luke, and

John," and in country places as late as 1618 alphabetical studies were begun at the crisscross row with the ancient prayer, or perhaps one might say charm, "Christ's cross be my spede and the Holy Ghost," "For feare the Divell should be in the letters of the Alphabet," adds the chronicler. But the first hornbooks taken to the new Puritan settlement in New England are said to have had the cross obliterated. After the hornbook came the "abce" or the "abcie," spelled also in several other ways. It comprised a series of little verses turning each on some word, which key words began with the several letters of the alphabet in succession. The device is well known in our later times. There were of old "latten abeesees" as well as English ones; the Latin were no doubt the more ancient. The primer, notwithstanding its name, was the third implement for learning put into the hands of a child. It contained at the Reformation prayers and religious meditations, but in some of its later forms it was much like a modern catechism. The primer came at last to include the contents of the hornbook and the "abcie"; such was the famous New England Primer which had its rise at the close of the seventeenth and passed through innumerable editions in the eighteenth century. The usual course was to pass the child out of the primer into the psalter—that is, to set him to reading Sternhold and Hopkins's version of the Psalms in meter. The rugged Bay Psalm Book was used as a reader in the days when

The Court and Country, 1618. Roxburghe Libr., p. 188.

Note 4.

Comp. Introduction to Ford's Reprint.

Comp. Caulkin's New London, 395.

CHAP. V.

approximate rhymes and a rough rhythm were the only alleviations of the child's task. But reading was also taught from little books "full of precepts of ciuilitie" done into verse "such as children will soone learne and take delight in thorow the roundnesse of the meter," as Schoolmaster Brinsley assures us. Rules of politeness in verse were centuries old in Latin, and were by this time common in English; one of these books was "The Schoole of Vertue," and there was a "Newe Schoole of Vertue" of French origin. To be polite, to "make his manners" by bow or courtesy to superiors, to stand reverently and modestly aside in the street when elders or people of dignity passed by, was one of the first and most important steps in early American education—it was the virtue of childhood, as it had been from the middle ages. But when the lad could read in the psalter without spelling the words, he bade adieu to school dame and English and was ready to be "entered" in Latin, as the phrase went.

Brinsley, *passim.*

Caulkin's Hist. of New London.

VI.

The grammar school.

By the term grammar school was meant in that day a school for beginners in Latin. One might learn some paradigms, and even more than this of Greek, in the higher grammar schools, and there were masters who added some driblets of preliminary Hebrew, the school thus including all the three learned tongues. But virtually its whole

CHAP. V.

force was spent on Latin, which was still the sacred language of religion and learning. Many of the pupils in the grammar schools had to be taught their English rudiments; beyond this the instruction was almost wholly in Latin. Lilly's grammar, with a ponderous and forbidding title, was in that language. The difficulty of this had at length brought forth some recognized English helps for beginners, such as posing books, or, as we should say nowadays, question books, on the accidence, and there were ponies intended for surreptitious use, in the shape of helps to construe Lilly's rules; but English was ostensibly left behind. The lad must understand when the master taught him in Latin, and he was supposed to converse only in Latin during school hours. Yet in spite of "ferula" and birch switches, and the risk of being distinguished as the "asinus" or donkey of his form, the pupil still contrived to speak much to his fellows in his mother tongue. The attempt to compel conversation in Latin was not wholly successful in England, and it always failed in America, even in Harvard College. Disputation had been for centuries the favorite means of rendering scholars expert in Latin and of vitiating their general education. The taste for polemics had pervaded the universities, and even the grammar schools, from the earliest times. Lads under fifteen were set to dispute in school Latin, often "thieving" their arguments on grave questions of philosophy or intricate points of grammar, and

Note 5.

Brinsley's Ludus, p. 24.

Note 6.

Brinsley's Ludus, 215. Wigglesworth in Sibley's Harvard Graduates, i, 267. Danker's Journal, 385.

Note 7.

Note 8.

CHAP. V.

Brinsley's Ludus, *passim.*

mingling their disputations with boyish sarcasms and rude ridicule, in the spirit of the gamecocks, in which masters and pupils took delight.

VII.

In the grammar school.

After seven or eight years in what Milton styles "the grammatical flats and shallows," the boy left the grammar school for deeper waters. Unless he had had an unusually good master the chances were that he could read his mother tongue but stammeringly—there were pupils who at some stage of their early Latin studies lost the art of reading English entirely. The lad of fifteen or more, on leaving the grammar school, was ignorant of numbers; some boys advanced in Latin did not know the numerals, Roman or Arabic, and could not find the chapter in the Bible, "much less the verse." The boy from the grammar school had learned to write and to make his own quill pens with the point next the middle finger slightly thinner and shorter than the other, and to make a ruling pen as well, "with a nock like that of an arrow." With this he could make two parallel lines, and he ruled his own paper thus and wrote between the two lines. "Penne, inke, paper, rular, plummet, ruling pen, pen-knife," were all included in the outfit for learning to write, and there was "a blotting paper" to keep the book clean. For doing his exercises the pupil used a piece of lead thrust into a quill, and he kept a piece of new

Brinsley's Ludus Literarius, 29, 47, and elsewhere.

wheat bread at hand for use in erasing pencil marks. The grammar-school boy rarely had occasion to write English, and many scholars from early neglect in the grammar schools were "too backwards to their dying day" in the art of writing the vernacular. The master and his usher were often inexpert in writing; in such cases a scrivener was sometimes engaged to teach the "Roman hand" and the beautiful "secretary hand" so puzzling nowadays to unpracticed eyes. There were also traveling scriveners who taught penmanship. The lad might be weak in his English when he left school, but he made amends for it by knowing how to write themes and even verses in Latin. The producing of Latin verses was a rather wooden handicraft; the grammar scholar used his Flores Poetarum for models, and he could borrow elegant ready-made locutions from a thesaurus of poetical phrases by Bucklerius. The Sylva Synonimorum was also very handy for "schollars of iudgement." When the word in mind would not scan properly, the verse carpenter could select another with the same meaning from this Forest of Synonyms. The ambitious young poet rummaged in Textor's Epitheta after decorative adjectives; for epithets, "if they be choyse, are a singular ornament," as Master Brinsley assures us. "Descriptions by periphrases" were to be had in Holyoke's Dictionary, and there was "Master Draxe his Phrases" and other books "to see how many wayes they can vtter anything in good

D'Ewes.

Note 9.

Ludus Literarius, 196.

CHAP. V.

Comp. D'Ewes's Autobiog., i, 102, 105.

phrase." One Latin verse was admired because its nine words could be arranged in a hundred and four ways, perhaps all equally prosaic.

VIII.

Writing schools.

A boy from the grammar school unable to write his mother tongue with any fluency and ignorant of the multiplication table was not fitted for the counting house, where his dexterity in cobbling Latin verses would avail nothing. For lads destined to these employments there were English schools of various sorts, including many old-fashioned "common schools" for all classes, which debarbarized their rudimentary English by teaching youths also to "congrue Latine." When appearing alongside the free schools such were sometimes called "inferior schools" or "trivial schools." With the rising importance of trade in the seventeenth century, "writing schools," so called, came into prominence. Lads, even of good families, who showed more aptitude for money-making than for learning Latin were sent to the writing school to learn "good hands and accounts." In these schools were taught an elaborate penmanship, arithmetic in forms somewhat fantastic, and the science of bookkeeping, complicated and intricated in that day by the multitude of varying monetary and metrical systems. Writing schools were private ventures, and in contrast to the severity practiced in the grammar school the writing school enforced

Comp. Ciuile and vnciuile Life, p. 21.

Comp. Willsford's Scales of Commerce, 1660, and arithmetics of the time.

CHAP. V.

no discipline whatever. Until the close of the seventeenth century such homely and useful schools were rarely if ever endowed. It was only by founding a Latin school that one could hope to gain the blessedness of a saint or the glory of a patriot. Such was the faith of Englishmen and of the founders of the early colonies in America. The vulgar utilities of English reading and writing and multiplying and dividing were much more suited to pioneers in America than Lilly's Latin grammar or even than what was esteemed the "rare and almost divine matter" of "Tullies Offices." But necessary and mercenary arts could not be made objects of sentiment by enthusiastic benefactors who wrote long letters to the Virginia Company ostentatiously subscribing them "Dust and Ashes," or laid their money when they were done with it at last on the altar of the venerated dead languages for the benefit of "poor scholars" who had been traditional objects of benevolence for centuries.

Lives of the Norths, ii, 293. Note 10.

Comp. Brinsley's Consolations.

IX.

Grammar school the universal remedy.

Valued at first as a means of producing clergymen, we find the grammar school in the fifteenth century esteemed in Scotland as a training place for public officials "for the king's use." After the Reformation it came to be regarded in England, Scotland, and Holland as a means for propagating Protestant doctrines and eradicating heresy. But as potable gold was the universal medicine and

Venice treacle the antidote to innumerable poisons, so the grammar school in that age of idealism became a cure for all heresy, heathenism, and barbarism. The greatest schoolmaster of James's reign, John Brinsley, laid at the feet of the Virginia Company the manuscript of his "Consolations for Ovr Grammar Schooles," intended especially for "all ruder places, namely for Ireland, Wales, Virginia," etc., "God having ordained schooles of learning," he declares, "to be a principall meanes to reduce a barbarous people to ciuilities." It was in this spirit that the Virginia Company allotted land for a college at Henrico to bring Indian children to a saving knowledge of Christianity and Latin grammar. For barbarous places "so nuzled vp in rudeness and superstition" it was thought there could be no help but in a Latin school. Benefactors seeking the conversion of the "infidell's children" sent books and maps and money for the new Indian college in Virginia. This was done dramatically after the manner of the time. A mysterious well-dressed stranger appeared in the open court of the Virginia Company, depositing there a box in which were found bags of "new gold" for the education of the Indians. Passengers on a returning East Indiaman, hearing news of religious destitution in Virginia, forthwith collected money; this, with other sums, was devoted to the founding of a collegiate school at Charles City. The students were to pass out of this "East India School," as it was called, to the college at Henrico, from the

Published 1622.

Brinsley's Consolations, 15.

MS. Records, *passim*.

Broadside, cited MSS. Comm., iii, 66. Records of Company, Oct. 24, 1621. Comp. Declaration of

privileges of which baptized youth were not to be quite shut out. To the endowment of the Charles City school the Virginia Company added a thousand acres of land and five apprenticed servants. The overthrow of the Company in 1624 involved the destruction of these schemes for transplanting the education then in vogue to America. Of all these benevolent projects there was a few years later not a bit of flotsam anywhere to be seen.

Col. of Va., 1622, pp. 51, 53.

Note 11.

X.

Symmes's and other free schools in Virginia.

Benjamin Symmes, a settler in Virginia, was the first of emigrant Englishmen to bequeath an educational endowment after the pattern set by English philanthropists in the ages before him. To found a free school in Elizabeth County, Symmes, who died in 1634, gave by will two hundred and fifty acres of land with an adjacent hay marsh and a herd of eight milch cows, which by 1649 had increased to forty. Interest-bearing and profit-sharing investments were not to be had. The usufruct of land and cattle, and sometimes the income from cattle alone, had been for centuries the commonest form of bequest for benevolent, religious, or superstitious purposes. One Henry Peasley founded a Virginia free school in 1675 with a gift of six hundred acres of land, ten cows, and a brood mare. Other public-spirited people gave to Peasley's school negro slaves in place of the obsolete tenants of old English endowments and the bond servants

Note 12.

Hening, vii, 41. Comp. also Neill's Educational Development of Va., 26.

CHAP. V.

Note 13.

Note 14.

given by the Virginia Company for educational uses. In the remaining parish records the existence of yet other free-school endowments in colonial Virginia can be traced. But the free Latin school of England was an exotic in Virginia. There was no town life, and there was small need of dispensing gratuitous Latin to thriving tobacco planters in a new country, whose clergy, such as they were, were imported ready made, and whose laymen at least did their talking and reading in mother English. The College of William and Mary did not get under way until the last years of the seventeenth century; there was no bishop on this side of the sea to induct men into holy orders; the primitive statecraft of the colony needed no other tongue than the vernacular, aided occasionally by Indian interpreters, so that the free Latin school of early Virginia was a short ladder with nothing but empty space at the top of it. Latin was studied merely as a gentleman's accomplishment. The abundant wild land, the cheap bond-servant labor, and yet cheaper slave labor, which became common in the last quarter of the century, tempted the young provincial of the Chesapeake colonies to land ownership and that culture of the soil by the hands of others that had been for ages the pursuit of the gentry of the mother country.

Comp. Reports of Clergy in Perry's Collections Va.

Of the character of the teaching in the few early Virginia grammar schools we know nothing. Little private schools early began to spring up at convenient points in the growing settlements which were stretched in a narrow, sinuous line along the margins of the watercourses and estuaries of the Chesapeake region. One may infer from the record that there were such schools before 1644, and it appears that the cost of a year's "scoleing" at that time was equal to that of two pairs of shoes. Forty years later, in 1684, there were so many of these little country schools that the mercenary governor, Lord Howard of Effingham, thought it worth while to exact a license fee from every schoolmaster. These schools had no relation to the parish authorities, but were established and conducted by the people spontaneously. "The children's fathers hire those schools and pay you out of their own pocket" is the quaint statement of a clergyman in a report to the Bishop of London in 1724. "To read, write, and cipher" was usually the whole course. "Care is generally taken by parents that their children be taught to read" certifies Parson Brunskill.

CHAP. V.

and Hugh Jones's Va., 70.

MS. Records of York Co., Va.

Beverly's Va., pt. i, 89.

Perry's Coll. Va., 268.

As above, 279.

XI.

The schools in Virginia being thus the offspring of the law of demand and supply, some of the endowed schools seem to have taught arithmetic instead of the dead languages, and one excellent private school in 1724 combined numbers with Latin and Greek. Virginia life in the first century after the settlement was extremely rural, not to say rustic; most of the planters had never seen a

Other devices for education.

Note 15.

CHAP. V.

Hartwell, Blair, and Chilton's Present State of Va., about 1697.

town, and even members of the House of Burgesses could not conceive of life as tolerable to people cooped up in a village where neighbors were so near that there was no range for a herd of cattle. The development of large landholdings began to produce a class of pretty rich planters in the last half of the seventeenth century who naturally wished to give their sons better advantages than they could get in the rough old field schools or the struggling free schools. Imitating the landed proprietors of England, these men brought their sons up under private tutors. The natural way to accomplish this in Virginia at that time was to buy a man trained in an English Latin school from among the redemptioners who were sold off the ship's deck for a term of years to pay their passage. This method of hiring a private tutor was in use in 1669 and probably earlier, and it seems to have prevailed in the Chesapeake region throughout the colonial period. No doubt some of the teachers who emigrated in considerable numbers in the prevalent fashion at the cost of a temporary loss of liberty were better instructed than many of the ordinary country teachers of the time. Before 1683 the brilliant William Byrd, who was perhaps the first man born in any of the colonies with a natural gift for felicitous literary expression, had been sent to England for education. As time went on, this recurrence to the sources of learning in the Old World was frequent among the rich in the Southern colonies.

Note 16.

Capt. Byrd's letter. Va. Hist. Reg., i, 64.

XII.

In New England the Latin school found an environment distinctly more friendly than was that of the colonies to the southward. The settlers were in the first freshness of their Utopian enthusiasm, and their church establishment was the very heart of their enterprise. In the Puritan mind preaching was really a sacrament above sacraments, though it was called "an ordinance." God was held to be present "in his holy ordinances" when they had "binn setled in a way of gospel order." It became therefore a matter of primary importance to educate preachers. For ages preparation for the ministry had consisted mainly in acquiring a knowledge of Latin, the sacred tongue of Western Christendom. Though the Latin service was no longer used by Protestants, and the Vulgate Bible had been dethroned by the original text, and though the main stream of English theology was by this time flowing in the channel of the mother tongue, the notion that all ministers should know Latin had still some centuries of tough life in it. The first professed aim of university and secondary education in that time was to raise up ministers; to fit men for the service of the state followed close after. In all early projects for schools and colleges in America these two were somewhat grotesquely intertwined, with a notion that a first step toward converting the heathen tribes was to make some of them bachelors of art. For this purpose the en-

Latin schools in New England.

Mass. Records, May, 1671.

CHAP. V.

dowment of the abortive Henrico College was undertaken in Virginia, and in 1666, after no little travail, Harvard succeeded in graduating an Indian.

XIII.

Mode of sustaining grammar schools in New England.

New Haven Records, 25th of 12th month, 1641, p. 127.

The English liking for free grammar schools, re-enforced by the Puritan passion for securing "teaching elders," caused Latin schools to be set up in many places "for the better trayning vpp of youth, . . . and that through God's blessing they may be fitted for publique service hereafter either in church or commonweale." The ancient English cow-and-calf endowment of education, which had been already introduced into Virginia, reappears in the Northern colonies. Of the many plans traceable in early New England, it is probable that nearly all had English precedents. In New Haven, Boston, Newport, and elsewhere one finds early proposals to sustain schools by the rental or usufruct of town lands, a method used in England and incorporated in grants to early Virginia plantations. John Eliot, the apostle to the Indians, had been a grammar-school usher in England, and his parish in Roxbury appears to have contemplated a free school as early as 1642, in which year ten shillings of rental was bequeathed toward its support. In 1645 all the householders in Roxbury made a perpetual annual subscription, amounting in all to twenty pounds a year, to sustain a free school for their children, "to fitt them for publike service

New Haven and Boston Records, *passim.* Tolman's Education in Rhode Island, p. 25. Comp. Dorchester Records, 54, 55, 1645.

Note 17.

both in churche and Commonwealthe." These rentals were made a lien on "not only their houses, but also their yardes, orchards, gardenings, out-houses, and homesteads." The few resources of a new country for a fixed income were probably all tried in turn by founders of New England schools. One finds among other things the rent of a ferry, of a wharf, of a shop, of a house, and of a gristmill devoted to education. The early Virginia tenant and servant endowment finds something like a parallel in the contribution to Harvard College of a hundred and fifty pounds, apparently out of a fund produced by the sale of indigent children sent out of England as apprentices. After trying other means, deficiencies were made up in some towns by a tax rate, and this method of sustaining town schools proved the most practicable and developed after generations into the modern system. In some New England communities the school tax was levied at first on schoolable children in the several families; often the rate was shared between property and progeny. In all these expedients there appears to be a resort to methods known in England.

CHAP. V.

Winthrop, ii, 264. Mass. Records, *passim*. Ellis's Roxbury Town, chap. iv.

Mass. Rec., 13, Nov., 1644. Quincy's Harvard Coll., i, 473.

XIV.

The religious motive.

The zeal for schools was somewhat more effective in New England than in the colonies farther south, because the communities were more compact and the local governments more vigorous. But it was also probably more effective, because

CHAP. V.

Note 18.

the main body of the people was religious, and schools in the seventeenth century were a part of the religious establishment. This trait education had inherited from the ages preceding. In some way even rough and rudimentary education took on a religious color in the eyes of the people of that day. Massachusetts ordained in 1642 that every child should be taught enough "to read and understand the principles of religion & the capitall lawes of the country." The preamble of the Massachusetts school law of 1647 makes it the motive of the act to thwart "the ould deluder Satan" by keeping the Scriptures accessible in the original tongues, that "the true Sence and meaning" might not "be clouded by false glosses of saint seeming deceivers." This law passed into the Connecticut code of 1650, preceded by this preamble with its uncouth rhetoric; the old deluder Satan still marches at the front, followed by the Papists, the saint-seeming deceivers walking softly in the rear, "false glosses" in hand. The broad and secular uses of education were not recognized as yet.

XV.

Motive of the school law.

By this curious law of 1647 the Puritan government of Massachusetts rendered probably its greatest service to the future. The act was not modern in aim, and for a long time it was inefficient, but from that quaint act there has been slowly evolved the school system that now obtains in the United States. The rush of Puritan immigration had virtually ceased about 1640, and the attention of the New England leaders was turned toward the thronging children in the prolific families of the settlers. The religious Utopia, such as the founders had imagined when they heard the voice of the Lord calling upon them to arise and depart out of the land of their fathers, was to be realized by the children born in "these ends of the earth." As early as 1642 there was alarm at the educational decline. Before 1645 there were agitations in favor of free schools in New Haven, Dedham, Roxbury, and other towns. In 1644 the Commissioners of the United Colonies of New England bestirred themselves to collect a peck of corn from each family for Harvard College, that the supply of preachers might not fail. But the graduates of Harvard were now finding benefices in England, where, sincc the rise of the Puritans to power, ministers with Puritan antecedents were much sought after. In 1646 the Massachusetts General Court sadly confesses "the fewness of persons accomplished to such imployments" as required education, and looks to the future with something like consternation. Six years later the records testify that Harvard students "as soone as they are growne vpp, ready for public vse . . . leave the country." Meantime "the first founders weare away apace." It was in the face of this disheartening exigency that the school law of 1647 was adopted.

Mass. Records, 1652.

XVI.

The school law of 1647.

This law, which has produced such far-reaching and unforeseen results, was confessedly a dam against the rising tide of ignorance. It was passed "that learning may not be buried in the grave of our fathers in the church and commonwealth." It ordained "that every township in this iurisdiction, after the Lord hath increased them to the number of fifty householders, shall then forthwith appointe one within their towne to teach to write and to reade." This ungrammatical sentence is the vital part of the law. Towns having a hundred householders were to establish grammar schools to teach Latin, or to pay a fine to the nearest towns having such a school. This provision for grammar schools, as the preamble implies, was intended to be the capital feature of the law, but it could not be enforced. On the other hand, the rude little schools for mere reading and writing, to be taught usually by some resident farmer, were possible in a new country, and they were realized in many townships during the next half century. Those country schools that pretended to the dignity of grammar schools were most of them shams or makeshifts to satisfy the law by such devices as covenanting that an incompetent master should teach Latin "as far as he was able," or that he should "teach English and carry them on in Latin as far as he could." Even where the teacher was fairly competent those desiring Latin came to be

Note 19.

distressingly few. In the matter of rudimentary schools a law could not achieve much. Townships might have something less than fifty householders with perhaps a hundred and fifty children, and yet have no school. One school in a territory of six or eight miles square was but a lean provision. Considering the number of voluntary schools already in existence the first effect of the law must have been slight indeed. Popular education under its provisions was rough and scant, as the surviving documents of the succeeding age testify all unconsciously. No new kind of school was introduced by the act, and the question of support was still left with each township, "as the maior part of those that order the prudentials of the towne shall appoint." Its importance lay in the requirement by a central authority that each local community of a certain population should sustain a school in some way, and its historical value consists in the principle thus established. The outcome of this law adopted, in what was the most religious as it was the most intolerant period of New England history, has been the development of a national system of secular education for many millions of children professing nearly every creed known in the wide world.

Note 20.

XVII.

Origin of the Massachusetts school system.

In human history nothing is educed from nothing; that which is exists by virtue of far-reaching roots struck deep into the mold of that which was.

CHAP. V.

Pioneers especially have no time to invent; necessity rarely brings forth anything better than imitation and adaptation. What makes the school act of 1647 of consequence is the legal obligation imposed on local communities to provide opportunity for education. For this England afforded no example. But New England was quite as likely to fetch a precedent from some Presbyterian country as to follow the tradition of England. She did not need to go farther than to Scotland. At the Reformation Knox desired "to purge the Churche of God from all superstition" and to disseminate the new doctrines in the remotest corners of Scotland. In his Buke of Discipline he demanded "That everie severall churche have a schoolmaister appointed, such a one as is able at least to teach Grammar and the Latin tung, yf the Town be of any reputation. Yf it be upaland . . . then must either the Reider or the Minister take cayre over the children . . . to instruct them in their first rudimentie and especially in the catechisme." Knox proposed this system sixty-seven years before the law of 1647; in both we have the same Latin schools in larger towns and rudimentary teaching in obscurer places. The Synod of Dort repeated the attempt in Holland in 1618. Knox's scheme and the Dutch imitation of it were but an expansion of the parish and cathedral schools existing for centuries before.

1560.

Note 21.

XVIII.

The decline in education.

The educational decline in all the colonies was inevitable and it was universal as we may see by the extant letters, wills, and records painfully written by men of the second and third generations. The violent aberrations of orthography from even the rather free standards of the time, the vagrant capital letters, the halting and confused march of sentences, suggest that brains, as well as hands, were numbed by the rude toil from which pioneers may not escape. The trees of the forest were a hostile phalanx to be broken, fields beset with stumps that defied the plow were to be subdued to culture; there were savages to fight and to flee from, towns and ships to build, with tasks of Hercules beside that left small room for learning. Frontiersmen find the Latin accidence dispensable. The generations of bad spellers and clumsy writers born to a new-world battle were much better trained for their environment than the most accomplished of the first comers. They had learned from boyhood to take bearings and lay a true course through labyrinthine woods, to handle with steady sureness the heavy firelock musket or the newer snaphance, and the long-barreled fowling piece, to swing true the felling axe, and to wield the heavy beetle, to hew a puncheon floor, to build a cabin of rough logs. They could balance and paddle on salt water and fresh in wind and wild weather the tottling canoe. Patience, courage, enterprise, and a nimble mental shiftiness could not but result from such a curriculum. But these men hardly knew more of literature than did the Greek heroes or the Hebrew patriarchs. In the rather well-written manuscript records of Virginia parishes of that time "the clarkes" record that the vestry "has made choyse on" one R. M. for a church warden; that the parson has "affeciated"; that A. B. has been "opoynted overseyear" of the highways; processioning of bounds is spelled "persestioning," sufficient is "sofitiant," and so on. It is entered that a certain person has been "making his redress to this vestry for helpe." A Maryland vestry clerk had no notion of mental reservation; he records that the vestrymen took the oath of abjuration "without equivocation or governmentall reservation." In New England it is amusingly pathetic to read the records of covenants with teachers written by town clerks who doubled the n in English or stipulated that the pupils should learn to "rite" or "wright." The awkward pronunciation of the pioneer scribe shows through his phonetic spelling when those to be taught appear as "childeringe," and one of the three r's in a contract with a teacher is sometimes "refmetick," sometimes "retmitick." Even the Boston clerk of 1652 bewrays his speech when he writes of the "pore scollers of Hervert College." Local government has its petty side; the New England towns had "tricks and shifts to evade the school laws." Few towns escaped fine for neglect of

Divers parish records of 17th century in original MS., Fairfax Seminary.

Printed records of several towns before 1700.

school laws in those days. In some of the towns there were children that traveled long roads to school; in one case it was eight miles. In New England, as in Virginia, many children learned to read in the old English way by home instruction. In Virginia the ability to read was perhaps about as common as in England at the same period, but there are cases of a man holding local office who was obliged to make his "signum" or mark in subscribing to a document; in Andover, Mass., in 1664, five out of eleven on a coroner's jury made marks. In other colonies than Massachusetts, Connecticut, and Virginia there was yet greater illiteracy. In Maryland half the adult males were probably unable to write their names during the whole seventeenth century. Harvard College ran down in the general decline. "The greater part of the people were devoted to the Plow," as a writer of the time explains, and "learning was forced to plod out a way to live." In the last quarter of the seventeenth century Harvard was a Latin and divinity school, slim in attendance, and inefficient in teaching, while it was kicked about as a political football in the strife between the factions of the Mathers and their rivals.

Shepard, 1672, and Ransom, 1709, in L. Swift on Election Sermons. Lincoln's Worcester, 248.

Bailey's Andover, 144.

Note 22.

Compare Quincy's Hist. Harvard, *passim*, and Danker's Journal, 384, 385.

Note 23.

XIX.

Decline of the Latin school.

Through all this period of darkness and decline the colonies of Massachusetts and Connecticut, and in a less degree the other New England

CHAP. V.

governments, except Rhode Island, preserved in form and something more that which has proved an invaluable legacy for the future—a system of schools sustained in part by enforced local taxation. The school that survived "the dark ages" of New England was no longer that brought from England. Supported partly by town rates the so-called Latin school was less able even than the English school to resist the intrusion of younger children. Such pupils gave trouble at Harvard, and at New Haven they "bothered the master of the grammar school by learning to spell English." Yielding to the demand of supporters, grammar schools came to give more attention to writing and arithmetic. But this innovation was admitted grudgingly at first. "It is scarce known in any place to have a free school for English and writing" was the objection raised in New Haven, but even New Haven only grumbled in yielding, and so by slow degrees it came to pass that the English studies at last drove the sacred Latin from the free school founded at first for it alone. In vain did the town meeting exhort the master to "bring his boys on to latting as fast as they were capable." Latin teaching barely survived at all by the aid of such hortation and of repeated legislation, local and general. Other important changes came by the irresistible pressure of circumstances. The remoter townsmen were taxpayers also, and they tired of sending their children over weary miles of snowdrifts to the town-

Town Records in Livermore's Republic of New Haven, 332.

Atwater's New Haven, 150.

ship schools or of teaching them at home. Thus as time went on "outskirt schools" grew up. In many cases, over the whole region covered by township communities the schools were rotated so as to be kept first in one neighborhood and then in another. In the eighteenth century we find New Jersey appointing men to look after the schools, and see that they rotated properly, so that all the inhabitants might have a fair chance. By such processes the town school gradually became the modern district school. An obligation to establish and to support schools, in part at least, from the public fund having once become traditional, one finds in the eighteenth century even dame schools and many writing schools maintained in part or wholly at public expense. Taking our stand at the point where the half-mediæval seventeenth gives place to the far more modern eighteenth century, we can see that the thousand-year-old exclusive instruction of the few was in process of slow transformation into a scheme of popular and universal education. As usual in such a metamorphosis, the change was made by insensible gradations; the continuity was without apparent seam.

Lincoln's Worcester, 249. Comp. Bailey's Andover, 519.

Budd, in Gowan, 102, note.

Temple's North Brookfield, 200. Judd's Hadley, 65. Boston Town Records, *passim.*

XX.

No such thing as public education not dominated by religion was known in the seventeenth century. From dame school to university all was ostensibly, perhaps ostentatiously, religious. In

Maryland and Rhode Island.

Note 24.

such a state of society, governments freely tolerating more than one form of religious belief could do little or nothing by state initiative for education; and in communities where there was a division of sentiment voluntary co-operation in schools was almost impossible. In Maryland the poor little arts of reading and writing were hardly known in some parts of the province, and it has been estimated that in the seventeenth century half of the adult males were unable to write their names. There were efforts to establish schools in the lifetime of the first generation; these were kept by one Ralphe Crouch, who was in some way connected with the Jesuits. Thirty-seven years after the first settlement the Catholic upper House of the Legislature proposed to found a government school, but the Protestant lower House promptly barricaded the way by proposing as a condition that all the teachers should be Protestants or that there should be at least one Protestant master in the school. The notion of a wholly secular and impartial rudimentary instruction had not entered the minds of men in any part of Christendom. One of those "schools for humanities" for which the Jesuit order was famous was begun "in the center of the country" in 1677, but without aid from the Maryland government. Rhode Island was similarly embarrassed, and there is no mention of schools in the early colony records. There were schools nevertheless. The early New England system of town schools came into Rhode

Compare Bozman, ii, 99. Md. Hist. Soc. Pub., No. 9. Johnson's Old Md. Manors, p. 6.

Sollers, in Steiner's Education in Md., 16.

Island by induction. Bristol, in 1682, established a school by dividing the expense between the parents of the pupils and the taxpayers, a method common in the adjacent colonies. But a retardation of educational development was the natural penalty of religious impartiality. One of the results of the English Revolution of 1688 was to make Maryland for a while a crown colony and rather intensely Protestant. In 1692 and in years following laws were passed for the promotion of "free schools" of the old Latin school kind, intended to produce candidates for holy orders who were to complete their training at the new College of William and Mary in Virginia.

Johnson's Higher Ed'n in R. I., p. 21.

Bacon's Laws, 1692–'94, xxxi; 1696, xvii; 1699, xvi; 1704, xxvii.

MS. Brit. Mus. H., 115.

XXI.

School and breakfast.

By comparison of such notices as we have of American schools with the English schools of the period, we can form a fairly clear conception of the outward traits of school life in the age of American settlement. We may dimly see the unwilling boy "with shining morning face" and a lambskin satchel setting out for school, breakfastless, in the dark winter mornings in time to begin his studies at the unchristian hour of six o'clock. Some schools postponed the hour of beginning until seven. The session ended at eleven, when the famished pupils went home to their first meal, though in a few schools there was a recess of fifteen minutes at nine o'clock, in order that those

CHAP. V.

Mulcaster's Positions, chap. xl. Brinsley's Ludus Lit., *passim.* Report on Burgh and Middle Class Schools in Scotland, 1867, p. 15. Knight's Colet, p. 362.

Note 25.

Note 26.

who lived near the school might snatch a hurried breakfast, a meal not generally reckoned with at that time. There was a custom in earlier times of allowing the fasting pupils to take some light food in school with bottles of drink, but if the custom survived into the seventeenth century it left no trace in educational literature. The session was resumed for the afternoon when the master rapped on the doorpost at one o'clock, and it continued until "well-nigh six at night," when the scholars, who must have been stupefied by an all-day confinement, heard the welcome word of dismission, "Exeatis." In a new country the rough roads and long distances must have made it next to impossible to begin in the dark at six in the winter. By 1719 the hour had fallen away in one place to "three quarters past seven." One finds the pupils of Christopher Dock, the Pennsylvania Dutch teacher, munching their "breakfast bread" along the road as they hurried to school at some unearthly time, and back-country schools in America retained cruelly long hours, with other cherished and venerable abuses brought from Europe, until the middle of the nineteenth century. In the early years of Harvard an hour was allowed at some time in the middle of the forenoon for morning bever, a light snack preceded by no breakfast. Half an hour was given to the afternoon bever, and an hour and a half each to dinner and supper. Small allowance was made for the activity of youth. There were no regular recesses for play

Bailey's Andover, 519.

Pennypacker's Hist. and Biog. Sketches.

Laws, Liberties, and Orders.

CHAP. V.

in any of the schools. On occasion a great man would lend his countenance to the school by a formal visit; at such a time he might crave a little grace for the prisoners of learning; a half holiday was granted at his request and in honor of his advent. Such playtimes were of old called "remedyes," but austere Dean Colet would not allow to the pupils of his new foundation of St. Paul's a playday at the request of anybody less than a king or a prelate. It was thought best to cut off this ancient privilege wholly at the little Virginia college; there were probably too many visitors of distinction; but one afternoon a month was set apart for play, and whenever a new student was enrolled "an afternoon extraordinary" was granted, "and no more."

Quincy's Harvard, i, 517.

Statutes, Knight's Colet, 308.

Ludwell MSS., i, p. 1. Comp. D'Ewes's Autobiog., i, 142.

XXII.

Ascham and reform.

On a certain day in 1563, during the prevalence of "the fever pestilence" in London, there sat at dinner in Secretary Cecil's chamber at Windsor Castle a group of distinguished men. Cecil turned the table talk to the recent flight of some lads from the neighboring school of Eton "for fear of beating," and condemned the harshness of schoolmasters. There were in the company of course some of those conservatives who rise up to defend any old-fashioned practice. But, as good luck would have it, there sat among the dignitaries of state Roger Ascham, the archery-loving, cockfighting, learned and gifted schoolmaster, who

CHAP. V.

had come to Windsor that day to read in Greek with the young Queen Elizabeth one of the orations of Demosthenes. Without title or political position it is fair to suppose that he sat far down near the foot of the table; but Cecil encouraged him to speak to the question, and Ascham gave his opinion strongly and no doubt eloquently against the barbarity of schoolmasters. Dinner ended, Sir Richard Sackville, who had held his peace while the debate went on, led Ascham away to a window for private speech with him. Sackville confessed to Ascham that the beatings of a "lewde Schoolmaster" had brought him to hate learning before he was fourteen years old. He entreated the queen's schoolmaster to write out what he had just spoken at the table. By this conversation Ascham was set on writing his famous work The Scholemaster. But neither the authority of Ascham nor of any other could at once abate the unsparing severity of school discipline which was popularly believed to be eminently beneficial to boys and of scriptural authority. Thomas Becon, the reformer, had complained that schoolmasters beat their pupils "like stockfishes." Mulcaster, the successor of Ascham, had no hesitation about flogging; he speaks somewhat gayly of "my lady birchely." Brinsley, the able and zealous advocate of school reform in the reign of James I, suggests several practical ways of avoiding brutal punishments, such as the use of rewards, and the keeping of a "black bill," or,

Note 27.

as we should now say, a black list; the unlucky scholars set down in this list were to be deprived of their rare playtimes. But even the humane Brinsley did not once dream of sparing the rod for serious offenders; he thought "ferula" a necessary remedy for bad Latin, and he used what he calls "little ierkes" with a small switch of "red willow." When little jerks with little switches would not serve, he recommends more serious flogging; the young rebel to be held over a form or up against a post "by three or four of his fellows," making sure "to hold him fast as they are enforced to do who are to shove or tame an vnbroken colt." This was the method of a conscientious and humane master; the brutalities of the unfeeling are not pleasant to imagine. There were others than Sir Richard Sackville who cursed some "lewde schoolmaster" for a failure to get learning, and some who attributed deafness to blows received in school. "It's a general plague and complaint of the whole land," writes Peacham, "that for one discreet and able teacher you shall find twenty ignorant and carelesse." The first master at Harvard went too far even for that age; it is not certain that he would have been dismissed for his barbarous punishment of students and the exceedingly short commons on which he fed them, but when he ferociously drubbed even his usher, beating him mercilessly with a hickory stick while two of his servants held the man fast, he lost his place, and set on

Ludus Literarius, *passim.* Comp. D'Ewes, i, 63, 64.

Brinsley's Consolations for Our Grammar Schooles, p. 43.

In Compleat Gentleman, 1660.

foot a reform in college discipline. A law was made limiting the punishment of students. If a student were not yet "adultus" he might get ten stripes for each offense. This was very mild; at Eton fifty-three stripes are recorded as given for a trivial fault at an earlier period, and the young John Milton had to suffer a beating from his tutor at Cambridge not very long before this. At Harvard an older student was not to be beaten at all.

Quick, app. to Mulcaster, p. 300.

Note 28.

XXIII.

Education of girls.

Sometimes, though rarely, such a phrase as "male childeringe" appears in a contract with a teacher, but it was always understood that children were boys only, girls did not count. There were no girls in the schools sustained by towns or by endowment at the period of American settlement. To read her Bible and psalm-book devoutly and to use her needle deftly were the only necessary accomplishments for a woman, and these could be got in a dame school or at home. The illiterate "her mark" is signed to papers in the probate office by many women whose fathers were men of education. "Probably not one woman in a dozen could write," says a well-informed New England antiquary. In England only "the first elementarie" was taught to a girl, and Governor Winthrop was convinced that much learning was dangerous to a woman's wits. The education of the most favored girl ceased at thirteen or four-

Note 29.

Dedham Historical Register, Jan., 1897, p. 18.

Judd's Hadley, 64.

teen, at which age she began to assume the responsibilities of a young woman and to blossom into a waiting candidate for wifehood.

XXIV.

Traits of schools.

An English writer recommends the middle of the day for teaching writing, because the fingers would then be warmer and nimbler, which suggests schoolrooms with no fire. In New England one finds the summer school sometimes kept in "the unfinished room" of a house which is spoken of as though a room unfinished was a normal part of a new-country house. The kitchen of a dwelling, with its great fireplace, was sometimes made a schoolroom in winter, or in its stead the "parlor"; the best room reserved for weddings and funerals, on which occasions the bare floor would be neatly strewn with sand. Even where there was a schoolhouse, as at Dedham in 1658, the schoolmaster was allowed to assemble the school in his own house "if the weather be extreme and unfit to travaill." In that climate there early grew up a custom of exacting a half cord or a "wayne load of wood for fewell" for each pupil. This was to be delivered at the schoolhouse in November, for no man of English origin in the first two or three generations after settlement knew that wood could be drawn much more easily on sleds over the snow.

CHAP. V.

XXV.

College ideals.

The direct influence in America of the advanced education of the seventeenth century was not great. No one with any sense of historic perspective will believe that the university men who lived or sojourned in Virginia in the early seventeenth century had any traceable relation to the group of Virginia statesmen that grew as from a congenial soil in the later eighteenth; it is equally fanciful to suppose that the existence of a considerable body of Cambridge men in early New England had anything to do with producing the literary forwardness of that region two hundred years later. But the university ideals of the time influenced directly the course of thought in the new provinces. Logic was the main study in all higher institutions, and the logic bequeathed by the schoolmen meant merely incessant practice of the art of dialectical disputation as a means of acquiring universal truth. In sermons and in conversation this verbal sword play was much affected and it rendered the wits nimble. But this highly valued "Aristotelian method" had for ages retarded the advance toward larger learning and broader views. Milton's disappointment in the university was great, and his contempt for its studies is delightfully Miltonic if not always discriminating. In his vehement complaint he ransacks "lofts of piléd thunder" for missiles with which to assail the curriculum of his time. It is "a pure trifling at grammar and sophistry," "an

Masson's Life of Milton, i, 197.

asinine feast of sow thistles and brambles"; the students are "mocked and deluded" "with ragged notions and babblements while they expect worthy and delightful knowledge." The universities in his opinion were "not yet well recovered from the scholastic grossness of the barbaric ages." There were university students of sound intellectual appetite, like Milton himself, who contrived to find fruit in fields set thick with the sow thistles of scholastic logic and the brambles of mediæval metaphysics. Others, on being abruptly thrust at fifteen years of age into these studies, took "such a distaste of what seemed to them a mere rattle of words, that they were very slowly, if ever, reconciled."

Note 30.

Lives of the Norths, iii, 283.

XXVI.

Harvard College.

In 1636 the Massachusetts General Court voted two hundred pounds toward "a schoole or colledge," and the next year selected Newton, the present Cambridge, as the place for it. This proposition might have proved as futile as the early proposals for a college in Virginia had it not been that John Harvard, a minister, dying in 1638, left a legacy for the proposed institution which thus had the breath of life breathed into it and became Harvard College. It was established on the most religious plan possible. The study of divinity was made the chief end of a student, prayer and religious consecration were prescribed academic duties; Bible reading twice a day and the faithful reporting of

Quincy's History of Harvard College, i, 515, 517.

CHAP. V.

sermons were enjoined. The test for the first degree was a student's ability to render the Old and New Testaments out of Hebrew and Greek into Latin "and to resolve them logically." For the second degree a summary knowledge of logic, natural and moral philosophy, arithmetic, geometry, and astronomy were added. There was here a slender recognition of mathematics in advance of the English universities. The modes of study seem to have been mechanical after the manner of the time. In the earlier years of the college each student was accustomed to transcribe for himself certain treatises in manuscript on logic and other studies made by Alexander Richardson of Oxford. In examining the list of subjects for graduating theses we are now and then refreshed by the intrusion of a question that has to do with human progress; the question of the circulation of the blood was discussed in 1660, and was again mooted in 1699, more than seventy years after Harvey had announced his discovery. For the most part the themes with which college graduates in that day busied themselves are grotesquely futile as, "whether privation is the cause of anything in Nature," "whether genus exists outside of intellect," and "whether a shadow moves." Behold philosophy! It was proved at Harvard commencements by reasoners with youth and courage on their side that the starry heaven is made of fire; that there is a stone which produces gold; and that the quadrature of the circle is possible.

Letter of Leonard Hoar, in Mass. Coll., vi.

The lawfulness and the possibility of curing wounds by sympathetic powder excited attention just before and after 1700, and the existence of a universal remedy was a question equally belated in agitating scholastic minds in America. We have in these questions the everlasting mark-time of mediæval philosophy, marching ostentatiously, but never moving out of its tracks.

Young's Subjects for the Master's Degree at Harvard, pamphlet.

XXVII.

William and Mary College.

After the Restoration Virginia began to feel an alarm like that which had startled Massachusetts earlier. It is probable that the deprived churchmen who occupied Virginia parishes during the Commonwealth were now returning to England to reap the reward of their fidelity to the king. It was feared that the "want of able & faithful Ministers" would deprive the colonists of "those great Blessings and Mercies that allwaies attend upon the Service of God," and the Assembly passed an act in 1661, and again in 1662, to found "a colledge and free schoole." But Sir William Berkeley, the governor, did not want either a college or a free school, and Berkeley, with a salary independent of the good will of the people, was more absolute in Virginia than his master Charles was in England. This pinchbeck Stuart detested ministers who were able to preach, and he abhorred printing presses. But the Virginia educational movement at the time of the Restoration was not

Purvis's Laws of Va., 1662. Comp. Hening, 1661 and 1662, pp. 25, 56.

CHAP. V.

Comp. Hening's Statutes, ii, 30.

wholly without result. If the proposed subscription for the college was ever taken, it probably was not collected, and the "houseing" ordered to be erected for the college is not again heard of. But at least two bequests to found new free schools were made in Berkeley's depressing reign. After the disorders and despotisms which followed the failure of Nathaniel Bacon's bold stroke for freedom in 1676 had passed away, a college subscription was set on foot in 1688 and 1689, and sums amounting to twenty-five hundred pounds were promised by wealthy Virginians and a few English merchants. The confusion resulting from the English Revolution of 1688 probably caused delay.

1691.

Two years more elapsed before the Assembly took action by ordaining an institution in three departments—a grammar school, a school of philosophy, and a school of Oriental languages and divinity.

1693. Note 31.

A charter was secured from the sovereigns. William and Mary, whose names the college took, gave freely out of the wild lands of the province, out of the royal revenues from tobacco, and gave outright the income from the fees for surveying land. The Virginia Assembly added an import duty on furs. In 1700, while the building designed by Sir Christopher Wren was yet unfinished, the college at the close of its first year held a commencement. The novelty of such an exercise attracted a large concourse of people to the new town of Williamsburg. Some of the great planters came in coaches, which vehicles were yet rare enough in America to be noticeable. Other visitors arrived in their own sloops, sailing in some instances from the upper waters of the Chesapeake, and in other cases on the open ocean from Pennsylvania and New York. Some even of the Indians gathered their blankets round them and strolled into the little capital to lend picturesqueness to this powwow of white men. The opening of an infant college was a notable break in the rather eventless monotony of a half-settled coast, remote from the great world.

Charles Campbell's Hist. of Virginia, 361, 362.

The so-called college, thus hopefully launched, drifted inevitably into the whirlpools and eddies of petty provincial politics; its revenues were a tempting bait to the ring of predatory colonial magnates and ambitious sycophants that surrounded a royal governor in that day. William and Mary College was but a grammar school for years after its start, and its development was tediously slow. But most of its resources were saved from plunder and waste, and at the outbreak of the Revolution it was said to be the richest institution of learning in America—for all of which it was primarily indebted to a single man.

Compare Hugh Jones's Present State of Va., 1724, 83, 84.

XXVIII.

Dr. Blair.

While Scottish example, as we have conjectured, had its influence in the founding of Harvard, the influence was more direct in Virginia, where the final success of the college was due to a Scotchman. Behind the measures taken to advance the project by the Assembly and governor in Virginia, by the king and queen, by the Primate and the Bishop of London, by Locke the philosopher, and by the executors of Robert Boyle, there is the moving hand of James Blair, one of the most pertinacious men ever born in a land of obstinate pertinacity. Having seen the subscription well made up in Virginia, Blair went to England in 1691 with a commission from the Assembly to procure the best charter possible and a royal endowment. The traditions of the court were dead against him. The government of Charles II had made a point of discouraging in Virginia printing presses, education, and other influences that unfit people for docile submission to tyranny. The colony was to buy English wares, to swell the customs revenues by producing the heavily taxed tobacco, and to buy negroes from the Royal African Company, in which not only great courtiers but royalty itself had held shares. When Blair argued the need of a college for the sake of the souls of the people, Seymour, the attorney general, replied contemptuously, "Damn your souls, make tobacco!" A less contentious man than Blair would have given up and gone home, a man less canny and persistent must have failed. He contrived to secure William's attention in the midst of the exigent affairs of a critical time, and he managed to gain the support of both the sovereigns. His manœuvres were worthy of an expert courtier; he played Archbishop Ten-

Am. and W. Inds., bundle 637.

nison and the Bishop of London and Queen Mary herself with skill, and won his suit handsomely. He carried back a charter for a *studium generale*, a place of universal study. After his return he fought triumphantly with petty courtiers and successive governors, breaking Sir Edmund Andros himself, who had contrived to survive for many years the infamy of a great variety of disgraceful conduct in his various governments. Dr. Blair was a man of versatile ability; his printed sermons passed through several editions, and he held his place as bishop's commissary at the head of the Virginia clergy for half a century. His discipline was mild, and he fought the battles of his order against encroachments, but his clergy disliked and opposed him. He resisted the oppressions of the royal governors, but the people were never attracted to him. He had no arts of conciliation, and he had no lubricating humor. He delighted to carry a measure by mere push of pike, and to his contemporaries he was a bundle of pugnacities. Every man born north of the Tweed was an object of prejudice, and Blair was accused, moreover, of having received nothing better than a Presbyterian ordination. Though no one seems to have questioned his honesty, it was complained that he "had large worldly concerns." He lived to an advanced age, and died rich in a land where many thriftless and often dissipated parsons got on but meanly. He was one of the chief benefactors of a colony that never showed him, young or old, living or

CHAP. V.

dead, the slightest gratitude of which there is any record. A single noble legacy made the obscure John Harvard immortal, but fifty years of resolute service and a liberal legacy to the college brought no honors to the founder of William and Mary. A good and public-spirited man, he was personally unlikable. But had Blair been less rugged, there might have been no "College Royal of William and Mary."

XXIX.

Colonies without colleges.

At the end of the seventeenth century there were efficient beginnings of higher education only in Massachusetts, Connecticut, and Virginia. New York was too much divided by the various nationalities of its people and too deeply interested in a trade reaching from Lake Ontario to the pirate settlements of Madagascar to have advanced beyond rudimentary schools. Pennsylvania and the Carolinas were too new, Maryland and Rhode Island too much subdivided in religion, and the eastward settlements of New England were too backward in development. Massachusetts had firmly established a college destined to an illustrious career, Connecticut was about to start into the new century with her Yale College, and Virginia was flushed with hope of a time when the grammar school at Williamsburg should grow into "a certaine place of universall study," as its charter proposed. These small beginnings were enough to mark the persistence in the Western world of the

English tradition in favor of higher education. In communities like the expanding English-American colonies of that time, necessarily materialistic in ideals and schemes of life, the mere existence of schools whose principal studies had no value that could be balanced against tobacco and codfish, pipe staves and beaver skins—studies whose value could not be reckoned in pine-tree shillings and pieces of eight—was of high import.

ELUCIDATIONS.

Note 1, page 208.

Schools before the Reformation.

"In the same year of our Lord's incarnation, 664," says Bede, "a sudden pestilence . . . ravaged the country far and near. . . . This pestilence did no less harm in the island of Ireland. Many of the nobility and of the lower ranks of the English nation were there at that time, . . . either for the sake of Divine studies or of a more continent life; and some of them presently devoted themselves to a monastic life, others chose rather to apply themselves to study, going about from one master's cell to another." Egbert, one of the Englishmen among the Culdees in Ireland, succeeded in escaping from the plague by vowing that he would say the whole psalter daily to the praise of God, and that he would every week fast one whole day and night. The account of his austerities in Bede, book iii, chap. xxvii, throws light on the ideals of life taught in the monasteries of the seventh century. In Tanner's Notitia Monastica he says of the Culdees: "The ancient British, Irish, and Saxon Monasteries, we find, were Schools and Universities of those times; they were not only Cells of Devotion, but also Nurseries of Learned Men for the use of the Church." To imagine anything like modern school or university instruction or learning in the monasteries of that early age would be misleading. In the Catholic monasteries and cathedral establishments organization was perhaps more perfect than among the Culdees. We get a view of higher and lower instruction as already established in a canon of A. D. 747, number 7, in Johnson's Ecclesiastical Laws. Some curious traits of the schools in the houses of the priests may be deduced from the canons in the

CHAP. V.

same work under A. D 960, numbers 10, 11, 51, and A. D. 994, numbers 19 and 20. "When the Monks were rooted out by the Danish wars," says Tanner, "an universal ignorance overspread the land, insomuch that there was scarce any one in England that could read or write Latin. But when, by the care of King Edgar and Archbishop Dunstan, Monasteries were restored, Learning found its former encouragement." Preface to Notitia Monastica. Fitzstephen relates that there were famous schools in three principal churches of London in the twelfth century. Furnivall cites a saying of Roger Bacon that there were schools in every city, town, burgh, and castle in the thirteenth century. Compare also Wright's Domestic Manners and Sentiments in the Middle Ages, 338 and ff. There is evidence of the survival of the teaching of children by the mass priest in the action of the corporation of Bridgenorth. When a more modern "Comyn Scole" was substituted at the beginning of the sixteenth century, a by-law was adopted which ordained that "there schall no priste kepe no scole save oonly oon child to helpe hym to sey masse." MSS. Commission, x, part iv, 425. There is an instance as late as Mary's reign of the restoration of an ancient endowment by town lands for the support of a priest "Habill to teache Grammar." Ibid., 533. In Collier's Ecclesiastical History, part ii, book iii, 165 (Lathbury's edition, vol. v, 29), we read: "The abbeys were very serviceable places for the education of young people; every convent had one person or more assigned for this business. Thus the children of the neighborhood were taught [Latin] grammar and music without any charge to their parents: and in the nunneries those of the other sex learned to work and read English, with some advances into Latin." Stow, in his Survey of London, notes that the Lateran Council in 1176 recognized cathedral schools, but in the Capitularies of Theodolf they are carried back to the end of the eighth century, and were, beyond doubt, still older. Johnson's Ecclesiastical Laws, 994, 19. Down to the end of the tenth century almost the only seminaries in Charlemagne's dominions appear to have been in cathedrals and convents. First Report of Cathedral Commission, xxv. It is to be noted that many of the English cathedrals were monastic institutions; in eight out of seventeen in the twelfth century the chapters were composed entirely of monks. Collier's Ecclesiastical History, book iv, cent. xii, 341 (vol. ii, 232, of Lathbury). On the origin of cathedrals and the colleges in the early Episcopia, see Report of Cathedral Commission, p. iv.

Schotel, in his Oud Hollandsch Huisgezin der Zeventiende Eeuw, p. 75, says of education in Holland: "In the earliest time most of the parish churches had their schools. . . . The school of the cathedral church [hoofdkerk] took the name of the great school. . . . In these last were taught not only Greek and Latin, but Dutch—that is, reading, writing, and ciphering, and not alone to the children of the well-to-do, but to the poor as well. They were all comrades in the school as in the street." Roger's Work and Wages, 165, 166, remarks on the widely diffused knowledge of Latin in the middle ages. Until the fourteenth century English was not even suffered to play tender to Latin in the schools, but in 1363 "it was ordeined that schoolemasters should teach their scholers to construe their lessons in English & not in French, as before they had beene vsed." Holinshed, ii, 678. Down to the Reformation Latin was taught before the reading of English, as we learn from Mulcaster, an Elizabethan schoolmaster. "Now," he adds, "we are returned home to our English abce." Positions, chap. v.

Note 2, page 209.

A definite number of scholars were to be sustained in each cathedral while living in commons. Whiston's Cathedral Trusts and Harrison's Description of Britaine, i, 235. The First Cathedral Report, p. xxiv, cites Cranmers Reformatio Legum that every cathedral should maintain a school for the mature education of youth. Chantry priests, whose support came from endowments for prayers for the dead, found their occupation gone when the government had forbidden all praying for the dead, and had indeed abolished purgatory. It was therefore ordained that such priests should "exercise themselves in teaching youth to read and write and bring them up in good manners and vertuous exercises." Bills were brought into Parliament in Edward VI's reign "for incouraging men to give lands for the maintenance of schools." Tanner's Notitia Monastica, preface, citing MS. authority.

Note 3, page 210.

By suppressing the alien priories, which were but offshoots of foreign monasteries, Henry V made a tempting precedent for Henry VIII, but Henry VI supplied the place of the schools lost with the suppressed priories in the preceding reign by founding various free schools in 1393 and 1394. See the section on Schooles and Houses of Learning in Stow's Survey of London, and Collier's treatment of this period in his Ecclesiastical History. Dean Colet's foundation of St. Pauls School in 1512 was "in place of an old ruined house," says Stow, and Christ's Hospital, in 1553,

CHAP. V.

was planted in the "late dissolved house of the Grey Friars," and "a school was ordained there." Many of the new free schools of the Reformation period were endowed out of the spoils of the monasteries. "For the most part the endowments were out of the tithes formerly belonging to the religious houses or out of chantry lands given to the king in the first of his reign, according to the intent of parliament therein, which was to convert them from superstitious uses into more godly, as in erecting great schools for the education of youth in virtue and godliness." Strype's Memorials (1822), vii, part ii, pp. 50, 51. Thomas Williams, Speaker of the House of Commons, in 1562 "took notice of the Want of Schools; that at least an Hundred were wanting in England which before his time had been." In giving this passage Strype adds, "being destroyed (I suppose he meant) by the Dissolution of Monasteries and Religious Houses." Annals of the Reformation, i, 292. The demand for Latin schools was no doubt increased by the growing ambition of the people in the new social conditions. No means were so convenient "to make Jack a gentleman" as to send him to the university to win the coveted title of "Mr." Even cobblers sought education for their sons. Hall's Satires, iv, II; Howell's Letters, 405, 406. Mulcaster thought that every child should learn to read English and also to write for his "necessary dealings." Positions, chap. 36. He refuses Latin to the common people because of the prevailing ambition to rise in England, but he adds significantly that "both clownes in the countrie and artificers in townes be allowed lattine in well gouerned states, who yet rest in their callings." "Factors or Marchants and the like, going beyond seas find it necessary and convenient to speak Latin," says Brinsley, Ludus Literarius, 211.

Note 4, page 213.

There was published in 1538 an A B C book, and it has been reprinted. The editor writes a preface wherein he says the Ten Commandments are not included. But they are included in rhyme—rhyme was the only amelioration of reading in that day. This is the authorized primer of 1538, though the editor says it is not. It has the A B C and the "a b abs," the Lord's Prayer in Latin and English, the Hail Mary in both tongues, and the Creed in both. Then there are parts of songs in Latin, "to help a priest to sing"—that is, for the child to help him to sing. This is followed, wholly in English, by an extended grace before and grace after "dyner." Then there is a grace for "fysshe dayes" and grace after dinner, and a short grace to be said be-

Note 5, page 215.

fore dinner and another to be said before "dyner" or "souper," a short grace after dinner and another after dinner or supper, then two graces after supper, then an Easter grace before and after dinner, then a prayer, then the Ten Commandments in rhyme, and then a series of rhyming precepts. The great number of graces before and after meat came from the habit of having children say grace. There were no breakfasts in Henry VIII's time, and no graces for such a meal.

Note 6, page 215.

One may be permitted to doubt the unbroken continuity of the master's Latin in many cases. The language in which the celebrated Harvey lectured to medical students on the circulation of the blood was probably better Latin than an ordinary schoolmaster's, but it is intentionally mottled throughout with English. Take this phrase for one example of a thousand: "Exempto corde frogg scipp eele crawle dogg ambulat." Prelectiones, 7. But Bacon says that pupils are to make paper books and to note the best sentences of the Roman tongue, and practice them in speaking and writing.

Note 7, page 215.

I have referred in the margin to Wigglesworth's complaint of the "boldness to transgress the college law in speaking English." Brinsley laments the remissness of his time in teaching English. Some colleges in the English universities made the constant use of Latin obligatory (Brinsley's Ludus, 211), but in all lectures and exercises were in Latin. Harvard students were quite unable to speak Latin when Dankers met them in 1689. It may safely be said that the colloquial use of Latin never found a lodgment in America.

Note 8, page 215.

Brinsley had "laboured and striven by Ferula and all meanes of severity" to improve the Latin of his boys, but he says, "I have not been able to make Schollers to vtter their mindes in any tollerable manner of ordinary things," etc., "without great severity." He confesses "they will not be brought to give overspeaking English." Ludus Literarius, 215. Theoretically, students admitted to Harvard could all speak Latin, but the requirements for admission were probably not strictly exacted. "When any scholar is able to read Tully or such like classical Latin author *extempore*, and to make and speak true Latin in verse and prose *Suo* (*ut aiunt*) *Marte*, and decline perfectly the paradigms of nouns and verbs in the Greek tongue, then may he be admitted into the college." Laws, etc., of Harvard, 1642–1646. Quincy's Harvard College, i, 515.

The rage for disputation in the schools had been even greater in earlier times before logic had been mainly relegated to the universities. Fitzstephen says in the twelfth century that upon holy days assemblies gather in the churches to hear these disputaitons of scholars, in which all the technical forms of reasoning and rhetoric taught by the schoolmen are practiced for display, and boys of the different schools "wrangle together in the art of versifying, and canvase the principles of Grammar." Stow's Survey, 705, with his quaint translation, 710, 799, edition 1633. In the sixteenth century this had been done away with, but Stow himself had seen assemblies of boys from various schools gathered in a churchyard to dispute on an improvised platform about the principles of grammar for the fun of the thing. As above, 64. When these gatherings ceased the boys from the rival schools of St. Pauls and St. Anthonys would provoke one another in the open street with the challenge to debate "Salve tu quoque, placet tibi mecum disputare?" To which the reply "Placet" being given, they fell to wrangling over tenses and constructions until often there ensued a general scrimmage of the two parties laden with satchels of books and piling themselves on one another in heaps to the obstruction of the streets.

Note 9, page 217.

The usher who was ultimately to be master of the free school at Charles City, Va., was apparently incompetent to teach writing and arithmetic. The Company gave him permission to take with him "an expert writer," who should be able to teach "the *grounds* of arithmetic, whereby to instruct the children in matters of account." But no other provision was made for such a man than to give him his passage free, leaving him to be paid by the parents. Abstract of Records, ii, 167. The form proposed for the organization of the school at Charles City, Va., was identical with that carried out in the grammar school of William and Mary College, nearly a hundred years later. There was in both a master, an usher, and a writing master. Compare Ingle's Letter, 1705, in Historical Collections relating to the Colonial Church, Virginia, 140. See the statute regulating the mendicancy of scholars of the university in 1388. Statutes at Large, ii, 302. Students appear to have continued to beg until forbidden by the statute of 1572 in the reign of Elizabeth. Compare also Jusseraud's English Wayfaring Life, 232, 233, and Wright's Domestic Manners, 339. The "poor scholars" were still made prominent in early appeals for Harvard College, and one is tempted to suspect, from the prominence given to Indian education at Harvard and in the early Virginia projects, that the "infidel" was substituted in part for the poor scholar as a means of stimulating liberality. A kind of mixed school, in which plebeian arithmetic jostled Latin grammar, existed in England and appeared early in America. For example, Dedham Records for 1663, 1670, iv, 67, 133. Bailey's Andover, 517. Compare p. 520 of Bailey, where there is a sort of confession that English studies are intruders in a Latin school, for a schoolmaster in 1723 is specifically bound as an additional duty "that he wold Teach boys to Read, Rite, and Cypher." Comp. MSS. Commission X, part iv, 138–140, where in 1695 a so-called writing school endowed by Sir John Moore is expected to fit boys for the university.

Note 10, page 219.

The old conception of education is struggling with the new. Of old higher education was the property of the few. In 1559 one of the measures suggested to Parliament was that the study of the laws, temporal or civil, be restricted to the sons of noblemen or gentlemen. Seven years later Knox sought to teach everybody their "first rudimentie" in order to render them Protestant. In 1616 the Synod of Dort tried to teach the catechism to all for purposes of religious indoctrination. In 1622 we find Brinsley struggling blindly with the principles of education, "God having ordained schooles of learning to be a principall meanes to reduce a barbarous people to ciuilities." It was just twenty-five years later that Massachusetts proposed to confound "the ould deluder Satan" by schools especially in Latin and Greek and Hebrew, but English schools were finally almost the only outcome of the act, the practical sense of the people gradually doing away with the superannuated Latin school. Of course, the clergy were educated in Latin. Justus Forward, of Belchertown, Mass., so late as 1763, writes D. D. (dies dominica) for Sunday, and several other days appear in their Latin dress. He says "studiebam" and "occupatus studiendo," "occupatus de iisdem," and "Daniel dragged ibidem," in his English diary. MS. in my possession.

Note 11, page 221.

The first Virginia Assembly, in 1619, petitioned in favor of the erection of a proposed "university and college." New York Historical Collections, iii, i, 342. The Company, with wise forethought, reserved liberal tracts of land for the support of churches and a local school in each plantation. Smith of Nibley MSS., New York Public Library. In Fuller's Worthies, i, 566, 567, it is said that Edward Palmer (whom Camden, in his Britannia, 1610,

CHAP. V.

folio 366, calls "a curious and diligent antiquarie," and who died in 1625) purchased an island in Virginia, called "Palmer's Island unto this day," and that he spent several thousand pounds in a fruitless endeavor to plant an academy upon it. Neill, in his Virginia Vetusta, says that the island in question was at the mouth of the Susquehanna, and gives for authority the Hermans-Faithorne map. I had the unique copy of this map in the British Museum examined, and received this report: "There is no island marked Palmer's Island on the map indicated at the embouchure of the Susquehanna or at any other point. There are marks of islands, but no name attached." That the island at the mouth of the Susquehanna was called Palmer's Island is to be deduced from the Proceedings of the Council in Maryland Archives, where an observation of its longitude is recorded in 1683. It was a wild and solitary place for a school.

Note 12, page 221.

In 1467 a testator left a cow to keep wax candles burning before the image of the Virgin in Felsham Church. In 1530 two cows were bequeathed "to the sepulchre light in Ampton Church to continew for evyr." In such cases the increase of the kine went to make the bequest perpetual. Bury wills, Camden Society, pp. 44 and 249. Dr. Fuller, the physician of the Pilgrims, gave "the first cow calf that my brown cow shall have to the church of God at Plymouth," and a ewe lamb was a common bequest to that church. Brigham, in Lowell Institute Lectures, 174, 175.

Note 13, page 222.

In the manuscript records of Christ Church parish, Middlesex County, Va., I find allusion to a free school already existing, for the benefit of which two cows have been bequeathed in 1691. As early as 1655 four cows were left in Isle of Wight County for maintaining and schooling orphans. In 1669 King Free School, in the same county, was established by bequest, and some other endowments can be traced, while there were those probably of which no record has been found. See two papers on this subject in the William and Mary Quarterly for 1897.

Note 14, page 222.

The boast of Sir William Berkeley, in 1671, that there were no free schools in Virginia—Hening, ii, 511 and ff., and Virginia Historical Register, iii, 12—has been repeated by superficial writers on the period. Berkeley adds, "Learning has brought disobedience and heresy and sects into the world." The passage is but a vivacious revelation of the state of mind of a willful and avaricious dotard, in whom contempt for the popular rights and the wishes of the people was hardening into that brutality which made his last years so terrible for Virginia, and brought about his own ignominious downfall. In 1671, when Berkeley wrote, the Symmes free school was in existence, the Eaton school was founded before 1646 probably, the King Free School endowment was made two years before, and four years later Peasley's liberal bequest was given for another free school. Both the Symmes and Eaton schools were in existence more than a century after their planting. An act had been passed in 1661 for the founding of a college which involved a free school. Berkeley probably knew better than any other person why the project slumbered. See section xxv of the present chapter. But the English system of free schools did not and could not obtain to any considerable extent in Virginia in 1671 or even later; physical and social conditions were against it. Compare Foote's Virginia, i, 11. In colony times the only Virginia school that rose to the dignity of the English free schools was the one attached to William and Mary College. Compare the inhibitions of printing in Virginia in 1682, Virginia Historical Register, iii, 13, and the utter prohibition of printing presses in Effingham's instructions of 1685. The allusions to schools in the seventeenth century that can be picked up from the remaining local records of Virginia are not many, but by comparing them with Beverley's statement of Effingham's course in licensing teachers about 1684, and then examining the replies of the Virginia clergy in 1724 to the Queries of the Bishop of London, we can form some notion of the voluntary education by means of "old field schools" that early grew up among the Virginians. As the bishop's query asks only about parish schools, some of the replies give negative information; but wherever the clergyman mentions the rustic schools they seem to be fairly numerous for a new country, to be taught by men and not women, and not to be above the level of the rough country school of the period elsewhere. "In most parishes," says Hugh Jones, "are schools in Little Houses built on purpose, where are taught English and writing." One private school for Latin and Greek flourishes in the same parish with two endowed schools of a lower grade. In one case a plantation was given to the incumbent of the parish on condition that he should sustain "a sufficient person" to teach reading, writing, and arithmetic. In Maryland, the ideal of Bray was a free school in every county, and one or two in the province for Indians. This does not account for the little schools. General View of the Colonies, prefixed to sermon of 1697, p. 7.

CHAP. V.

Note 15, page 223.

In Ciuile and Vnciuile Life, 1579, 1586, Roxburghe edition, p. 21, the country gentleman is made to say, "Wee gentlemen in the Country, vnlesse our sonnes proceed in the study of the common lawes, Diunitie, or Phisicke, doo hold them learned ynough if they can write and read English, and congrue Latine." Note that he must "congrue Latine"—that is, after a fashion put it together. This probably represents the education thought fit for his son by the Virginia planter a hundred years later. Even so much Latin probably could not always be had.

Note 16, page 224.

There were some convicts who were capable of teaching, but the convicts were not usually of the kind to supply teachers, and in Virginia in the seventeenth century there were fewer of these than of indentured servants known as "free-willers" who had embarked of their own accord, and the "kids" who had been "trapanned" aboard ship by craft or force. The schoolmasters no doubt usually belonged to the class of voluntary or involuntary redemptioners, and not among the petty criminals who were sold for seven years. The will of Colonel John Carter, in 1669, specifically provides for the purchase of a bond servant who had been "brought up in the Latin school," to teach his son Robert, afterward the famous King Carter of Virginia. See quotations from the records at Lancaster Court House in a letter from Mr. Wilson Miles Cary in The Nation of April 22, 1897. Boucher long afterward says that two thirds of the schools in Maryland were taught either by indentured servants or by convicts. Causes, 184, 189. I think the convicts much the smaller of the two classes. Boucher would have mentioned the fact had it been the other way.

Note 17, page 226.

The general responsibility of a corporate town as such for the support of its school, where there was one, was a trait of English life, carried over to the rustic municipalities or "towns" of New England, and gradually changed to our more local system. Compare, for example, what Brinsley says in 1622 in speaking of badly managed schools: "That it were better to turne the maintenance given to the schoole to bear the charges of the towne for other duties and seruices then so vnprofitably to employ it." Consolations for Our Grammar Schooles, 43.

Note 18, page 228.

The rough life of the frontier has always been dangerous to morals and manners. The remedy proposed in Massachusetts was rather traditional than practical. It was ordained in 1642 that children when tending cattle were to employ their time at spinning on the rock or distaff and knitting tape, and boys and girls were forbidden to converse together. Such an order was doubtless without any result. In 1645, after the news of the great Virginia massacre had startled New England, boys were ordered to learn the use of small guns, half pikes, and bows and arrows, thus reviving old English customs and customs as old as the Roman law, no longer of any value. Compare Ridley's View of the Law, 1634, p. 48.

Note 19, page 230.

In President Chauncy's Commencement Sermon of 1655, p. 38, what may be called the unattainable ideal of the time is thus expressed: "In cittyes and greater towns schools should teach the Latin and Greek tongues, and Hebrew also, which ought to be had in great account with us for the Old Testament sake."

Note 20, page 231.

In the platform of Church Discipline adopted in 1648, vi, 6, the school is regarded as "lawful, profitable, & necessary for training of such in good Literature or Learning as may afterward be called forth unto office of Pastor or Teacher in the Church." This hesitating indorsement of the school is backed up by half a dozen texts of Scripture. In re-enacting the school law the Connecticut General Court of 1673 omitted the epithet "old deluder" before Satan, whose character was well enough known by this time, and in 1692 the diabolical preamble disappeared entirely from the laws of Massachusetts. Compare also the New Hampshire law of 1715. In 1673 Connecticut made it obligatory on county towns to have a grammar school, "for the use of the county," under penalty (after 1677) of ten pounds. In 1678 Connecticut took the lead of Massachusetts by making it obligatory on every town of thirty families to have an English school. In 1684 the surplus money of the treasury was to go to the grammar schools. All this legislation testifies to the increasing difficulty of maintaining the so-called Latin school. Massachusetts in 1671 increased the fine for neglecting schools to ten pounds, and ordered it paid to the nearest town having a grammar school. To cite no other evidence of the struggle to keep alive grammar schools, the New Hampshire law of 1721, in something like desperation, makes the failure for a single month on the part of a town of one hundred families to provide a Latin school punishable by a fine of twenty pounds, to be collected from the personal estate of the selectmen. This was no doubt in depreciated currency. See Weeden's Economic History of New England on the decline, and in some cases the extinction, of New England Schools.

CHAP. V.

Note 21, page 232.

From the Third Report for the Commissioners on Education in Scotland for 1867–'68 we learn that schools for Latin, to which were subsequently added "Lecture" schools for English, existed in the chief towns from a very early period. Several of these schools are known to date from the twelfth century. All the chief towns had schools before the beginning of the sixteenth century. "The statute of James IV (1496), which ordains that barons and free-holders who were of substance should put their eldest sons and heirs to the 'scholes fra they be six or nine year of age, and to remain at the Grammar Schools quill they be competentlie founded and have perfite Latine,' is conclusive on this point." These schools were closely connected with the cathedrals, monasteries, and religious establishments; the teachers were ecclesiastics "or in some way connected with the cathedrals and monasteries," and they were sometimes sustained by altarages. "The scholars . . . were no doubt originally those destined for the church. Gradually, however, sons of gentry and of barons . . . were sent . . . to these schools, and from the beginning of the second or more flourishing period of the history all the higher middle classes took advantage of them." It is interesting to find that not only the grammar but the elementary schools existed in Scotland in 1494. In that year the chancellor of the diocese of Glasgow orders that no one without his license should teach "scholares in grammatica aut juvenes in puerilibus." Light is thrown on the condition of Scottish schools just before the Reformation by Andrew Melville's account in McCrie's Life of Knox, 475, 476. The repeated legislation in 1616, 1633, 1646, and finally in 1696, shows how slowly the plan was put in force. Report of Commissioners, p. 8. It is worth remarking as illustrating the force of historic continuity, even in time of revolution, that Knox's reader or minister teaching the rudiments in an "upaland" town is only a Protestant reproduction of the older priest in small parishes combining teaching with "praying for the people," such as we have already mentioned above as existing in former ages in England. It would carry us too far afield to note here the rather futile efforts made in the seventeenth century to make Knox's ideal actual in Scotland, or to discuss the Scotch school establishment of 1696, etc. It is sufficient that the plan set forth in 1560 remained a fixed ideal and tradition in Scotland, as the plan of 1647 did in New England. In 1704 most of the parishes in Scotland had each a Latin school in name, but the masters were nearly all incompetent. The schools were not free, but, as in many New England towns, the fees of the scholars eked out the teacher's living. Proposals, etc., in Harleian Miscellany, Park's edition, i, 500 and ff. Some towns, as Polworth in 1652, had no salary for the teacher except his "quarter payments" from the pupils. MSS. Commission, xiv, App. iii, p. 94. Comp. p. 128. As in Scotland, so in Holland, the reformed clergy early sought to strengthen their position by means of schools and a system of catechetical instruction. The plan proposed by the Synod of Dort in 1618, probably with a purpose of extirpating Arminianism as well as Romanism, was to establish schools for teaching "Christian doctrine" "in towns and country places where none have existed." In these schools the children of the poor were to be gratuitously instructed by orthodox teachers, well versed in the catechism. Two whole days in the week were to be given up to teaching the catechism. The resolutions are translated in De Witt's Historical Sketch of the Parochial School System of Holland preceding Dunshee's History of the Dutch Church School in New York. Of the state of the schools of Holland in the seventeenth century a notion may be formed from Schotel's Oud Hollandsch Huisgezin, Hoofdstuk, x, from which I have quoted in a preceding note. Compare also a brief summary in English of Schotel's chapter in Geddes's History of the Administration of John De Witt, 33–37. Some of the mistresses of Dutch bye schools or shop schools (byscholen, winkelscholen) could not read, but taught the catechism orally, and the school teaching was generally of a primitive sort. But the Synod of Dort had made a declaration resembling that of Knox in favor of schools in every parish, and this unattained Dutch ideal would be likely to have weight also in New England. Rude and imperfect as was the system launched by the Massachusetts law of 1647, it made "writeing and reading," not the catechism, as in Holland, the corner stone of the country school.

Note 22, page 235.

A letter written by Governor Dudley to the Society for the Propagation of the Gospel in 1701 says of Massachusetts, Connecticut, New Hampshire, and Maine, "I am of opinion that there are no children to be found ten years old who do not read well, nor men of twenty that do not write tolerably." Such a condition probably has never existed among the people of so large a region in any part of America from the Glacial epoch to the present time, and, considering the character of the astute politician who expressed this opinion, one should not take it too seriously. It is said by Upham, the industrious historian of Salem, that very

CHAP. V.

many people could not read in the ancient capital only nine years earlier, and that schools were in a bad condition.

Note 23, page 235.

In the Blue Book for 1867 the Report on Burgh and Middle Class Schools in Scotland, from which I have already quoted, referring to the Buke of Discipline, says that by the colleges which Knox proposed for every notable town he intended "grammar schools on the model of those more ancient seminaries in which the 'trivium' or course of three sciences were taught," p. 5. A passage in the same report on p. 7 suggests the source of John Harvard's inspiration: "Cambuslang, where the Rev. John Harrison, minister of the parish, endowed a Grammar School in 1602; with Prestonpans, where a trilingual school for the teaching of Latin, Greek, and Hebrew was founded about the same time by the Rev. John Davidson, who endowed it with all his fortune, including his books." That it was early found difficult to exact Hebrew of the Harvard students is apparent from the extracts from Wigglesworth's diary in 1653, given in Sibley's Harvard Graduates, vol. i, under the name of the diarist.

Note 24, page 237.

A multitude of illustrations might be cited. "That ye education of youth may be carried on sutably to Christs ends, by ye counsail of the teaching elders in this colony," is the phrase of the New Haven Colony Records in 1660, vol. ii, 373. A very notable entry in the town records of New Haven in 1723 directs that a certain piece of land be used "for the educating of children of Congregational or Presbyterian parents only, and for no other use whatever, forever, hereafter." Atwater's New Haven, 151.

Note 25, page 240.

Meals were hard to reckon with in the reigns of Elizabeth and James. It seems clear that most people of position in Elizabeth's reign ate their first meal at about noon. Harrison, in Holinshed, i, 287, says: "Heretofore there hath béene much more time spent in eating and drinking than commonlie is in these daies, for whereas of old we had breakfasts in the forenoone, beverages or nuntions after dinner, and thereto reare suppers generallie when it was time to go to rest. . . . Now these od repasts thanked be God are verie well left, and ech one in a maner, (except here and there some yoong hungrie stomach that cannot fast till dinner time) contentes himself with dinner and supper onelie."

Note 26, page 240.

In 1555 the burgh school in Aberdeen began at seven o'clock, according to the report on Burgh and Middle Class Schools in Scotland. There was an intermission of an hour at nine, "when all were directed to hasten to breakfast." The school was then resumed from ten to twelve, and again from two to six. But most English schools were held unbrokenly from six to eleven and from one to six, and even at a later period, as we may infer from Brinsley. In another Scottish school, that at Elgin in 1649, work began at six and continued till six, with two hours' intermission—one for breakfast and one for dinner. Report as above, p. 15. I can find no trace in later schools of the bever taken in the schoolroom, which must have been the custom in the reign of Henry VIII. The statutes of St. Paul's School, as drawn by Colet, say: "Also I will they bring no meate nor drinke, nor bottel, nor use in the school no breakfasts, nor drinkings in the tyme of learnynge in no wise," etc. Knight's Life of Colet, 308. The hours of St. Paul's School were from seven to eleven and from one to five. This, with the difference between Aberdeen in 1553 and Elgin in 1649, as given above, and some other facts I have noted, cause me to suspect that the longest hours came in only with the new zeal of the Reformation period. But Colet's statutes are very severe in refusal of holidays, etc. "Yf the master grantith any remedyes he shall forfeit xl s. totiens quotiens," etc. The holy days of the Church were interruption enough in Colet's time. As late as 1763 I find in Justin Forward's diary that he visited Hatfield's school, and advised a "vacancy," which was granted. Manuscript in my possession.

Note 27, page 242.

John Brinsley was a clergyman of Puritan tendencies, and a brother-in-law to the famous Bishop Hall. He has been less cited than his forerunners Ascham or Mulcaster, but he appears to have had practical ideas on the subject of school management in advance of both, and his books are most instructive to the student of the history of education, especially his Ludus Literarius and his Consolations for Our Grammar Schooles. The latter has a special interest for us, because it was written to promote the welfare of the schools projected for Virginia, as well as those in Ireland and Wales. It was submitted to the Virginia Company for approval before its publication. Among the reforms advocated by Brinsley were a somewhat later hour of beginning schools, a recess for breakfast in the middle of the forenoon, and another in the middle of the afternoon, and a large attention to the teaching of English.

Note 28, page 244.

The passage in Brinsley's Consolations, p. 43, is suggestive: "When our scholars coming to man's estate shall cvrse vs for

CHAP. V.

that by our blowes they were made dunses or deafe . . . or to hate all learning." "They think themselves the best schoolmasters when they teach little and beat much," says Becon. He says one might think them "vexed with some infernal fury." It should be remembered, in mitigation of censure on the schoolmasters, that in a civilization like that of the sixteenth and seventeenth centuries, discipline without corporal punishment would have been more difficult than in our later time. The pupils regarded their master as a natural enemy. This was hit off by a Dutch schoolmaster of that time, whose sign before his door showed a portrait of himself sitting in the midst of his uproarious and unruly scholars with a crown on his head and this legend below: "Het gekroonde hoofd-sweer" (The crowned headache). Schotel's Oud Hollandsch Huisgezin, 76. From this antagonism came the practice of "barring out," or, as it was called in this country, "turning the master out." There was an early instance of this turning out at William and Mary, in which the boys received encouragement from Governor Nicholson himself, and fired blank cartridges at Dr. Blair, the president. This custom seems to have died in England only in the nineteenth century. It lingered long enough in this country for the present writer to have partaken of a "treat" of apples served by one master to buy exemption from it, and to have had the bitter experience when about twelve years old of leading in an actual conflict of the kind, when the resolute master with stalwart help from without broke down the door casing and carried the house by storm. Addison at the same age was more successful at Litchfield in an enterprise of the kind, according to Dr. Johnson. The practice was very common in the seventeenth century. See the Gentleman's Magazine of 1828, part ii, pp. 402–408. The custom of "taking the school" was set down as an old one in Aberdeen in 1568, when the boys secured three days of vacation. In 1604 the boys again "took the school" with guns and other weapons, and foraged for "puir folke's geir," such as "geisse, foullis, and ultheris vivaris." Burgh Records of Aberdeen, xxviii.

Note 29, page 244.

Mulcaster, like his predecessor Ascham, was an admirer of the classical attainments of Queen Elizabeth, and so inclined to advise a higher education for women than was customary. But tradition was against him. "I set not yong maidens to publike grammar Schooles," he says, "a thing not used in my countrie, I send them not to the vniversities, having no president thereof in my countrie." He says that maidens "taught to read and write, to sing and play, to speak daily spoken tongues, and of best reputations in our times" compared well with men. Positions, 166. The Puritans naturally regarded Elizabeth's rule with disfavor, and her masculine acquirements seemed to them rather unscriptural. Anne Bradstreet was an example, however, of an educated woman in New England, though a reluctant Puritan, and An Cotton of a cultivated woman in Virginia. "For the first fifty years after the settlement very little is on record in respect to schools, and from the numerous instances of persons of the second generation who could not write their names, it is evident that education was at a low ebb. Female instruction in particular must have been greatly neglected, when the daughters of men who occupied important offices in the town and church were obliged to make a mark for their signature. Yet the business of teaching was then chiefly performed by women. . . . Every quarter of the town had its mistress, who taught children to behave, to ply the needle through all the mysteries of hemming, overhand stitching, and darning up to the sampler, and to read from A B C through the spelling book to the psalter. Children were taught to be mannered and pay respect to their elders, especially to dignitaries. In the street they stood aside when they met any respectable person or stranger, and saluted him with a bow or courtesy, stopping modestly until he had passed. This was called 'making their manners.'" Miss Caulkin's History of New London, 395. "Children who did not attend school were taught to read at home, and nearly all could read, females as well as males. Writing was considered much less important, and it was not judged necessary that females in common life should learn to write." Judd's History of Hadley, 64. Compare Bailey's Andover, 13, footnote. Judd adds that girls were not permitted to attend public schools in Boston until 1790, and that the permission was not granted in Northampton until 1802. Mrs. Grant says that in Albany women could usually read in Dutch the Bible and a few Calvinistic tracts, but not English in 1704. Memoirs of an American Lady, I, 33. Needlework was added to this. She adds with unnecessary detail, "This confined education prevented elegance." In Philadelphia in 1722 "flourishing on muslin and embroidering petticoats" was taught to young ladies along with French.

Note 30, page 247.

D'Ewes complains of the morals of the university: "Swearing, drinking, rioting, and hatred of all piety . . . did abound . . . generally in the university . . . so as I was fain to live al-

CHAP. V.

most a recluses life." It is characteristic of the age that D'Ewes finds consolation in reflecting that the religious opinions of his licentious, riotous, and impious fellow-scholars were uncorrupted by "Anabaptisticall or Pelagian heresies," and that there was no bowing toward the altar. Autobiography, i, 141. Libertines and blackguards in abundance, but no Baptists, Arminians, or High-churchmen, thank God!

Note 31, page 250.

The charter of William and Mary College in English is recorded in a beautiful contemporary handwriting in the manuscript book of Virginia Instructions, in the Library of Congress. It is printed with Hartwell, Blair, and Chilton's account of Virginia, and the copy of the latter in the Library of Congress is annotated by some critic, who notes slight variations in the sense of the English version of the charter from the Latin original. The phrase "studium generale" has a sense hardly appreciated by those who copied it from the ancient charter for William and Mary. See Heinrich Denifle, Die Universitäten des Mittelalters bis 1400, 1–29, for an exhaustive study of this word. On page 15 he says: "Der Dominicaner Ricoldus, de Montecrucis schreibt an der Wende des 13 und 14 Jhs. in seinem Werke gegen den Alchoran, er sei zu den Sarazenen nach Bagdad gereist, 'ubi generale ipsorum sollempne habeter studium.' Wie im Occident der Ausdruck studium generale im Sinne von Lehren Austalt für die studierenden der Christenheit genommen wurde, So wendete der Dominicaner derselben für das Hauptstudium der Sarazenen an." Blair's instructions from the General Assembly read: "You shall make it your business to peruse the best Charters in England . . . having Regard alwaies to the Constitutions of this Government." P. R. O. Am. and W. Ind. Bundle 637.

CHAPTER THE SIXTH.

LAND AND LABOR IN THE EARLY COLONIES.

I.

ENGLISHMEN were accustomed to a land system the most intricate the world has ever seen. The feudal law in its passing had left behind a mass of technicalities, and the evasions of that law had given birth to a multitude of fictions. In many cases instruments of conveyance were ostensibly instruments to do something else, and they were often not registered, but kept secret. There was a jargon of land-law terms mastered by conveyancers, that made it sometimes difficult to transfer land. In the century preceding colonization there came in the custom of piling up whole vocabularies of conveyance in one deed, with endless tediousness of repetition of clauses and provisos. The statutes were stuffed at the same time until the reader "was made giddy by a continual recurrence of the same form of words in the same endless period." Law came into disrepute as something hardly comprehensible and a source of endless entanglements to the lay mind. Lawyers were forbidden in the colonial courts. In Virginia mercenary lawyers—that is, lawyers who took fees—were almost wholly forbidden until 1658, when they were totally ejected.

CHAP. VI.

Direct ownership of the soil.

Reeves's Hist. of Law, iv, 506-508.

Reeves, iv, 560.

Note 1.

Note 2.

The New England colonies had a like prejudice, and would not suffer a single lawyer to becloud the acts of the early courts. When Massachusetts came to framing a working Constitution in 1641 there was a rivalry between Ward and Winthrop, educated as lawyers, and Cotton, who wished to proceed on a theological basis. The lawyers triumphed, but they did so by holding to the severe simplicity of old English law. The laws were not even called laws, but liberties; a man had the liberty of being hanged in certain cases. Somebody saw the absurdity, and appended a note explaining that liberty meant law, and the experiment of using this term for laws was not again tried in Massachusetts. The Dutch had but one lawyer among them, and they pretended to be unwilling to give either side in a case the exclusive benefit of his skill. They refused him permission to practice. Thus it came to pass that the earliest laws were simple and direct. Decisions were based on common sense and the merits of the case, as seen by the magistrate. There were other forces that held land laws to simplicity. There was little land in America that had come through feudal tenure. Even the king as a source of title did not usually appear in the deed. In the later seventeenth century lawyers and conveyancers began to be sought after; their services could no longer be dispensed with. The colonial laws and deeds after the Restoration became somewhat more intricate, and affected the English in their style. But the habit of passing land easily had become fixed, and though deeds might take on English forms and abound in repetitions, landholding remained substantially the same, the simple and direct ownership of the soil.

II.

Livery of seizin.

Note 3.

There was one trait of land law that had survived from the middle ages—that had survived apparently from nobody knows what remote antiquity. It made so dry a matter as the transfer of land picturesque and dramatic. This was called livery of seizin—the delivery of possession. The seller stood on the tract to be conveyed and taking a bit of turf from the land, and, if there were trees, plucking a twig and thrusting it into the turf, passed it into the hands of the buyer. The custom was capable of many variations. Judge Sewall, of Boston, received seizin of six hundred acres of forest by "turf, twig, and splinter," as if to embrace all the possibilities of timber land. In the history of Salem it is recorded that John Rush took a twig from a growing tree and a bit of green turf and said, "Here, son Thomas, I do before these two men give you possession of this land by turffe and twigg." In turning over the primitive records in Virginia one finds that "livery and sesen was made of a turffe of the earth of the within written land." In other cases "twigg and turff" marks another form. Sometimes the livery is marked by a different form and personal estate is

H. B. Adams, Cape Ann and Salem, 78.

MS. York Records, 1645.

Ibid., 1641.

CHAP. VI.

Surrey, Va., MS. Records, 1652.

included. One Colonel Henry Browne, wishing to give his whole estate for the benefit of his wife and creditors, delivers to them "one silver spoone, part of premises as a voucher to lead to intent, purport," etc. When a house was to be delivered the seller took hold of the ring of the house door and formally gave it into the hands of the new owner. The ground with its appurtenances was thus handed over in a manner suitable to illiterate times and restricted territories. But land in a new country became an article of frequent merchandise. Tracts of wilderness, remote and sometimes unsurveyed, could not be given by livery of seizin. In Maryland the mere certificate—the warrant entitling the holder to take up land—came presently to be passed about as current money. And, indeed, the custom of livery of seizin probably went out of use in America more rapidly than in England. In Virginia, the most conservative of the colonies, it was still somewhat in vogue in 1748, when it is recognized in a statute. Perhaps this was a mark of oncoming decrepitude. For a thousand years and more it had existed without legislation; when it became necessary to mention it in statute law the usage had passed its prime. In England to-day the seller often passes a ferule into the hands of the buyer of land without leaving the court room. So does the faint shadow of ancient custom stretch itself across modern life, growing more attenuated until at length it vanishes, no one perceiving where it left its last trace.

Note 4.

III.

Communal holding primitive.

One mode of holding land, the oldest known to the English world, dating far back of the feudal system, seems very curious to modern eyes. It did not much attract the attention of lawyers in its time. Questions regarding it were settled almost wholly in the petty court of manor or township, and the great jurists had no call to discuss it. As a general rule it was a subordinate kind of land-holding. The town community was tenant, as a whole, to the owner of the manor. The manor ownership might be litigated, might be taken away by violence, but the town held of the lord of the manor, whoever he might be, from time to which the memory of man runs not. If the owner-ship of the land came into question, it was as a whole. In this way it escaped almost entirely the notice of the land courts and of the older writers on the law of land. But as it went out of existence the township community began to attract the attention of the learned. Who should have the commons? What rights had the lord of the manor and the people under new conditions? And then inquiries were made by the curious into the origin of the commune, and presently a great literature has grown up about it mostly in a life-time. Efforts have been made to connect it with similar forms in other countries. The great fact coming out in all this discussion is that the town commune was very primitive. It can be traced in

England back to the fifth century. It disappears in the prehistoric past in its full vigor. A considerable portion of the surface of England was cultivated in this way in the seventeenth century, and it shows how far human development can be carried without breaking an ancient shell of society.

IV.

The village commune.

What was this village commune? Setting aside the disputed points in its ancient history—whether the commune was a combination at first of serfs, or whether it was a free mark—it seems probable that it once held all its territory in common, and that at the earliest period the arable land was allotted annually. The advancement of civilization relaxed the severity of this communism. Little patches were dealt out permanently to residents, or at least to shareholders, but the division of land retained marks of the older order. The land of a single owner was scattered over the lands of the town apparently as last divided. The meadow, the pasture, the mast land, and the woodland remained an undivided common when William Marshall began the study of it in the latter part of the eighteenth century. The fences and gates were kept up by the proportionate care of the several cultivators, and the rents of the lord were paid by the "town" as a whole. In New England, where there was no lord, a town registry was established, and the town held the disposal of land in

Note 5.

its own hands. "The furlongs"—that is, the "furrow-longs"—were held by each household, were fenced in a common field, and often for the first years of settlement were held undivided and allotted year by year. Each person had his "home-lot right" and "acre right" in the undivided meadow, forest, and upland. These were at first sold as a unit, and were termed "an accommodation." The times of planting and of turning in of cattle were sometimes regulated in "field meetings" or "side meetings," after the immemorial usage of the English township. The common fields were in primitive towns but three. Two were in different sorts of grain, the third was taking its year of rest as a sheep and cow pasture. Each cultivator had to raise the crop decided on by the majority in the side meeting or field meeting. It was an animated scene in a common field when all the commune was planting or harvesting. There were New England towns that went back to the original norm of the town, and cultivated the land by dividing it annually until the town should fill up. Then when the town was fuller, they divided their arable land, giving each an equal chance. Society was prone to fall apart in a new country. The town community held it together in common helpfulness.

Note 6.

V.

The commune in England.

Agricultural villages were yet flourishing in England in the seventeenth century. Very many

CHAP. VI.

had gone down before the cupidity of sheep-raising landlords, but the greater part were yet in full vigor under one and another shelter. Some seem to have kept a stiff proportion of their ancient rights. We find ducking stool and pillory in one rustic town; in Queen Mary's days there remained a prison and gallows in another. Persons seeking justice outside the borough for any matter occurring in the borough should lose their entire freedom—that is, their right of property in the community. Even in Connecticut one finds the right to appeal to higher courts was hampered and jealously watched. In England the townships in James I's time looked to overlords for protection. Some were resolutely independent.

Gomme, English Village Communities, 163.

Ibid., 77.

Ibid., 79.

VI.

The commune in America.

That the New-Englanders were largely born to the commune is evident. They were mostly farmers, and farmers in that time were frequently found in village communes. Perhaps the small farmer was more susceptible to Puritanism; perhaps the condition of the towns was favorable to the spread of Puritanism. Threatened with inclosure of their "wastes"—their mast land, their woodland, and their meadow—these villagers embraced the religion of the discontented. In New England the origin of the commune was soon forgotten. In the time of the Revolution we find John Adams proposing to inquire who among the

Note 7.

fathers of Massachusetts suggested this mode of settlement. He had no notion of its English origin. From the first, Plymouth was organized somewhat on the communal model. Salem, after trying independent holdings awhile, adopted the same plan. The great migration of Winthrop seems to have brought along with it the plan of the village community as the very best one on which to settle Puritan churches and congregations. If it was predetermined, it was a masterstroke of policy; but whether it was a matter of forethought or not, the townsmen must many of them have been acquainted with it. Nearly the whole of New England adopted the same plan. From I know not how far east clear down the coast to Connecticut and Long Island, and down the Jersey coast to Delaware, the people organized in this way. One never hears any other plan proposed. The phraseology of the town community was theirs. The swineherd or hogreeve went through the town blowing an early morning horn, the cowherd, the goatherd, the gooseherd, the shepherd were all present, as needed in various New England towns. There were water bailiffs, there were drummers to call people to meeting and to make announcements, there were overseers of chimneys and of chimney sweepers, perambulators, cullers of staves and corders of wood, firewards and haywards or hedgewards, and all the half a hundred other occasional officers of the town. Their names passed easily from one to

Note 8.

another, like coins worn smooth. One thing they missed—it was the lord and his rents. But when a Connecticut town moved to Newark they easily spoke of the quitrents as the lord's half-penny. It would have been the lord's penny in England.

VII.

Distribution of land.

The land was distributed with more or less equality in some towns and with more or less inequality in others. The houses stood rather compactly about the meeting-house. Every man had his home lot, his share in the cultivated field, his right to feed his cows in the common pasture and in common fields when crops were off, and so on, duly awarded him. A part of the fence or a gate, a pair of bars or "a lift" was assigned to him to keep up. The town owned the realty and divided it according to its by-laws and its own good pleasure. There were town cows sometimes, there was always a town bull, and a town horse was kept at Salem. Town sheep were not uncommon; a herd of two thousand paid all the corporate expenses of a certain town in Connecticut. The town sometimes kept packs of dogs to hunt wolves with. The tradespeople who wished to settle within the bounds of the town made bargains with the "selectmen" or others having charge of "the prudentials of the town" for a monopoly. Its mill sites and other privileges were disposed of in this way, the townspeople agreeing

Note 9.

Conn. Rec., i, 30.

CHAP. VI.

Note 10.

to help build the mill; to a blacksmith they gave a monopoly. The ideas prevailing were rustic; we read of one village which had reached a transition stage and which was alarmed lest the community should be "ruinated" by the influx of people. It is to be remembered that no New-Englander, unless from choice, was solitary. He was always a member of a community and therefore civilized. Thus grew New England.

VIII.

Political importance of the town.

The word town underwent a change in New England, or at least a provincial sense became the main sense of the word. It did not mean at first a town, but a group of farmers engaged in agriculture on a particular plan. The New England village was almost precisely the same at the outset as the English farming community. But it was in a new country where there is a chance to change, where change is inevitable. In the first place, the township in Massachusetts took on governmental functions. It became the political unit; this was its capital change. Deputies were elected to the Legislature from the "towns," large and small. The counties sank into insignificance, the towns were the sources of power. In the next place, the town boundary was also the boundary of the parish. The parish in Massachusetts was of primary importance. And, in the third place, the rulers, finding themselves freed from some of the cares of

CHAP. VI.

government by the autonomy of the towns, made even the farms attachments to the several towns. The town meeting, from being a side meeting to assign a date for the putting in and out of cows, became a place where the very sources of political power lay. The leading magistrates were outvoted by the representatives of the towns over and over. This was unexpected in a day when the magistrate was reverenced as the appointed of the Lord. The magistrates offered strong resistance, but the stronger resistance of the commons would not down. Efforts were made to overrule the lower House, but the deputies, having got the bit in their teeth, carried things their own way, and then the government fell into the hands of the towns, or rather, as has been said, into the hands of the churches, whose members did all the voting.

IX.

Society in the South.

The custom of granting farms in the first generation to prominent citizens in return for the assistance given in colony planting was discontinued. In the rivalry between independent towns and farms the towns by natural selection won the day. The prominent man, a little more eminent than the others, was content to take a larger share in the town instead of a separate grant. After the first generation there were fewer men of distinction engaged in planting towns, and hence fewer occasions for special grants. The New-Englander became exceedingly fond of the town system; he did not think of doing without it. Everywhere that New-Englanders went in the first and later generations the town system went with them. But it did not elsewhere acquire any such prominence as in Massachusetts and Connecticut. There were no political privileges, and the church was not of the prevailing order. Long Island, New Jersey, and certain regions in the Delaware Bay all had the inevitable town plan. One or two churches moved away into South Carolina and Georgia, where their village plan was lost in the larger agriculture of the South. If we had the evidence that is perhaps lost, we should find that the township or village community could be found germinating in the Southern colonies. Such a sub-colony as that of Barkly or Berkley, to which an "incorporacion by some vsuall or fit name" was promised, must have contemplated common lands and other elements of the commune. That and its rustic ally the hundred, and its civic type the borough, were the form in which nearly all the local government of England was cast. But nearly all the men of Barkly perished at the hands of the Indians or otherwise. Indian massacres, the growth of a staple demanding much land, and the consequent rapid development of territorial greed, soon destroyed every vestige of the town in Virginia. A "hundred" in 1660 proved that a "commons" had been granted to it in 1631. If we look to Maryland it is hard

Note 11.

Note 12.

Smith of Nibley MSS., 57.

Note 13.

CHAP. VI.

Johnson's Old Md. Manors. Kilty's Landholder's Assistant, ch. v.

to make out whether manors with "courts leet" established there very early had jurisdiction of commons, as is probable from the usual organization of a manor. But the circumstances were most unfavorable to the community; the great staple of tobacco set people's teeth on edge to become rich out of it. Cultivation almost from the start began to change its character. Great and greater shiploads of bond servants, free-willers, kids, and convicts were unloaded in Virginia and Maryland and sold for four years' service. For half a century or more large estates with white bond servants were the rule. In 1670 there were three times as many white bond servants as blacks in Virginia. Within ten or fifteen years after that, as the century drew to a close, Virginia ceased to buy white servants in any numbers, and plantations worked by black servants became the rule.

De Vries and Geo. Donne's MS. Bodleian Library.

X.

Contrast between the North and South.

A very usual method of holding land in England was by the manorial system. The manors were entailed to the eldest son or other heir of the manor lord. But parts of these manors were village communities from the most ancient times. In New England they made village communities without any lord of the manor, and quitrents were left out of the count. The granting of farms quite independent of the town contemplated another English mode of landholding. But just as agricultural villages were crowded out in Virginia, so were independent farms driven to the wall in the Northeast. An order went forth that farms should belong to the towns in which they were situated. It was inconvenient to have them separate. The Church was the drilling ground to keep the people strictly in line with advanced Protestantism. The farmer could have no rights in common fields, his cattle were foreign to the pasture, his pigs had no right to pick up nuts from the common woodland, he had no acre rights when dividends were made, but he must attend the town church and pay the dues levied upon him for the clergy and other town burdens, and all burdens were put directly on the town. Individuals were unknown, the town was the taxpayer and the landowner. Sometimes, as at Salem, the town bought out a man's holdings, his "accommodation," exchanging therefor a farmstead carved out of the great unappropriated wilderness. But the favorite method of settling land came to be in a colony or town. By this means the ecclesiastical power was greatly augmented. The minister was usually the one educated man in the parish. He knew some Latin and Greek, and he had even a smattering of Hebrew. He was educated in what was the only branch of knowledge affected by minister or layman—theology. His dominance over the unlettered was tolerably complete. On the other hand, the Southern planter, with long stretches of woodland between him and his neighbors, could cultivate his wide fields in almost entire independence; his code of morals even was mostly his own, but his public interests were as extensive as his county or his province. This state of society begot self-reliance, and produced more leading statesmen than the other; but the people lacked the New England cohesion and susceptibility to organization, without which the statesmanship of the Revolution would have been vain. The Southerner, from his isolation and from other causes, became hospitable, eager for society, and in general spontaneously friendly and generous; the New England people became close-fisted and shrewd in trade; it is a trait of village life. But the benevolence of New England was more effective than that of the South, because it was organized and systematic. The village life of the extreme North trained the people to trade, and led to commercial development, and it made popular education possible. The sons of the great planters at the South were averse to commerce; they were also the most liberally educated and polished in manners of all the colonists; but the scattered common people could have few schools, and were generally rude and ignorant, even when compared with the lower class of New-Englanders, who stood a chance of getting some rough schooling, besides a certain education from the meeting-house and the ever-recurring town debates.

XI.

Strangers forbidden.

A stranger might in old New England find a constable at the door some morning to warn him to leave. He was not expected to go, but his landlord must give security that he would not be chargeable, or at least the town was quit of him. People attracted by the superior medical skill of Boston physicians were thus warned. St. Clement's Manor, in Maryland, at its Court Leet, orders John Mansell "to remove his inmate or give security." The towns had done so from the most remote times. Even in the Salic law, a thousand years before, no person was suffered to remove from one villa to another. A trace of this is found in the Connecticut law that "noe Inhabitant shall have power to make sale of his accom̄odation of house and lands vntil he have first propounded the sale thereof to the Towne . . . and they refuse to accept of the sale tendered." The town community is dead in New England, though its methods of government remain, and even in the West and South there are traces of it in the language. In the old common field, strips were allotted from year to year, but one piece of land belonged to nobody. It was called "Jack's Land." Here the plowman left his plow, his hoe, his seed to the hospitality of an undefined somebody called Jack. The author of "Wonder-working Providence," a New England captain, calls Ireland "Jack's Land." It was nobody's country; one man and one party after another might take

Old Md. Manors, 15.

Seebohm, The Salic Law, 359, 360.

Rogers, Work and Wages, 107.

1 Conn. Rec., 351, 1660.

CHAP. VI.

possession. Curiously enough, the word survives in America in an old game, played on a slate, where all drawn games are credited to "Jack," and are marked in a division called "Jack's Land." It is the very last attenuated ghost of the ideas of the ancient commune.

Note 14.

XII.

The Virginia parish.

MS. Records of various parishes, in Fairfax Seminary.

Note 15.

Accomac Records, 1632.

In Virginia and the South the parish vestry took the place of the township in New England. Virginia was the Southern model as Massachusetts was the Northern. In the extant parish records of Virginia the vestry makes a contract for building a church, ordains a referendum for locating a church, and employs and dismisses a minister, builds a paling fence about the church, and "distreynes" for tithes. The vestry also opens roads, appoints overseers of roads and holds them to account, levies fines for bastardy and concubinage and for disorder in church, orders the land processioned, relieves the poor, binds out "orphants," appoints side men or collectors, and objects to the admission of non-residents lest they be chargeable. The parish also in one case elects a "select vestrye" from each of three precincts. In 1694 Petsoe Parish divides itself into eight precincts for the processioning of land. Here is nearly everything that was done by the New England town transacted by the vestry of a Virginia parish. The parish in Virginia stretched far—usually over an entire

Records of Petsoe Parish, in Fairfax Seminary.

county; in New England it was restricted to a town.

The processioning of land was observed by the Virginians between Easter and Whitsunday. They made formal processions about the bounds of their several tracts, renewing the marks in the line trees. When a division line had been thus marked three times it was no longer open to question. In Massachusetts, Connecticut, and Long Island the townships, as landholders, were "to go the rounds" at regular intervals. Each individual owner of plowland and mowland within the town must trace his boundary every winter if his adjacent neighbor exacted it. The colonists were thus following a custom whose origin was lost in the obscurity before written records.

XIII.

Inheritance.

The leadership of the great families was sustained in New York and in the colonies south of Pennsylvania by primogeniture—the prerogative of the eldest son to inherit the landed estate in case the father left no will. Custom followed the law, and fathers who willed their property usually left most or all of the land to the eldest son, as belonging to him by prescriptive right. To primogeniture the aristocratic colonies added the dead hand of entail, by which the land was sent down for generations in the line of the eldest male. Even a clumsy fiction, called in law "common recovery," by which the entail might be broken in England, was forbidden by statute in Virginia, and was not accounted applicable to the other colonies.

The Pilgrims at Plymouth and the Massachusetts Puritans had belonged to that politico-religious party in England which sought the abolition of certain old abuses. As early as 1636 Plymouth enacted that land should be held after "the laudable custom, tenure, and hold of the manor of East Greenwich"—that is, in an ancient Saxon way preserved at the coming of William the Conqueror by the county of Kent. One characteristic of this tenure was that it divided the lands equally among the sons in case there was no will. Massachusetts, which expressly abolished many of the worst features of feudal tenure, by name, gave to the eldest son a double portion according to the Mosaic code, but divided the rest among daughters as well as sons. This system prevailed throughout New England. Primogeniture had come to be esteemed a natural right, and the Massachusetts leaders felt obliged more than once to defend themselves from the charge of having "denied the right of the eldest son." They answered by showing the comparative insignificance of land in a new country, and took refuge behind the example of Moses. Pennsylvania took the same middle course of sheltering innovation under the law of Moses by giving the eldest son a double portion. The laws of some of the colonies made the

Plymouth Records.

land liable, to a greater or less extent, with personal estate for the debts of the deceased, which robbed the eldest of a part of his "insolent prerogative"; but it was not until the shock of the Revolution that primogeniture and entail were swept away, under the leadership of Jefferson and others. But land was so abundant that a thrifty younger son often earned in a lifetime a better portion than his elder brother. The eldest son's double portion in New England survived the Revolution for some years. A very ancient mode of inheritance prevailed in some English boroughs, called among lawyers "borough English." By this custom the lands descended to the youngest son. It found no lodgment in the laws of the colonies, so far as I know; but in New Hampshire it was a widespread custom to leave the homestead to the youngest, who remained at home and cared for the old age of his parents. This reasonable form of the custom of "ultimogeniture" lingers yet in certain parts of the country, as, for example, in some of the northern counties of New York. The other custom of a widow inheriting a third of her husband's estate is even more widely prevalent, and is a matter of law in most of the States.

Note 16.

Belknap's New Hampshire.

XIV.

Serfdom and apprenticeship.

The problem of England in the days of James I was how to be rid of its poor. They had, many of them, been turned out of a living by the inclosure

CHAP. VI. Note 17.

of commons in the mania for sheep husbandry, and some of them had had the villages pulled down about their ears. They were sent a-wandering, living as they could live by hook or by crook. Necessity made many of them rogues, and the desire to have done with rogues was so intense that England hanged its thieves out of hand. Henry VIII thought to be rid of such vermin of society, and he hanged, if we may believe Harrison, two-and-seventy thousand, including "great theeves, pettie theeves and roges." In Elizabeth's reign three or four hundred felons were eaten up annually by the gallows, and James I merrily carried on the work of extermination; one reads of "twenty hanged up at a clap," in one place. But the vagabonds did not grow fewer.

Harrison in Holinshed, i, 314.

Recent serfdom had left its mark on the poor man. He had been freed, not from benevolence, nor from any motive having regard to the personality of the serf. Wickliffe and others had taught that it was meritorious to free a man from bondage who was a Christian—that is, who had been baptized. This scruple fitted to the churchly conscience of the age; it grew more and more exigeant. "We think it pious and meritorious with God to make certain persons absolutely free from the yoke of servitude who are at present under villenage to us," said Henry VIII. Elizabeth and James, less scrupulous on this point, proposed to sell to those whose blood was tainted with slavery the privileges of freedom. It was not till the

Note 18.

eighteenth century had dawned that Chamberlayne's State of England, an annual publication, could drop its set phrase, "but few now in England," and say, "Now slavery is entirely thrown away and every Servant Man or Woman are properly hired Servants." But the habit of regarding the peasant as a recent serf had its influence in the treatment of him.

Chamberlayne, 1696–1702.

Note 19.

The "spirit," who was later called a crimp, was on the watch for him. Did they need more soldiers in Flanders? The spirit, by means best known to himself, packed off the poor man to Flanders. He was equally ready to ship him to any other country for a reward. The Virginia colony began to ask for people. The wilderness was hungry for laborers. The spirit shipped little children by the score down the Thames and off for America. Parents followed the vessels all the way to Gravesend, but the law would not help them; Virginia wanted laborers. Sometimes a parent could pay enough to get the lad released. Men were carried also to that abode of hopelessness. From the first there were two general classes: free apprentices and convicts mostly for petty crimes. "Apprentices," says Chamberlayne, "are a sort of servant that carry the mask of Pure villains or Bond slaves, differing however in that Apprentices are slaves only for a term and by covenant."

XV.

Servants in the colonies.

From the outset there were in New England as well as in Virginia apprenticed servants, who had been bound for a long term before leaving England, and were treated as a recognized species of property. Winthrop speaks of the "money" the three hundred servants had cost that they were enforced to set free for want of food. Cradock and others who did not come to New England sent servants to take care of estates for them. In 1629 De Vries, the Dutch traveler, saw English men and women staked and lost at cards, and he bluntly told the Virginians that he had "never seen such work in Turk or Barbarian." George Donne, the author of a manuscript in the Bodleian, saw servants brought to Virginia by the shipload after 1630, and he describes the horrors of the traffic, their insufficient food, their ragged and barefoot condition, and their landing far from their destination and being forced to march the rest of the way in their enfeebled state. Nearly all the emigrants that came between 1620 and 1650 were bondsmen. This does not imply that they were not some of them educated, for many Latin-school men were obliged to sell themselves to the crimp. After the Restoration servants were sold in great numbers to Virginia. Fifteen hundred a year is the estimate of Berkeley at a time when Virginia contained but two thousand black slaves. As the term was for four years, there were six thousand

Donne's MS.

See note 16, chapter v. Compare Diary of John Harrower; Am. Hist. Rev., vi, No. 1.

white slaves always in bondage there. Before 1650 the term of some was ten years or more, and that of many was seven or eight years. After the restoration of the Stuarts in 1660 the term of service was permanently reduced to four years.

XVI.

Fate of servants.

English laborers bound themselves to serve a term of years, fairly hoping to better their condition in America; and men in domestic or other trouble would sell themselves for a term of service in the plantations, plunging into the abyss and trusting to luck to come up in better plight in a new world. Husbands forsaking their wives lost their identity in the transport ship, and wives fleeing from unbearable husbands were swallowed up in the flood. Runaway children and fleeing apprentices were greedily welcomed by the crimps; felons and prison breakers pursued by hue and cry were quickly safe on board. In those days of slow communication, renegades of every sort were as utterly lost to their old lives in America as they could have been had they migrated to the moon. It was an age of flogging; criminals, soldiers, sailors, pupils, children, and now and then even wives, were thought the better for scourging. One ought hardly to be surprised, therefore, at the numerous and cruel whippings of English servants, women as well as men, who were scourged naked with hickory rods and washed with brine; the punishment continuing sometimes at intervals for hours, or being renewed day after day. There were also in use, by masters and overseers, thumbscrews, sweatings, and other such devil's devices. The food allowed was sometimes a scant diet of Indian meal. The sick servant was neglected lest the doctor's charge should exceed the value of his remaining service; and one thrifty master in Maryland required a servant, sick of a mortal disease, to dig his own grave in advance, in order to save the other men's time. In 1705 Virginia prohibited the secret burial of servants and the whipping of "Christian white servants" naked, without the consent of a justice. Great numbers fled away from the sharpness of bondage, taking the risk of cruel punishments and an extension of their terms if captured. During the existence of New Netherland, Dutch servants broke away to New England or Maryland, while English servants from both directions made their way to the Dutch territory. With New England the Dutch had at one time a treaty for the return of those "who carried their passports under their feet." To get away on shipboard, to seize a shallop and make off to a neighboring colony, and represent themselves as shipwrecked mariners, and to fly to the Indians, were favorite devices of runaways. So great was the number of fugitives that "inferior persons" were always liable to arrest on suspicion. North Carolina was filled with runaways from Virginia. In 1663 a dangerous conspiracy of indentured servants

Danker's Journal.

was discovered in Virginia, and a general fear of the class, among whom were many desperate characters, probably prompted much of the severe treatment inflicted on bondmen. The Pilgrims found that servants led astray "the unstaid and young." The Massachusetts colonists before starting essayed at considerable cost to sift their servants, excluding a corrupt element; they even sent back two boys who had shown vicious propensities on shipboard. But the large proportion of penalties meted out to servants during the first years of the colonies shows how slight was the effect of the sifting process. Even in the colonies where the convict element was shut out, many of the servants were obtained from dangerous classes, such as "sturdy beggars, gypsies, and other incorrigible rogues, idle and debauched persons." They could "eat till they sweat and work till they freeze," in the quaint words of a traveler in New England. It was probably from those who had been servants that the sea rovers fitting out in the colonies found recruits. The pirate James, when short of hands, lay off the Virginia coast and captured transport ships, many of the convicts and servants in them preferring to risk a halter in cruising "on the grand account" to pining in colonial bondage. In some instances the criminal transports rose and slaughtered the crew, taking the ship into some out-of-the-way harbor and escaping. The degradation of the women servants was a continual source of evil; laws were made to correct their immoralities, and other laws

CHAP. VI.

to prevent these "Christians" from intermarrying with the heathen Africans. In all the colonies there were those brought as servants, even as convicts, who rose to wealth through industry and frugality, two virtues on which a new land pays high premium. Some founded families that attained to honor and influence.

XVII.

Convict servants.

The severity of English penal laws occasioned evasions of all kinds; for Anglo-Saxon people prefer to reform an abuse by avoidance rather than by direct abolition. The old provision for "benefit of clergy" was stretched to an absurd comprehensiveness. The need for men in the colonies offered a new opportunity for merciful evasions of the death penalty in cases of minor felony. It became common to pardon thieves on condition of their accepting a seven years' term of service in the colonies, and the English State-Paper Office has many curious petitions for this commutation. As early as 1622 a horse thief indicates that he much prefers service in Virginia to hanging. At a later period a husband is found petitioning on behalf of his wife, condemned to death for stealing three-and-sixpence, that she might be transported to any plantation. After the Restoration it was enacted that justices, at their discretion, might send "loose and disorderly persons" to the colonies, and at intervals a hundred or so of "Newgate birds" were taken in a close lighter from Blackfriars to Wool-

State Papers, *passim.*

wich, where they were put aboard ship for America.

Bristol was the chief center of the colonial trade; here even the small traders and sometimes the peddlers had ventures in the colonies. Bristol, therefore, naturally took the lead in the servant trade, and most of the great officers of the city became involved in kidnapping. When, in Bristol, a man was on trial for some small crime, the petty officers would persuade him to beg for transportation in order to escape being hanged. These transports were then assigned to the mayor and each of the aldermen in turn, who sold them to the plantations, and grew rich from the spoils of the poor and the desperate. In the most paradoxical scene in judicial history the worst of judges, George Jeffreys, himself reeking with corruptions and cruelties incredible, is found arraigning aldermen of this opulent city for their share in this trade. Ordering the scarlet-robed mayor from his seat on the bench to a place in the prisoner's dock, he cried, with brutal exultation, "See how the kidnapping rogue looks!" He ranted at the aldermen in words too vile to be reprinted. Yet the selling of condemned men and the condemning of men that they might be sold were practiced openly at the court of James II at this very time. The ladies of the queen's bedchamber and the queen herself eagerly snatched at the profits from the sale of the rebels of Monmouth's rebellion, whom Jeffreys had just then condemned; even

CHAP. VI.

William Penn begged for twenty of them for the Philadelphia market.

XVIII.

Introduction of slaves.

In 1619 a "Holland man-of-war," short of water and food, put into the James River, and cast anchor before the only English settlement on this side of the globe. The captain was forbidden to land, but as he threatened to throw overboard some slaves captured in the West Indies, Captain Kendall, commanding at Jamestown, exchanged some "presents" for them. These fourteen "negars" were the first slaves in English America. The opening of new settlements and the lighting upon new staple products produced a demand for unskilled labor which the English "spirits" or crimps could not adequately supply. Negroes were therefore brought from the West Indies, and afterward direct from Africa or Madagascar. The labor of slaves increased the ability of the colonies to "take off" English goods; it is therefore not surprising that a Committee on Foreign Plantations, soon after the Restoration, declared that "black slaves were the most useful appurtenances of a plantation."

The English serfs had received their freedom chiefly on theological grounds as fellow-Christians, with some additional weight thrown into the scale by their being fellow-Englishmen. But freeborn Englishmen were by custom sold into severe bondage for long terms, and even sent beyond seas in large numbers; there could, therefore, be no repugnance in the minds of the colonists to the enslavement of blacks, who were not only pagans, but so different in appearance as to seem to be another species, not entitled to human consideration. At least, if they came from Adam, they were by some theological experts identified with the cursed descendants of Cain, for Ham was thought to have found a wife in the land of Nod.

XIX.

African slavery.

Slavery is more ancient than historic records. In the centuries of warfare between Christians and Mohammedans, the practice of enslaving captives outlawed by their "infidelity" had prevailed. Negroes were easily confounded with the Moors, and thousands of blacks were annually brought into Europe for sale as early as the middle of the fifteenth century; and a century later, in 1553, one finds four-and-twenty of them brought as far as England. From Spain first, and then directly from Africa, black slaves had been carried to the Spanish colonies to develop the mines. The Royal African Company of England announced to Charles II, in 1663, that the very existence of the plantations depended on an adequate supply of negro servants; and though their declaration was due to cupidity, it was at least true that all rich and successful American colonies up to this time had possessed slaves. So late as 1735 the Lords

Commissioners of Trade declared that the colonies "could not possibly subsist" without an adequate supply of slaves. Indeed, the first effect of the introduction of slaves was a rapid advancement in subduing forests and opening sources of wealth.

For nearly sixty years after the beginning of negro slavery here, there seems to have been no scruple or question about it. The lifelong bondage of negroes was tacitly justified by their heathen condition. When, in 1677, the question was first raised in an English court, Africans were held to be slaves by the custom of merchants and "as being infidels." This notion was so general that very many planters resisted efforts to instruct their slaves in the Christian religion, lest baptism should emancipate them. To remove this obstacle the Virginia Assembly had enacted, in 1667, that the conversion of a slave should not invalidate the owner's claim to his services, and similar laws were afterward made in most of the other provinces. But these laws were merely of colonial authority, and were not sufficient to overcome the scruple of covetousness. A proposal from England to encourage the conversion of the negroes "would not go down" with the New York Assembly in 1699. Philanthropic exertion for the negro was at first wholly religious, seeking his conversion not so much for the good of the negro as for the glory of Christianity. The attention of James II having been called to the pagan condition of the negroes, he resolved at the council board, in 1685, that all the slaves in the plantation should be christened; the thought of baptizing them in a mass by royal order, whether they would or no, was no doubt doubly pleasing to him as a zealot and as a lover of arbitrary methods. Efforts to convert the slaves in the seventeenth century were few and languid, the most notable being those of the superannuated Eliot, in Massachusetts. There were a few individuals who, like William Penn in 1700, had "a concern for the souls of the blacks"; but many held them to be quite without souls, and hence not proper objects of concern.

XX.

Anti-slavery movements.

The first voice in America to speak against the perpetual bondage of man to man was heard in a memorial of some Friends of Germantown in Pennsylvania. This protest, in vigorous broken English, was addressed to the Philadelphia Yearly Meeting in 1688, and it opened an agitation which resulted, seventy years later, in bringing the Philadelphia Quakers to a conclusion opposed to slaveholding. In the fundamental law of Massachusetts and Connecticut, villanage and other feudal servitudes were prohibited, and in 1646 the Massachusetts General Court actually undertook to send back to Africa negroes who had been kidnapped by a slaver, and to send with them a letter of apology and explanation. But the Calvinist reverence for the law of Moses was a less elastic standard than the "inward light" of the followers of Fox. If the early Puritan, bound to the letter of Scripture, was less likely to run into aberrant fanaticism than the Friend, he was also less quick to gain new and modern views of duty. Refusing to participate with "man-stealers," the textual conscience of the Massachusetts forefathers did not shrink from selling Indians captured in war into chattel slavery, or from buying slaves who appeared to have come into bondage otherwise than by downright kidnapping. These nice distinctions could not be kept up, and thousands of negro slaves were sold into New England without any question for conscience' sake. The scruple about human liberty with which the Puritan forefathers had come to this country had been swiftly forgotten. Some merchants of Boston were engaged in the Guinea trade, of which, however, Newport was the great center. Before the anti-slavery writings of the Quakers, Hepburn, Burling, Lay, and Sandiford, had appeared, an influential but rather timid voice, that of Judge Sewall, was heard opposing the importation of slaves to Massachusetts. He had been led by the narrow theological spirit in which he was bred into grievous mistakes in the witchcraft trials, but he was an honest and even a scrupulous man. Fond of popular favor and shrinking from censure, it cost him a struggle no doubt to give to the press, in 1700, his little tract against the slave trade, entitled The Selling of Joseph. Its influence was probably not great.

So closed the seventeenth century. The progress in humanity had been very slight. The number of bond servants was constantly increasing; the black tide of African slavery was ever swelling. No voice worthy of the name was yet heard in protest.

ELUCIDATIONS.

Note 1, page 273.

"'Fine and recovery,' 'conveyance to uses,' 'lease and releases'—all the circuitous forms that evasion had been compelled to assume—survived, together with the whole storehouse of factitious science that had grown up round them. Once launched into existence, the system of private and unregistered conveyance had generated a science and a vocabulary applicable to the numberless 'estates' created in law, which made every title a matter of intimate personal history; hence arose the necessity of investigations requiring the most practiced and recondite knowledge of the old body of statute law which feudalism had left behind it." Hoskyns, The Land Laws of England, in Systems of Land Tenure, p. 183.

Note 2, page 273.

See the note on p. 482 of Hening, vol. i, on the alternate forbidding and licensing of lawyers in Virginia. In 1642 the new governor had things his own way and admitted attorneys; in 1645 mercenary attorneys were expelled, in 1647 the act was made stronger, in 1656 all acts against mercenary attorneys were repealed, and in 1658 a vote of total expulsion was taken.

Note 3, page 275.

"The particular usages of the Saxons, however, were very similar to the present. The twig and turf were the simplest method of livery, and by the twig and turf did they give seizin to the purchaser. When grants were made to the church, a twig was usually laid on the altar. This occurred so frequently that it would be useless to cite instances in its support. A tree growing on a soil was regarded as a part of it, hence a branch of it served to give seizin. . . . When Ulphus, king of Deira, gave lands to the church of York he 'took the horn, wherein he was wont to drink, and filling it with wine, kneeled before the altar' and deposited it as a symbol of possession. . . . In the time of

CHAP. VI.

Henry III, William Earl of Warrenne and Surrey, on a grant made by him to the priory of St. Pancrace, delivered seizin by the hair of his head." Watkins, Law of Tenures, pp. 81, 82, note xxxiii. See the article on Charter Horns in Andrews's Old Church Lore.

Note 4, page 276.

In some parts of England and Ireland tenures are by the custom of some manors conveyed by a bit of rush, straw, or hay. I have this by report as to Ireland, and in the present day. See also the custom of Yetminster, Dorset, in Watkins on Copyholds, 544.

Note 5, page 278.

Private property in a strip in a common field came in only when fields become permanently arable. Nasse, 11. North Devon common lands were cultivated one or two years and then left to pasture in the latter part of the eighteenth century. Marshall's Rural Economy, 259. New England had land in considerable quantities reallotted every year at first. Land was still allotted thus in England in some places. It ought to be remarked here that Rhode Island was first organized into towns, and for a long time was a congeries of independent towns. From the vices of that system the State has not yet recovered. First Assembly of Rhode Island, 15. Rehoboth, on account of its remoteness, was for a long time virtually independent, and was built in a semicircle. Newman's Rehoboth, 15, 16. In Stiles's manuscript I have seen an account of a town built in a circle about the church.

Note 6, page 279.

Mr. Seebohm calls attention to the animated scene in the common fields at the time of planting, as described by Piers Ploughman in the prologus:

> "A faire field full of folke fonde I there bytwene
> Of alle manner of men the mene and the riche
> Worchyng and wanderyng as the world asketh."—Text B.

Note 7, page 280.

Mr. Ashton, in his Humour, etc., of the Seventeenth Century, gives this:

> "A Lord, that purpos'd for his more availe
> To compass in a Common with a rayle,
> Was reckoning with his friend about the cost
> And charge of every rayle, and every post;
> But he (that wisht his greedy humor crost)
> Said, 'Sir, provide you Posts, and without sayling,
> Your neighbours round about will find you rayling.'"

And this other:

> "There be many rich men, both Yeoman and Gentry,
> That for their owne private gaine hurt a whole country;
> By closing free commons, yet they'le make as though
> 'Twere for common good, but I know what I know."

Note 8, page 282.

A penny an acre was the result of knight's fee system as shown by Seebohm very ingeniously, p. 39. Towns paid quitrents as a whole in New York State. There is never any separation of a town into severalties in any State. The town processions the land, pays taxes, etc. Livingston and Smith's Laws of New York, vol. ii, 237--249. In the Grants and Ceremonies of New Jersey of Leaming and Spicer, 1664, it is provided that the lots shall be of certain sizes, "excepting Cities, Towns, and the near Lots of Townships. By 1672 towns were becoming common, and the regular laying out of Land, Rules for building each Street in Townships and Quantities of Ground for each House Lot, the same is left to the freeholder or first undertaker thereof." The antiquity of the swineherd may be appreciated by the mention of him in the Thorold Rogers in the Middle Ages, Work and Wages, 83.

Note 9, page 282.

The law that each cultivator was accountable for a portion of fence, and must pay the damage done by cattle intruding, was as old as the laws of Ine in the seventh century, and probably much earlier. This equitable law existed in New England, New York, New Jersey, etc., a thousand years after. Compare Seebohm's Village Community, 110.

Note 10, page 283.

Of primitive town government no better outline is afforded than that found in Connecticut Records, i, 30 (1639):

"The Townes of Hartford, Windsore, and Wethersfield, or any other of the Townes within this jurisdiction, shall each of them have power to dispose of their owne lands vndisposed of, and all other comodityes arysing out of their owne lymitts bounded out by the Court, the libertyes of the great River excepted, as also to choose their owne officers, and make such orders as may be for the well ordering of their owne Townes, being not repugnant to any law here established, as also to impose penaltyes for the breach of the same, and to estreat and levy the same, and for non-payment to distrayne, and yf there be noe personall estate, to sue to the Court to sell his or their house or land, for making satisfaction. Also each of the aforesayd Townes shall have power by a generall consent once every yeare to choose out 3, 5, or 7 of

CHAP. VI.

their cheefe Inhabitants, whereof one to be chosen moderato^{r}, who having taken an oath prouided in that case, shall have a casting voice in case they be equall, wch sayd p^{r}sons shall meett once in every 2 monthes & being mett together, or the maior part of them, whereof the moderato^{r} to be one, they shall have power to heare, end and determine all controversies, eyther tresspasses or debts not exceeding 40s. provided both partyes live in the same Towne; also any two of them or the moderato^{r} may graunt out summons to the party or partyes to come to their meetings to answere the actions; also to administer oath to any witnesses for the clearing of the cause, and to give judgment and execution against the party offending. But yf eyther party be grieved att the sentence, he shall haue liberty to appeale to a higher Court, p^{r}vided it be before iudgment and execution be graunted. But yf it fall out there be noe ground for the appeale, the Court to confirme the iudgment and give good cost and fine or punish the party appealing."

Note 11, page 285.

Of town communities in "Delewer" Bay in 1670 the following is from Denton's Brief Description of New York: "These persons being thus qualified settle the place and take in what inhabitants to themselves they shall see cause to admit of until their Town be full; these associates thus taken in have equal privileges with themselves and they make a division of the Land suitable to every man's occasions, no man being debarr'd of such quantities as he hath occasion for, the rest they let lie in common till they have occasion for a new division, never dividing their Pasture-land at all which lies in common to the whole Town." There is some ambiguity in Denton's description, and the towns may refer themselves to New Jersey and New York. An instance of village community of French origin is found in Parkman's Discovery of the Great West, p. 7. Here there are town lots with arable land outside of the manor and an annual rent to the lord of the manor. Parkman's authority is Abbé Faillon's La Colonie Française in Canada.

Note 12, page 285.

In enumerating "The Common Land of the companie," Sir Edwin Sandys says, "three thousand in each of the fower old Burroughes." Here the borough is made the local unit, as was frequently the case in England—a district with common lands. The Records of Virginia, p. 15. In New England the town became the borough for representation; in Virginia the borough or hundred began, but the unit soon drifted into the county with which the parish was almost always coterminous. Bacon's Laws of Maryland, 1694, provide for the laying out of a common for a new town. This was the usual course of procedure. Long before this time it is probable that manors were given up. Copley to Lord Baltimore, April 3, 1638, in Calvert papers, makes a strong statement of the difficulty of maintaining them in Maryland.

Note 13, page 285.

Charter to Throckmorton, Yeardley, R. Berkley, and Smythe, in Smith of Nibley MSS., 57: "And shall also within the said terme of seaven years grant to the said Adventurers . . . letters and grants of incorporacion by some vsuall or fit name or title with liberty to them and their successors from tyme to tyme to frame and make orders ordinances and constitutions for the rule . . . and directynge of all persons to be transported and settled vpon the land hereby intended to be granted," etc. This bears date February 3, 1618 (1619), and was no doubt the model on which many grants were made at that time. It indicated a liberal gift of local autonomy hardly to be realized without the granting of township government or of government by the borough or hundred. The colony of Virginia was to have no jurisdiction except in case of "tryals of matters of Justice by appeale or otherwise." This was precisely the case with the more independent towns in England. Gomme's English Village Communities, generally.

Note 14, page 290.

But the uninclosed vacant lots on which speculators planned to build, and on which cattle were pastured, took the name of commons and held it all the way into the interior. Commons they are to-day, but the title and the thing are passing into swift forgetfulness. Boston Common remains a part of the original common land of the town, and there are some others.

Note 15, page 290.

The same men were reappointed by the Petsoe Vestry in 1699, "oversears of the highways" for another year, "they having not perform'd the offiss thare unto belonging the year Past."

Note 16, page 293.

Harrison marks this difference in descent in Elizabeth's day: "Burrow kind" where the younger is preferred before the others, "which is the custome of manie counties of this region"; also the woman to have the third of her husband's possessions.

Note 17, page 294.

Nasse cites the statute of 1488, chaps. xvi and xix as marking the beginning of inclosures of commons. The last was "An act

CHAP. VI.

against pulling down of townes." It had no doubt begun somewhat earlier. In 1513 a law of Henry VIII prescribes that the "pulling downe and destruction of townes within this realm, and laying to pasture lands which customably have been manured and occupyed wyth tythage and husbandry," should be restored. So the succeeding acts of 24 and 25 Henry VIII. The reformer Becon denounces the "wrong they have done to the poor commons, as by making common pastures several to themselves," etc. Fortress of the Faithful, 598. The character of Latimer's sermons against the abuse is well known. In 1549 the peasantry rose in an endeavor to restore the commons. Harrison says in 1577 that some "daily do make beggars inough whereby to pester the land espieng a further commoditie in their commons, holds, tenures, dooth find such meanes as therby to wipe many out of their occupiengs, and turne the same unto his private gaines." Holinshed, i, 308. In 1607 riots are noted against inclosures of commons and wastes. Nichol's Poor Laws, 232. There is a sermon on the Rainbow preached at Paul's Cross in 1617 by Bourne, in which he graphically says: "Depopulators have inclosed fields, townes, churches, and all, pulling those down which their religious forefathers did build up, stopping doores with thornes and their windows with brushes; yea, covering their roofs with thatch; nay, leaving them naked or else turning these holy places into barnes or sheepcoates or other prophane uses," p. 47. See also Stafford's A Brief Conceipt of English Pollicy, 1632. Harleian Miscell. ix, 199. The extracts that might be quoted are all but innumerable, but Marshall in 1786 shall end these where he says that the spirit of inclosure is such that in half a century more an open field or undivided common may be rare. It was the cry of oppression at first, when the change to sheep farming was made. Selden says Depopulatio Agrorum is a great offense in the common law. And yet this revolution in agriculture, so unjustly enforced, was beneficial to England. The peasants thrown out to beg lived or died according to their shiftiness. The cruel law of natural selection destroyed those unable to adapt themselves; human advancement is pitiless and unforgiving.

Note 18, page 294.

Chamberlayne's State of England, All the volumes after 1710 say of villanage, "But this kind of tenure is in a manner out of use." I am aware that this brings serfdom further down than the authorities by a hundred and fifty years. The copy I consulted lacked the volumes between 1702 and 1708, but the change takes place in that interval. Serfdom went out before this time; it had practically been out of use for long generations.

Note 19, page 295.

Servants hired or apprenticed "were subject to be corrected by their Master or Mistress, and resistance by a servant is punished with some severe penalty," says Chamberlayne. A fatal blow from a servant to a master was petty treason, and brought on him capital punishment. He had no redress for ill treatment. The hired servant as well as the apprentice might be sold for his unexpired time. He must work for a price fixed by others, and no man would hire him without the permission of his former master. He was a slave for a time in all but name. Any combination on the part of the employed looking to a strike was treasonable.

NOTE.—I have reserved the Carolinas and Pennsylvania until they can be fully treated. Their history in the seventeenth century is short.

INDEX.

CHARLES ALEXANDER NELSON.